Contemporary
Austrian Writings

The German Library: Volume 74

Volkmar Sander, General Editor

CONTEMPORARY AUSTRIAN WRITINGS

Edited by Ingo R. Stoehr

continuum

NEW YORK • LONDON

2007

The Continuum International Publishing Group Inc
80 Maiden Lane, New York NY 10038

The Continuum International Publishing Group Ltd
The Tower Building, 11 York Road, London SE1 7NX

The German Library is published in cooperation with Deutsches Haus,
New York University.

Printed in the United States of America

Library of Congress Cataloging-in-Publication Data
Contemporary Austrian writings / edited by Ingo R. Stoehr.
        p.   cm.—(The German library ; v. 74)
Poetry English and German on facing pages; prose and theatre pieces in English.
        ISBN-13: 978-0-8264-1508-0 (hardcover : alk. paper)
        ISBN-10: 0-8264-1508-3 (hardcover : alk. paper)
        ISBN-13: 978-0-8264-1509-7 (pbk. : alk. paper)
        ISBN-10: 0-8264-1509-1 (pbk. : alk. paper)
    1. Austrian literature—20th century—Translations into English.   2. Austrian
literature—21st century—Translations into English.   I. Stoehr, Ingo Roland.
            II. Title.   III.   Series.
                PT3823.C66   2006
        830'.809436—dc22   2006037240

Acknowledgments will be found following each work,
which constitutes an extension of the copyright page.

Contents

Contents · vii

Drama

ELFRIEDE JELINEK

Prose

THOMAS BERNHARD

BARBARA FRISCHMUTH

NORBERT GSTREIN

ELFRIEDE JELINEK

GERT JONKE

MICHAEL KÖHLMEIER

PETER ROSEI

MICHAEL SCHARANG

JOSEPH ZODERER

JOSEF HASLINGER

Introduction

Referring to the contemporary literatures written in Austria, Switzerland, and Germany (before 1989–90, this would refer to two Germanies) as "German" is at best editorial shorthand for titles, although there is nothing self-evident about it. But neither is what constitutes Austrian literature self-evident. Two recent literary histories about Austrian literature since 1945 illustrate the issue. In *Österreichische Literatur 1945–1998: Überblicke, Einschnitte, Wegmarken* (Haymon, 1999), Klaus Zeyringer proposes seven hypotheses on Austrian literature, one of which states that "Austrian literature is literature in the context of the changing state and cultural space of Austria" (p. 56). Wendelin Schmidt-Dengler makes the same point in his *Bruchlinien: Vorlesungen zur österreichischen Literatur 1945 bis 1990* (Residenz, 1995), when he emphasizes that the years 1866, 1914, 1918, 1933, 1934, 1945, 1955 have a different significance in Austrian history from Germany (p. 12). At the same time, both Zeyringer and Schmidt-Dengler take great pains to assess the larger picture that locates Austrian literature within German–language literatures, which share more than just a literary market. On the other hand, each "national" literature is not monolithic but diverse in itself.

The selection in this anthology, the final one published in The German Library in 100 Volumes, surveys the diversity of styles and approaches in Austrian literature. It does not, however, include writers from ethnic or national minorities, with the possible exception of Michael Donhauser, who is originally from Liechtenstein. Austrian literature after 1945 can also be thought about in terms of different literary centers (typically, Vienna, Graz, Salzburg, and Klagenfurt) with distinct literary identities. This collection does not emphasize this approach, although the selected texts include works by poets associated with the Vienna Group, as well as poems by Alfred Kolleritsch, who has been the main force that made the city of Graz a literary center by bringing authors together as a collective and by founding *manuskripte*, the literary magazine he edits.

An "open" approach seems best suited to avoid fossilizing stereotypes of a specific Austrian "character." Stereotypes about literature of Austria (such as the multicultural heritage of the Austro–Hungarian empire, the focus on "language play," the motif of the village) may contain the proverbial kernel of truth. Even if they do, however, they are part of what Zeyringer calls a "literary-historical field" that is subject to change.

The texts in this anthology are chosen present a snapshot of the Austrian literary-historical field and invite the readers to venture onto this playing field to explore trends in contemporary Austrian literature for themselves. Extending such an invitation is one of the true pleasures of an editor (something with which I am familiar as editor of the bilingual literary magazine *Dimension*², from which several of the selections are taken).

One of the abiding clichés associated with Austrian literature is the centrality of language in terms of both reflecting on language itself and foregrounding the linguistic medium. Austrian authors indeed seem drawn to this theme, perhaps even more strongly than their colleagues in other German-speaking countries. During the 1950s and early 1960s, the "Vienna Group" (Friedrich Achleitner, Konrad Bayer, Gerhard Rühm, and Oswald Wiener) and more or less loosely associated writers, such as the writers represented here (H. C. Artmann, Ernst Jandl, and Friedericke Mayröcker), took language apart and reassembled it to play with its possibilities. But this does not mean that they all did it the same way nor that they did not evolve as individual writers. For example, Jandl focused at first as much on linguistic experiment as on emotional effect, and over the years, his poetry grew increasingly personal.

Any text constructs a world out of language. The (self-)generative power of language is emphasized, for example, in the short text by Gert Jonke. Considering story worlds as linguistic constructs raises the issue of realism, that is, to what extent literature may refer to reality and even voice social criticism. Michael Scharang has emphasized social criticism but does not restrict himself to Austrian reality, as the excerpt from his novel about the United States shows. Peter Rosei and Barbara Frischmuth mix realism with elements of science fiction and fantasy. Whereas the first of Rosei's texts evokes a Kafkaesque eeriness, Frischmuth's short story is, with all its fantasy elements, an epistemological fable about how one's "knowledge" of the world can lead to disastrous consequences.

Social criticism lies at the heart of the literary endeavors of Thomas Bernhard, Gerhard Roth, and Elfriede Jelinek. All three authors are critical of their state; they share the assumption that the former involvement with Nazism—or, rather, an insufficient coming to terms with that involvement—has defined contemporary Austrian identity. While the issue of Nazism is the key to Roth's novelistic cycle *Archive des Schweigens* (Archives of Silence), his earlier *Winterreise* is still more focused on an individual's lack of social belonging. To make his point, Roth uses Italy and sexuality as symbols of hope and failure. The protagonist's trip to Naples, Rome, and Venice does not bring liberation, and the use of sexuality has made the novel controversial. Jelinek's musical tragedy *Clara S.* is also set in Italy, but at the time of Italian fascism, which allows her to directly connect male domination with fascism in the catastrophe that ensues from the encounter between Clara Schumann and the Italian poet Gabriele d'Annunzio, who demands sexual favors in exchange for financial help for the Schumann family.

The excerpt from Jelinek's novel *Children of the Dead* underscores another cliché, that is, the importance of the village as a literary motif and subject matter. Although this critically evokes a conservative poetics of regionalism (the *Heimatroman*), it is more in keeping with the *Anti-Heimatroman* and the *New Village Story*. Jelinek's "Prologue" permits the reader to understand that nothing is what is seems; the idyllic mountain village is just facade. The "Epilogue" completely lifts the facade from the underlying strata of Nazism. Norbert Gstrein's text also fits within the *Anti-Heimatroman* with its reporting "from below," that is, from the viewpoint of the villagers, who may not quite understand everything about their honorary consul.

The reproach that potentially all of Austrian literature may carry a strain of provincialism is symbolically, and actually, connected to the village as a literary motif. Of course, it may be argued that, like politics, all literature is local, and the village is simply a placeholder for the world. However, it may be more helpful to look at how individual texts expand the village boundaries. For example, Jelinek's *Children of the Dead* is not even realistic when it plays with vampirism. The village that celebrates the turtle festival in Joseph Zoderer's novel is not even located in Austria but in Latin America.

Austrian literature is as much part of German–language literatures as it is of what Goethe called a *World Literature*. It is not only about the world (that is, choosing setting or subject matters from around the globe, as in the texts by Scharang and Zoderer) but *of* the world. The latter means that Austrian literature is in the mainstream of global traditions. For example, Michael Donhauser experiments with the Japanese poetic form of the haiku; Michael Köhlmeier revisits the Homeric *Odyssey* in a postmodern parody and pastiche; and Raoul Schrott reconceptualizes the history of the world in a poetic project that encompasses the history of writing as easily as the history of natural sciences.

Many texts in this volume voice personal concerns and observations; most selections, however, have a political dimension. Each text, however, does so in a different way. For instance, the literary techniques of Jelinek and Koehlmeier include postmodern elements, and Jelinek is more directly political. The texts by Robert Menasse and Josef Haslinger are the most recent and, indeed, take the reader into contemporary events. While strongly political, they blend private and political aspects in a new, critical realism. Haslinger's story, especially, is another example of how nonprovincial Austrian literature is: it tells the never-ending story of the psychological pain caused by war. But the story is not about a war of our parents' generation; it is about the effects of a war during our own lifetime in what we now call the "former Yugoslavia."

Austrian literature is about love and death, sexuality, politics, war, history . . . and life itself, as all literature is. Of course, when authors sit down to write, they usually have something to say—why should they even bother to start writing if they were not saying something in a new way, a different way, a way that makes what is written stand out as it never did before. The writers represented here all approach the world and express it in their own way—and that way has a great deal to do with each writer's individuality and literary-historical field, which is Austria.

I.R.S.

Contemporary
Austrian Writings

H. C. Artmann

jetzt kommt es darauf an . . .

jetzt kommt es darauf an ob ich auf meinem
seiltänzerseil den richtigen fußhalt finde

ich bin kein jäger kein hasentöter sechzig
kinder möchte ich zeugen keine hasen töten

unter meiner oberhose trage ich die unterhose
ich besitze eine rote eine gelbe eine lila

ich besitze ein oberhemd unterhemd keines
einen apfelbaum besitze ich leider nicht

ich liebe mädchen ich lehre sie neue sprachen
ich bin ein sprachenlehrer für die mädchen

ich beherrsche das feine nahuatl das quiché
das aymarà das guarani das araucano o ja

ich bin ein spezialist für indianische idiome
ich gebe es zu es bedarf viel guter balance

mein seiltänzerseil trage ich in einer tasche
meine tasche ist nicht von mäusen angenagt

ich komme eben aus stockholm und reise strax
nach paris ich komme nicht weit an diesem abend

H. C. Artmann

now it depends . . .

now it depends on my finding the right foothold
on my tightrope-walker rope

I am not a hunter not a rabbit-slayer sixty
children would I beget not slay rabbits

under my outerpants I wear my underpants
I own one in red in yellow in lilac

I own an outershirt no undershirt
nor an apple tree unfortunately either

I love girls I teach them new languages
I am a language teacher for girls

I have mastered fine nahuatl, quiché
aymarà, guarani, oh yes araucano

I am a specialist for indian idioms
I admit it requires a good balance

I carry my tightrope-walker rope in a satchel
my satchel has not been chewed on by mice

I just arrived from stockholm and travel straight
to paris I won't get far this evening

ich bin kein jäger kein hasentöter sechzig
mädchen möchte ich packen und keine hasen töten

ich lecke den wind wie eine blaue briefmarke
für den nächsten eilbrief an meine liebste

aus der luft springe ich auf die place vendome
wie ein behender akrobat aus federn und draht

plötzlich im letzten sommer bin ich in malmö
auf einer vespa fahre ich krabben aus ich tus

wenn frischer seewind an deine knöchel kommt
verblauen dir die socken wie eine hübsche ferne

durch die leutnantsgasse rollt ein faß äther
das ist gut abgedichtet da läuft nichts aus

die krabben sind sauberenthülste schöne tiere
enthülste krabben werden keinen flieder fressen

der seewind trägt ein interessantes telegramm
er weht aus dem fischhafen ich folge ihm hurtig

plötzlich im letzten sommer kaufe ich eine mütze
ich setze sie auf schief gerade und in den nacken

durch die leutnantsgasse rollt ein leckes faß
ein seemannsleben aus feingestanzten blechankern

die krabben werden in weiße duftende sahne getan
alle nachbarn nehmen ziegelsteine aus den wänden

meine vespa läßt den morgen wie glasperlen klirren
der flieder ist ein zartbewegter salzstreuer o ja

in allen ziegelwänden der stadt entstehen löcher
die nachbarn gucken sie erwarten sich ein telegramm

I am not a hunter not a rabbit-slayer sixty
maidens would I grab and not slay rabbits

I lick at the wind like at a blue stamp
for the next express letter to my beloved

I appear on the *place vendome* out of thin air
like a nimble acrobat of springs and wire

suddenly last summer I'm in malmö
riding on a vespa I deliver shrimps I do

when fresh sea breezes come against your ankles
your socks turn blue like a scenic overlook

a barrel of ether rolls through *leutnantsgasse*
it's well-sealed nothing leaks out

the shrimp are cleaned-shelled beautiful animals
shelled shrimp will never eat lilacs

the sea breeze carries an interesting telegram
it blows from the fish harbor I follow briskly

suddenly last summer I buy a cap
I put it on askew straight and pushed way back

through the *leutnantsgasse* rolls a leaky barrel
a sailor's life of finely-wrought tin anchors

the shrimp are put in white fragrant cream
all the neighbors take bricks out of the walls

my vespa rings the morning like glass beads
lilac is a finely shaken saltshaker oh yes

in all the brick walls of the city holes appear
neighbors peep they expect a telegram

Translated by Michael P. Elzay

© *Dimension* 14 (1981): 27–29.

Ernst Jandl

Gedichte

ETWAS AUF DEM BODEN

etwas auf dem boden
ins auge fassen
etwas ins auge gefaßtes
vom boden aufheben
etwas vom boden aufgehobenes
in der hand halten
etwas in der hand gehaltenes
aufmerksam betrachten
etwas aufmerksam betrachtetes
zu boden lassen
etwas zu boden gelassenes
fortkriechen sehen

GUT KLEID

ich haben ein hut an
gut hut
ich haben ein jacken an
gut jacken
ich haben ein krawatten an
gut krawatten
ich haben ein hosen an
gut hosen

Ernst Jandl

Poems

SOMETHING ON THE FLOOR

catch sight of something
on the floor
lift something caught in the eye
from the floor
hold something lifted from the floor
in your hand
observe something held in your hand
carefully
drop something carefully observed
to the floor
watch something dropped to the floor
creeping away

GOOD CLOTHING

I having hat on
good hat
I having a jackets on
good jackets
I having a ties on
good ties
I having a pants on
good pants

ich haben ein schuhen an
gut schuhen
ich haben ein hemmed an
gut hemmed
ich haben ein kurz hosen an
gut kurz hosen
ich haben ein socken an
gut socken
ich darunter sein nacket
gut nacket

DER GELBE HUND

der hund wischt sich am hund den mund gern ab
nämlich am hund der er nicht selber ist
wenn aber er allein und hund nur selber ist
wischt gern an sich den mund er selber ab

so hält auch gelb sich lieber auf bei blau
grau grün rot lila—steht jedoch nur gelbes
korn vorn vor gelber villa, gelben himmel darüber
ist auch das gelb sich selbst am leibsten lieber.   23.10.78

WIEDERGEFUNDEN

ein blatt
darauf
maschinengeschrieben
maus

sonst nichts

vor tagen
wochen
unbestimmter zeit
kam das da drauf

von mir

ich weiß   17.1.78

NACH ALTEM BRAUCH

keiner schließlich
hat es gewollt

I having a shoes on
good shoes
I having a shirtie on
good shirtie
I having a shorts on
good shorts
I having a socks on
good socks
I being naked underneath
good naked

THE YELLOW DOG

the dog likes to wipe his mouth off on a dog
that is on a dog who he himself is not
but if he is alone and only a dog himself
he likes to wipe his own mouth off on himself

just so yellow would rather hang around with blue
gray green red lilac—but then if only yellow
grain stands before the yellow villa, yellow sky above
even the yellow likes itself the best.   23/10/78

REDISCOVERED

a page
on it
typewritten
mouse

nothing else

days ago
weeks
indefinite time
it got on there

by me

I know   17/7/78

ACCORDING TO THE OLD CUSTOM

nobody, after all
had wanted it

jeder schließlich
hat es getan

das hört sich an wie lüge
und ist es auch   9.8.78

DAS BLEIBEN

das bleiben kann ein sitzenbleiben
oder ein stehenbleiben sein
es kann auch ein liegenbleiben sein
ein zuhause bleiben oder ein draußen bleiben
es gibt so viele arten von bleiben
aber keine hält ewig
das ist manchmal gut
aber manchmal schade   25.10.78

KORRESPONDENZ

so schreibe ich nur noch karten
auf denen ein ja oder ein nein
anzukreuzen ist
briefe schreibe ich nicht mehr.
wenn ich dadurch einen freund verliere
bestand diese freundschaft nur aus papier
von dem ich ohne dies genug besitze.

REKORDE

als ich klein war
wollte ich groß werden
wie mein vater
1 meter 64
war sein rekord

als ich erwachsen war
wie mein vater
war mein rekord
1 meter 72

everybody, after all
had done it

that sounds like lies
and it is too   9/8/78

REMAINING

remaining can be remaining seated
or remaining standing
it can also be remaining lying
remaining at home or remaining outside
there are so many kinds of remaining
but none lasts eternally
that's sometimes good
but sometimes too bad   25/10/78

Translated by Laura A. Lindgren

CORRESPONDENCE

so now i write only postcards
on which a yes or no
is to be marked with a cross
i no longer write letters.
if that means the loss of a friend
that friendship was made only of paper
of which anyway i have quite enough.

RECORDS

when i was small
i wanted to be tall
as my father
1 meter 64
was his record

when i was grown up
like my father
my record was
1 meter 72

1 meter 70 messe ich
laut meinem reisepaß
vom 6. februar 1991

er gilt
bis zum 6. februar 2001
meinem nächsten rekordjahr

From Ernst Jandl: poetische Werke. hrsg. von Klaus Siblewski.
© 1997 by Luchterhand Literaturverlag, München, a division of
Random House GmbH.

1 meter 70 is my height
according to my passport
of february 6th 1991

it remains valid
till february 6th 2001
my next record year

Translated by Michael Hamburger

Friederike Mayröcker

Zugeschüttetes Gesicht und andere Gedichte

ZUGESCHÜTTETES GESICHT

was wird sein wenn
ich schon bald vielleicht statt in den Büchern
zu lesen nur noch über die Buchrücken meiner Bibliothek
werde streichen können weil ich mich zurückentwickelt haben
    werde
in jenen Zustand meiner Kindheit in dem ich noch nicht
zu lesen imstande war also Analphabeth war
und mir habe vorlesen lassen müssen von meiner Mutter
oder sonstwem
also eingegangen sein werde
in einen Zustand in dem ich nicht mehr
zu lesen imstande sein werde
also mir abermals werde vorlesen lassen müssen von wem frage ich
    mich
und wieder geworden sein werde Analphabet

MEINE MUTTER MIT DEN OFFENEN ARMEN

wenn sie mich grüßte wenn ich zu ihr kam

meine Mutter mit den zärtlichen Worten
wenn ich sie anrief daß ich nicht kommen könne

meine Mutter mit dem abgewandten Gesicht
als sie noch sprechen wollte aber es nicht mehr konnte

Friederike Mayröcker

Buried Face and other poems

BURIED FACE

What will happen when
soon perhaps instead of reading books
I can only caress their backs in my collection
having reverted to the state I was in
as a child, still unable to read,
hence was analphabetic,
and had my mother read aloud to me,
or some other person,
thus when I've gotten
in a state where I cannot
read any more and
once again will have to ask someone to read to me I wonder who
when I again will be analphabetic

MY MOTHER WITH HER OPEN ARMS

greeting me when I came to her

my mother with her gentle words
when I called to say I could not come

my mother with her face averted
when she wanted to speak again but could not

meine Mutter mit den geschlossenen Augen
als ich zu spät kam sie ein letztes Mal zu umarmen

BIN JETZT MEHR IN CANAILLEN STIMMUNG

ich freue mich nicht wenn mir jemand gepreßte Blumen
oder 200 Millionen Jahre alten Lavasand sendet
ich freue mich nicht über Blumen an meiner Tür
über Blumensträuße wenn jemand mich aufsucht—
solche Zeichen haben für mich jeglichen Sinn
verloren, sind mir leere anspruchsvolle Gesten geworden.
Weiß ja nicht wo und wie ich mich befinde, nur,
daß das alte PIANO PONY mein Komet ist und mit mir weint.

ANRICHTESCHRANK, STILLEBEN AM MORGEN

konstant tomatenrot zerknüllt / *verknallt* : verknalltes Herz
und Wangenrot auf der Kredenz die rote Stoffserviette
als Bällchen Bäckchen rundgeknäult / auch Tritonfarbe
zart gerunzelt sanft gefältelt : UN =
ZEITIGKEIT VON KNOSPE . .   von roter Herkunft küchengelb
verflochten : krauses Mandarinen Haar, und
fliegenblau und fliedergrün die wunderbare Welt

SERAPHIM, ODER VOR EINER REISE

wessen Augendeckel, Ohrläppchen—
deck-chair mitten im engen Zimmer (wehend)
draußen Regen, vom hochgelegenen Fenster Hotelfenster
in einer fremden Stadt träume ich DAS GEWIMMEL
in den *squares* in den *avenues*—:
ICH BIN ANGST!   habe geträumt eine Serpentine
einen Seraphim einen Berg hinauf zierlich unbeleuchtet oder
mit kleinen Lämpchen wie in der Erinnerung sommerlicher
Lauben, mit Mutter zufuß unterwegs, manchmal ein
Scheinwerfer spürt uns auf, immer der Abgrund links oder rechts
Havelock Trenchcoat Burbury, die englische Küste bei Dover ich
habe geweint irgendeine englische Königin will uns
empfangen—   ich verstehe das alles nicht
sehe den Sprung in der Tasse, nagende

my mother with her eyes closed
when I came too late to hold her one last time

AM NOW IN A DIRTIER MOOD

I'm not glad when somebody sends me pressed flowers
or lava dust 200 million years old
I'm not glad to find flowers at my door
or about bouquets when somebody pays a visit—
such signs have altogether lost for me
their sense, they're empty importunate gestures.
Don't know where I am or how I feel, only that
the old PIANO PONY is my comet and weeps for me.

SIDEBOARD, STILL LIFE IN THE MORNING

constant tomato red crumpled / *crushed*: heart with the hots,
and cheekred on the credenza the red cloth napkin
as a ball and little cheek squeezed, rotund / also Triton color
delicately wrinkled, gently puckered: NOT
THE SEASON FOR BUDDING ..   originally red, threaded with
kitchen yellow : curly tangerine hair, and
flyblue and lilac-green the wondrous world

SERAPHIM, OR BEFORE A JOURNEY

whose eyelid, earlobe—
deckchair in the middle of the narrow room (windy)
rain outside, from the high window Hotel window
in a strange city I dream: THE TURMOIL
in the *squares* in the *avenues*—:
I AM FRIGHT!   dreamed a serpentine
a Seraphim, a mountain, up, daintily unilluminated, or
with little lamps reminiscent of summery
bowers, on a walk with mother, sometimes a searchlight
picks us out, always the abyss to left or right
Havelock Trenchcoat Burberry, the English coast near Dover
I've been crying, some English queen or other plans
to receive us—   I understand nothing of it,
see the crack in the cup, gnawing

Angst und Tränen. Sie hält mich ab in die Tiefe zu
springen/(schreiend): *ich kann nicht mehr /*
(es scheint und bemoost die Wirkware)

HINEINVERSÄUMTE HINEINVERSÄUMENDE NACHT

für NIEMAND

Novembermorgen im Fenster
drüben die grünen Luken
meistens ist der Stengel einer Pflanze der Weg
menschlicher Salamander mit gläserner Augengallerte
der winterschlafende Schmetterling unter der Heizung
rührt sich nicht mehr
das Brotpapier raschelt—
irgendwo hinter obskuren Gardinen
stehen sie schon zusammengerottet hämisch grinsend ohne
     Erbarmen
warten auf meine endgültige Niederlage
und daß ich hinstrecke auf dem Erdboden darniederliege
daß sie dann auf mich springen auf meine Weichteile und mich
     zertreten
während ich stutze und frage—

HAUSALTAR: HIERONYMUS BOSCH

1 geschwärzte Nadel: das abgeschnittene Haar auf dem Seifenrest
auf dem Boden der Fliesenküche zerquetschte Beeren
in der Flickkiste die nach Tabakrauch stinkende ausgebesserte
     Wäsche,
das feucht verquollene Strumpfzeug: 1 verfaulte Birne
zum Geschenk gemacht der Näherin vor 1 Woche—
heute wieder Juligestirn, sage ich, die eckigen violett getönten
Schatten an der Hausfront gegenüber, unwillkommen
was GEMEINHIN Musik genannt aus einem der offenstehenden
     Fenster
diese Hitze ist metaphysisch, sagt eine Freundin und leiht
dem strahlenden Morgen ihre rauchige Stimme ..
                                        für Cathrin Pichler

fright and tears. She stops me from jumping
into the depths/(shrieking): *I give up /*
(*it shines and covers with moss the knitwear*)

NIGHT NOT GONE, NOT GOING INTO

for NOBODY

November morning in the window
the green skylights opposite
mostly the stem of a plant is the way
human salamander with glassy gelatin eyes
the hibernating butterfly beneath the heater
motionless now
the bread wrapper rustles—
somewhere behind obscure curtains
they've ganged up wickedly grinning pitiless
they're waiting for me finally to be defeated
for me to stretch out supine on the ground
to jump on me trample my soft parts and crush me
while I boggle and question—

DOMESTIC SHRINE: HIERONYMUS BOSCH

1 blackened needle: hairsnipping on the soap
remnant, squashed berries on the kitchen tile,
in the sewing box the patched clothes stinking of tobacco,
the stocking bloated with damp: 1 moldy pear
1 week ago presented to the seamstress—
today the July stars, I say, the jagged shadows
violet on the house front opposite, unwelcome
music AS THEY call it from one of the open windows
this heat is metaphysical, a friend says and loans
the radiant morning her smoky voice ..

for Cathrin Pichler

Translated by Christopher Middleton

© DIMENSION² 4.2 (1997): 273–277.

Michael Donhauser

Zwölf Haiku

Drei Lose: was wohl
hätten wir gewonnen—
—um Mitternacht.

In den Rosenstrauch
wiederkehrt mit der Hitze
der hohe Sommer.

Einsam der Ginster
geistert: Geste, verwehrte
tut nicht dergleichen.

Lästige Wespe
werde dich bald vermissen
beim Nachmittagstee.

Regenbogenstück
unter jenen DREI SCHWESTERN
ich lache, durchnäßt.

Das Reifenzischen—
zweifacher Zweifel: wohin
mit welcher Sprache.

Am Teich von BELBO
unsere nackten Körper
—das Libellenblau.

Michael Donhauser

Twelve Haiku

Three lotto tickets:
What on earth could we've won—
—now at midnight.

Into the rose bush
Accompanied by the heat
Full summer returns.

Alone, the broom bush
Roams ghostlike: gestures, denied,
Do not measured up.

A bothersome wasp
I'm going to miss you soon
At the afternoon tea.

Piece of a rainbow
Right below those THREE SISTERS
I laugh, soaking wet.

The hissing of tires—
Double doubt: where to go now
Using which language.

The pond of BELBO
There are our naked bodies
—the blue of dragon-flies.

Kastanienallee
das Meer in deinen Blättern
—spätsommerlich.
(Murazzano 30. 8. 1992)

Nachtlandstraße—
Trauerflor: Verkehrstafeln
im Scheinwerferlicht.

Abendwind, kühler—
bleiche Spätsommersonne—
kaltes, weites HERZ.

Weiche Müdigkeit:
diese Jungbaumallee dort
so vormittäglich

Zersiedlung: Wälder
gelber Herbst und Dahlien
dann ein Frachtbahnhof.

Roads lined with chestnuts
The whole ocean in your leaves
—a late summer's mood.
      (Murazzano August 30, 1992)

Country road at night—
In mourning: the traffic signs
Well-lit by head lights.

Evening breeze, cool—
A late summer's pallid sun—
Cold, wide open HEART.

Gentle tiredness:
The avenue with young trees
So late-morning-like.

Urban Sprawl: Forests
Yellow autumn and dahlias
Then a freight depot.

Translated by Ingo R. Stoehr

© DIMENSION² 2.2 (1995): 299–301.

Alfred Kolleritsch

Gedichte

DEM ENDE ENTGEGEN

Sie klopfen an,
das alte Leben tönt zurück,
die Hammerhände
faustfroh,
das Letzte zu zertrümmern,

die Erde und das Meer vertrauen,
was in sie verschwindet
dem Tod an (jenem Anfang).

Wo sie getrennt sind
und sich widersprechen,
ist unser Augenblick vermutbar.

TAUTOLOGIE

Mit jedem Satz, verklemmt in die Zeile,
eingefault in die Schrift,
ist mitgenannt, daß wir
allein sind auf der Halde.

IN DER WELT

Ausgenagt ist die Spur,
einst schien es,

Alfred Kolleritsch

Poems

TOWARD THE END

They are knocking
—old life resounding back—
hammer hands
fisthappy
to smash the last thing;

what vanishes in them
earth and sea entrust
to death (that beginning).

Where they are divided
and contradict one another
our moment may be presumed.

TAUTOLOGY

With every sentence, jammed in the line,
molded into the writing,
mention is made that we
are alone on the slag heap.

IN THE WORLD

Gnawed out is the trace,
once it seemed

das Angeschaute
behielte die Augen,

ohne ihr Gesehenes
weicht das Erscheinen aus,
das schöne Wiesenkleid
fliegt weg im Wind,

überstürzt
das Gesagte
sein letztes Bild,

so trieb es auch
das Gedächtnis fort,
den Rest,

auf diese Weise
bewahrt,
ist nichts da,
aber so viel.

ABSCHIED

Schön zusammengekehrt sind die Schritte
zu einem Weg,
und schon zeichnen die Vögel
Horizonte, weit drüben warten die Wälder.
Was werden die Felder uns geben?

Unnahbar aber sind die Häuser,
tiefe Gärten,
von einem Arm zu anderen
nicht meßbar,
das Gewachsene
lügt in den Gärten.

Wir gehen fort
mit den Wolken,
als hätten sie Zeichen,
Geliebtes
hinterläßt eine Spur,

as though what is gazed at
maintained the eyes

without what they see
appearance recedes
the meadow's beautiful dress
flies away in the wind

what is said
overwhelms
its last image
likewise it drove off
remembrance,
the rest

preserved
in this way,
nothing *is* there,
yet so much.

LEAVETAKING

The footsteps are nicely swept together
into a path
and birds already mark
horizons—forests are waiting far over there.
And what will the fields have to yield us?

Unreachable, however, are the houses
deep gardens
from one arm to another
immeasurable
what has grown
is telling lies in the gardens.

We go away
with the clouds
as though they had signs;
what is beloved
leaves a trace,

vielleicht den schiefgewachsenen Zweig
im Ort? Dort, wo sie den Platz haben,
zu warten, zu trinken,
ohne Scham auch den Steinen
dankbar zu sein, ihrer Härte,
dazustehen im Wind
oder im Abendrot,
ohne angekommen zu sein.

KEIN WEG

Wenn dieses eine Wort fehlt,
das man nicht sagen kann,
das die anderen Wörter bindet,
umverteilt auf sich,
ausartet,
geht die Welt über
in Sätze,
reihen die Netze,
geknüpft, daß sie
das Unfangbare vergessen,
das andere Wasser,

gelehnt an Vielfältiges,
flußabwärts
ziehen wir aneinander vorbei,
tauschen die Lügen aus,
unsere Wahrheit,
und wenn Felder sind,
leergefrorene,
spielt der Rauhreif
die Botschaft zu,
ein einziges Weiß,
es leuchtet die Pupillen an,
und ein Stern davon
geht durch die Stirn,

aber auch das Schweigen
ist keine Erfahrung.

perhaps the branch grown awry
in the township? There, where they have room
to wait, to drink
without shame to be grateful
even to the stones, for their strength
to stand there in the wind
or in the dusky red
without having arrived.

NO PATH

If this one word is missing
—the one that cannot be said,
the one that binds the other words,
spread around upon itself—
if it degenerates,
the world will transform
into sentences;
the nets—knit so that
they forget the uncatchable—
will line up
the other water

leaning on the many things
downstream
we move past one another
exchanging lies
—our truth—
and if there are fields
frozen empty,
the hoarfrost
will deliver the message,
a singular white,
it shines at the pupils
and from it a star
passes through the forehead

but even silence
is no experience.

16

»Die Dauer drängt zum Gedicht«,
das Gedicht braucht sie nicht,
es vergeht und ist.
Im Entgegenfliegen
wilder als sonst,
bliebst du bei mir, ja,
du bist es, Billie Holiday!

17

Schamlos zu sein, überlegen nackt,
unbekannt, unheimatlich,
aber im Land, auf dem
du und ich Schwellen verbrauchen,
das Glück zu pflücken,
warum nicht?
Zwei Welten in der Übung
für eine.

35

»Der Nationalismus ist der Orgasmus
der Kollektive«, sagtest du,
»der Orgasmus trennt, schnippt
das Denken weg.« »Er vernichtet
das andere«, erwiderte ich, »er hat
nur sich selbst, schafft das Einzige
und das Eigentum, *ich* heißt er,
wie der Tod.« Hoch in der Luft
lösten die Schwalben Knoten, Figuren
der Einsamkeit vor dem Nichtsein
der Wolken. Dann verstanden wir nicht,
was Musik ist, genährt vom Schönen.

16

"Permanence presses toward the poem,"
the poem does not need it,
it passes away and is.
In flying toward it
wilder than usual,
you would remain with me, yes,
it's you, Billie Holiday!

17

To be shameless, supremely nude,
unknown, without home,
yet in the land on which
you and I use up thresholds
picking happiness
why not?
Two worlds in rehearsal
for one.

35

"Nationalism is the orgasm
of the collectives," you said,
"orgasm divides, clipping
away thought." "It annihilates
the other," I replied, "it has
but itself, creating uniqueness
and property; 'I' is its name,
like death." High up in the air
swallows were unraveling knots, patterns
of solitude before the nonbeing
of the clouds. Then we did not comprehend
what music is, nourished by beauty.

Translated by Christian Rogowski

DER KREIS

Der Sprung
hinaus über die Wiederholung
ins Weglose,
ins Nichtgezeigte (so lag vor Mykene
das Laub verdeckt im Dunst),
war keine Rückkehr, kein Erstes
drohte im Schatten,
nichts war aus dem Schlaf
zu wecken, Wörter
flatterten leer.

Unbeschützt umwächst
uns die Wildnis, jetzt
mißraten die Städte,
verfault das Meer, kein Spaten,
kein Netz findet
lesbare Spuren, ohne Anlaß
ist eines mit sich selber eins.

Musik bricht auf, Bienenschwärme
tragen die Geschichte, das Erkalten
und Bleiben. Töne, Glockenschläge,
genährt vom Vergehen, durchbrechen
die Dauer, Feuer brennt,
im Gehör entstehen und verschwinden
Quartette, Variationen,
schnelle Erlösungen. Welches
Opfer. Marylin Monroes Lebensgröße
im Coronadohotel, verurteilt
zur Vergangenheit, aber todlos.

Die Ebene ringsum ist ein Kreis,
im Schnee sich löschende Fährten,
Lebenswolken, zerfasert am Himmel,
und dann Hügel, auf ihnen einzukehren,
nichts außerhalb, kein Anfang und Ende,
wenn das Eine ist
sichtbar als Wein. Leuchtende Ruhe,
die, gefunden, verschwindet.

THE CIRCLE

The jump
beyond the repetition
into the pathless,
into the nondescript (thus the leaves lay
hidden in the mist before Mycenae),
was no return, no first deed
lurked in the shadows,
nothing could be awoken
from sleep, words
flapping empty.

Unprotected the wilderness
grows around us, now
the cities go awry,
the ocean rots, no spade,
no net finds
readable traces, without cause
one is identical with oneself.

Music sets out, swarms of bees
carry the story, the cooling down
and the staying. Sounds, strokes of the bell,
fed by passage, break through
duration, fire burns,
quartets, variations,
quick redemptions originate and
disappear in the ear. What
sacrifice. Marilyn Monroe's lifesize
in the Coronado Hotel, sentenced
to the past, but deathless.

The plains all around is a circle,
traces are erased in the snow,
clouds of life, shredded in the sky,
and then hill to make a stop,
nothing outside, no beginning and end
when the One is
visible as wine. Shining calm,
which, once found, disappears.

VERIRRT

Das Gedicht war im Haus,
in der Vermengung der Räume
dachte es, es erfand dich dort,
wo ich abwesend war,
verbannt in Sträucher
und Bäume,
in die maßlose Vielheit
der Wälder.

SPRACHE

Die »Arbeit« der Sprache
draußen. Sich selbst redend,
Narziss
im Gekreisch der Städte, fluchend,
bebend im Sterbebett,
auf der Zunge der Küssenden.

Mit tausend Wellen
schüttet sie Schaum, Fontänen,
Blasen zerplatzen,
verwirrend erhält sie die Welt
und weist ab.

Mit ungehorsamen Gliedern
versuchen wir's im Gekräusel,
mit Nachttau im Gesicht,
ungerettet
und zerbrochen.

VON DEN LIPPEN

Sie verhüpfen sich in die Sprache,
wühlen sich ein, verraten,
was zu sagen ist, als wäre
das Spiel selbst ein Spiel.

GEDENKEN

Wenn ich zu mir
zurückkehre,

LOST

The poem was in the house,
in the mixture of the rooms
it thought it had invented you there
where I was absent
exiled to shrubs
and trees,
in the boundless multitude
of forests.

LANGUAGE

The "work" of language
outside. Speaking himself
Narcissus
in the screeching of cities, cursing,
trembling on his deathbed,
on the tip of the tongue of those who kiss.

With thousand waves
it pours foam, jets,
bubbles burst,
confusing it receives the world
and rejects it.

With disobedient members
we attempt it in ruffles
with night dew in our faces
unsaved
and broken.

OF LIPS

They lose their way, hopping into language,
did themselves in, betray
what has to be said as if
the game were itself a game.

REMEMBRANCE

When I return to
myself,

auf dem Grab des Vaters
stehend
(das Maß Erde
zwischen Sohle und Kopf
zeigt,
daß man lebt),
enträtselt das Wolkenbild
sein Gegenmaß.

Eine Tanzfläche,
übersät mit Gräbern,
lockt das Verschwundene,
sich selbst auszusprechen.

Ich spreche mit Toten.
Sie erhalten die Welt
und begehren Sätze,
hinab zu ihnen.

Zwei Fersengruben
warten über dem Schädel des Toten,
der mit dem Schotter kämpft
gegen das Verschwinden.

EINBLICK

So fliegen die Bälle,
die Bahnen nehmen sie mit
und erfinden den Flug,
das dachte ich,
als du bereit warst,
tief verhüllt von dir selbst.

standing
on my father's grave
(the measure of earth
between sole and head
shows
that you're alive),
the cloud formation deciphers
its countermeasure.

A dance floor,
strewn with graves,
tempts that which has disappeared
to pronounce itself.

I talk with dead people.
They preserve the world
and desire sentences
spoken downwards to them.

Two hollow heels
wait above the skull of the dead
who fights the gravel
to avoid disappearing.

INSIGHT

This is how balls fly,
their trajectories carry them along
and invent the flight,
that's what I thought
when you were ready,
thickly disguised from yourself.

Translated by Ingo R. Stoehr

Raoul Schrott

PHYSIKALISCHE OPTIK I

er kam aus dem november · der hagel brachte
  ihn herab · all das wasser auf den flügeln
die nähte und die grate einer gußform

  die im regen hing bis der wind sie kappte
und er dann an die scheibe schlug wie ein bügel
  der aus seinem schloß schnappt · der ahorn

dort und seine äste · so schwarz war er
  eisengrau der bauch · nur ein paar federn
zum schwanz hin heller doch kaum scheinbarer

  als seine schwere nun plötzlich am balkon
in die sich die krallen hakten · norwegen
  oder die tundra · kein anderes land dachte

ich mir ließ diese tarnung zu und dem schnabel
  nach zu schließen war es wohl ein sperling
augen dunkel wie mangan und ein ring

  ganz weiß und schmal fast wie abgeschabt
von diesem schauen · flüsse im winter wegwärts
  ein erzeinschluß in den pupillen · das herz

ein flacher kiesel unter hagelschlossen
  zurückgelegt in den oktober · aufgehoben
war er leicht und das wort »vogel« eine vokabel

unklarer herkunft und von irgendwo im norden

innsbruck, 22. 10. 96

Raoul Schrott

PHYSICAL OPTICS I

it came out of november · the hail brought
   it down · all that water on the wings
the seams and fins of a cast

   that hung in the rain till cut by the wind
it struck against the pane like a shackle
   snapped from a lock · that maple

there and its branches · it was that black
   its breast iron gray · a few feathers brighter
towards the tail though hardly more apparent

   on the balcony now than this sudden gravity
its claws still clung to · norway
   or the tundra · no other land i thought

could warrant this disguise and judging
   by the beak it had to be a sparrow
eyes dark as manganese and a ring

   pure white and small as if scraped thin
by all that looking · rivers in winter along the way
   inclusions of ore in the pupils · its heart

a flat pebble among the hailstones
   handed back to october · picked up it felt
light and "bird" a word of obscure

origin and from somewhere in the north

innsbruck, 22.10.96

DIE ERFINDUNG DES ALPHABETS II

ihn ausbrennen den fels · das feuer ins fleisch
setzen bis es sich schwarz in die adern frißt
wir stickten den brand mit bloßen händen sagten

nicht ding und auch den namen nicht · mensch
war eine silbe · sie hatten wir in blöcke gefaßt
die wir aus dem härtling schlugen seinen falten

und decken und im offenen lagen · im tausch
mit der sonne trockneten wir holz · gepreßt
in die löcher wurden pflöcke daraus · so bauten

wir uns am ende den tag · so wurde er morsch
das grüne mark in den gruben verschleißt:
man kratzt bloß wurzeln heraus · wir tränkten

die keile mit essig · sie quollen auf wie frisch
gebrochener papyrus der den berg innen spleißt
das war das gezähe der gruben und wir holten

sprache brocken um brocken fast wie im rausch
zum stollenmundloch · göttern die man nicht heißt
körpern verwachsen aus vogel und hund dankten

wir mit unserem buckel · narbig wie ein erdfrosch
den nur regen aus seiner asche lockt · er frißt
sich satt · wir aber atmeten staub und meißelten

wort um wort ohne vokal · nichts als geräusch
aus dem tauben gestein · geliebte die du auch haßt
herrin des türkis und seiner schlacke von mitlauten

serabit al-khadim, 21. 2. 95

EINE GESCHICHTE DER SCHRIFT VI

vor aufgang ist der wind ein irrläufer
von nordwesten gegen die nacht · ich
schreibe dir diesen brief von einem
haus aus salz · den ziegeln der etesien
die in den see brechen · so baue ich die
worte · als ob du bei mir wärst und die

THE INVENTION OF THE ALPHABET II

firing the rock · setting the flame
into its flesh until the veins burn and blacken
we damped the blaze with our bare hands calling

it neither thing nor saying its name · man
was a syllable we cut into boulders broken
from bedrock its thrusts and folds lying

open under the sky · bartering with the sun
we dried out wood · shoved in
the holes it turned into pegs · pitting

the day against rock until it wore thin
the strip's green marrow went rotten:
roots were all we hacked out · wedges soaking

in vinegar · they swelled in the stone
like freshly cut papyrus splitting it open
such were the tools we mined with lugging

language lump by lump in a sort of delirium
to the mouth of the pit · gods you couldn't
name bodies half dog half bird saw us scraping

and bowing in gratitude · with our scarred skin
like the toad only rain tempts from the ash · it will eat
its fill · we though were breathing the dust chiselling

word after word without vowel · just the din
from the barren rock · beloved and sullen
lady of turquoise—and a slag of consonants jarring

serabit al-khadim, 21. 2. 95

A HISTORY OF WRITING VI

the wind before dawn is a missive
from north-west erring against the
night · i write these lines to you
from a house of salt · etesian tiles
crumbling into the lake · that is
how i build with words · as if you

braune decke auf dem bett dir ihre
falten über den schlaf die schulter
werfen würde · du richtest dich auf
gehst zur tür · unter den strünken und
palmen rinnt das wasser über die
gräben und der mond setzt einen
beistrich in einen tümpel seine sichel
zerkratzt bis aufs email und rußig wie
ein topf über dem feuer · davor dein
rücken und eine linie des lichts hoch
zum knie · an deinen sandalen war ein
riemen lose und zog spuren in den sand
wie ein kiel der zu den buchstaben
immer bloß ansetzt · und dann wieder

gabroon, 8. 1. 96

DÄMMERUNGSERSCHEINUNGEN II

der marmor der wolken · und dein kopf
aus dem dunkel gehauen mit schmalen
strengen gesten · die strähnen gerafft im
nacken die augen wie der schatten von
eukalyptusblättern die auf den stuhl
dort an der mauer fallen und die stirn
hell unter beiden händen · auf den fliesen
der terrasse hält die nacht still wie ein
insekt im spreiz der beine die zitternden
fühler aufgerichtet · vier fingerspann
über dem horizont liegt ein segment der
dämmerung · der bogen eines flügels der
sich schwarzblau mit dem wind schließt
und öffnet wieder · erdlicht · und nichts
mehr nun das sich berühren ließe · deine
lippen straff der geruch von kaltem holz
und die stille in der du dein hemd auf die
linke schulter ziehst · der morgen ist
etwas das über die hügelkuppe kommt
weit und unaufhörlich in indischem
rot · wir aßen orangen im dunkeln

vathi, 24. 8. 97

were here the brown blanket on the
bed casting its folds over your
sleep your shoulders · you sit up
and go to the door · water runs
through the ditches under the
palms and the stalks of bushes and
the moon writes a comma in a pool
its sickle scratched to the enamel
and blackened like a pot on the fire
before it your back and a line of
light rising to your knee · the loose
strap of your sandal dragging in the
sand was like a quill always poised
to write a letter · and then again

gabroon, 8.1.96

TWILIGHT PHENOMENA II

the marble slabs of the clouds · and your
head hewn from the dark with gestures
lean and hard · the strands of hair gathered
on your neck eyes like the shadows of
eucalyptus leaves that fall on the chair by
the wall and your brow bright beneath both
hands · on the tiles of the terrace the night
stands as still as an insect its legs apart
raised antennae trembling · at four fingers
breadth above the horizon lies a segment
of the dawn · the curve of a wing closing
bluish-black on the wind and spreading
again · earthlight · and nothing now that
could be touched · your lips taut the smell
of cold wood and the lull in which you
draw your shirt to your left shoulder · the
morning is something that comes over the
crest of the hill vast and unending in
indian red · we ate oranges in the dark

vathi, 24.8.97

FIGUREN II—*DIE AGLAURIDEN*

mohnfelder zwischen den grauen mauern
durchbrochene gassen manchmal plätze
der schlaffe fittich der hitze · ihr schritt
über die lücke der steine · der linke fuß
vorgesetzt der rechte noch im begriff zu
folgen berührt bloß mit zehenspitzen die
erde · sohle und ferse fast schon im lot
der glanz ihres schreitens behende und
in sich ruhend zugleich · doch von woher
kommen die statuen · sie nähern sich nicht
sie kommen zurück und suchen heim · die
wiedergänger des augenblicks · einmal
vorüber ist das kleid angehoben über dem
knöchel in der hand eine kanne voll wasser
aglauros und ihre schwestern · unter den
pinien des vesuv die eidechsen die man
mit einer grasschlinge fangt · ich habe es
oft und oft geübt an ihrem kleinen finger

pompei, 15. 2. 98

ISAAC NEWTON—*PRINCIPIA*

es war ein dienstag · der weiß gestrichene tisch
und die stühle standen im rasen und ich saß
zum essen mit meinen stiefschwestern · es war warm

und wegen der pest die fakultät geschlossen · ein glas
wasser neben dem teller und der ausgelöste fisch
verursachten ekel mir: der dünne darm

das schwarz gestockte blut · wir sprachen belangloses
ihre münder sah ich lautlos sich bewegen
und hinter ihrem rücken so etwas wie einen flügel

bloß beschnitten an den rändern · ein absichtsloses
streifen fast als wollte ein engel ihre gedanken erwägen
dann fiel ein apfel plötzlich von seinem ast

und die welt war in sich aufgehoben · die hügel
das haus der zaun · kein anfang fand
mehr zum ende an vorbestimmter stelle—er widerstand

FIGURES II—*THE AGLAURIDS*

poppy fields between the gray walls
alleyways opening up now and then
a square the limp wing of the heat
her step over the gap in the stones
the left foot moving forward the right
about to follow the tips of its toes
barely touching the ground · her sole
and heel almost perpendicular the
radiance of her stride nimble and
composed · but where do these
statues come from · they do not
approach they come back and only to
haunt · the revenants of the moment
once she had passed her dress
rides up above the ankle a jug of
water in her hand · aglauros and her
sisters · under the pine-trees of
vesuvius the lizards one snares with
a noose of grass · i have practiced it
again and again on her little finger

pompeii, 15. 12. 98

ISAAC NEWTON—*PRINCIPIA*

it was a tuesday · out on the grass
chairs and the table painted white where i ate
with my stepsisters · it was warm

and the faculty shut for the plague · a glass
of water and the gutted fish upon the plate
were but nauseous to me: that black coagulum

and thin intestine · our talk was idle
i saw them mouthing soundless words
and behind their backs something like a wing

though its edges clipped · as if a passing angel
tried to weigh their thoughts with its caress
then an apple fell and everything

that was the world was held · the gateway
the house the hill · no beginning now could
meet its end at the appointed place—it withstood

seinem natürlichen drang nach ordnung · eine last
lag auf den dingen und von ihrer masse ging eine schwere
aus die sie voneinander abstieß · ins ungefähre

woolsthorpe, 1666

ÜBER DAS ERHABENE VIII

gott so hieß ein generalleutnant
der britischen armee · das XIII. korps am südflügel
der sich weit über das netz der karte spannt

wie eine wetterfront auf den vorhügeln
des el taqa-plateaus: die keilförmigen spitzen
eines kolkraben der seine fittiche auf den sand senkt

ohne in die luft zu gehen · die straße schwenkt
vor dem stacheldraht ab und die skizze
zeigt wo noch mehr sperren liegen

ein lkw führt zerborstene blöcke von den steinbrüchen
der kriegsgräber auf die rampe · ein schuttriegel
wie ein panzer auf diesem kargen stück

feld · wenn dann beim abladen
die minen in den abraum explodieren ziehen schwaden
von rauch aus flachen krypten

kleine kammern für den sturzregen wo das geschwader
der vögel nach aas sucht · wie engel in ägypten

naqb el khadim, 2. 2. 96

WILDSPITZE

mit der sinkenden sonne geht die farbe
des firns vom gelb über ins glühen zur schneide
gedrängt vom aufsteigenden schatten · die narbe

des abends die sich über dem eingeweide
der erde erst schließt wenn das licht diesen rand
mit seiner klinge ausbrennt · stumpf wie kreide

breitet die kälte sich unter dem felsband
aus · auf den schlacken des schnees glimmt sie
im dunkeln noch einmal auf und der wundbrand

such natural urge for order · a burden lay
on things and from their mass there came a gravity
forcing them apart · to indefinity

woolsthorpe, 1666

ON THE SUBLIME VIII

gott: that was the name of a lieutenant
general in the british army · the XIII corps
on the south wing that soars

over the local grid like a weather front
in the foothills of the el taqa-plateau: a raven
with wedge-shaped wingtips swooping down on the sand

it doesn't go off but alights · the track
meets barbed wire and veers away
the map showing other barriers too · a truck

carrying shattered boulders from the quarry
of the war graves up to the embankment · a block
of rubble like a wall of armor on this barren

strip of land · when the unloading resumes
the mines explode in the dirt below plumes
of smoke rising from the shallow crypts

small chambers for the pouring rain where squadrons
of birds for carrion · like angels in egypt

naqb el khadim, 2.2.96

WILDSPITZE

with the sinking sun the firn's color
fades from yellow to a glow the rising shadows
force to the arête · the scar

of an evening that will not close
over the bowels of the earth until the light
sears this edge with its blade · the cold's

advance is blunt as chalk below the weight
of the crags · on the slags of snow it flickers up again
in the dark before the gangrene of night

der nacht beginnt · als wäre diese agonie
nie wirklich gewesen: die stille · dann kippt alles
wieder zurück in den grauton einer photographie

die abstufungen eines einzigen intervalles
von zeit · die ärmel streifen am anorak · die hände
verschrammt · kauernd · der laut eines windfalls

wie vor einem hörsturz · die winterwende
man hält nicht lange aus am gipfel · es ist als wäre
da ein anderer körper und das licht ohne ein ende

die gegendämmerung hält in der schwere
des erdschattens noch aus die strahlen nun zur garbe
gebündelt: den tropen einer inszenierten atmosphäre

wildspitze, 26. 2. 98

LA ZISA

und kehrten zurück in den umhegten garten · eden
die gipfel weit um die bucht in der farbe der narzissen
und mitten in diesem saal des sommers der *sebihl*
eine quelle aus marmor · rippen die kehl um kehl hervortreten
als würde wasser über wasser fließen
um sich in die vier flüsse zu ergießen · es ist still
bäume voll orangen und widergespiegelt auf der fayence
der reglos blauen becken deine silhouette · ein bild
das in sich selbst besteht: diese licht an den tag gelegte absenz
glast · hoch darüber in den kapitellen
pfaue die ihre federn ausstellen · das fleisch unverweslich hielt
ihr rad die sonne in den augen · und zurückstehlen
wollt ich die dir: das ist es was worte tun · blendarkaden
offene fenster für den wind und einen klaren blick
über kuppeln · in der nische vielleicht
einer der den becher reicht akrobaten schachspieler im mosaik
amphoren im sand über den gewölben im schatten
safranfäden in der hand · etwas das sich dir niederneigt
und weg · alles vollkommne immer nur im werden

WENDEKREIS DES STEINBOCKS

zeugenberge · blöcke und brocken glänzend schwarz
tags zuvor hatte ich sie im feldstecher hinaufjagen gesehen

finally sets in · as if this agony had never been
real: silence · then the complete reversal
to a photograph's gray in-betweens

gradations of a single interval
in time · sleeves brushing against the anorak · hand
grazed · hunkered down · the sound of a windfall

as if before a hearing loss · winter has turned
and on the summit one cannot hold out for long · as if
the body there was different and the light without end

for a while the counter-twilight endures
in the gravity of the earth's shadow gathering its rays
into sheaves: the tropes of a rehearsed atmosphere

wildspitze, 26.2.98

LA ZISA

and we returned to the enclosed garden · eden
the peaks for around the bay far in the hues of narcissi
and amid this court of summer the *sebihl*
a marble fountain · ribs rippling one by one
as if water welled on water
to flow into the rivers four · how still it is
trees full of oranges and mirrored in the faience
of the calm blue pools your silhouette · an image
inhering in itself: the lucidity of this absence
agleam · high above on the capitals peacocks spread
their feathers · with imperishable flesh
fans kept the sun in their eyes · i tried
to steal it back for you: that is what words
can do · open windows for the wind blind arcades
and a clear view over cupolas · in that niche perhaps
one offering the cup chess-players in mosaic acrobats
amphorae in the sand over arches in the shade
threads of saffron in the palm · something bowing
to you and then gone · all perfection only ever becoming

TROPIC OF CAPRICORN

relict mountains · blocks of black and shining
slabs · i'd seen them through binoculars the day before

flanke an flanke innehaltend witterung aufnehmen
und wieder weiter durch diesen glast seitwärts

sich schlagen · es waren schwere tiere das auflohen
ihrer mähnen das einzige was sie vom fels abhob
den wind an der wange kletterte ich in diesem abwegsamen
den klüften entlang · geröll das frost gesprengt

und sand zerschliffen hatte und so liegen blieb
in jenem flüchtigen gleichgewicht das eine zeit bedingt
die nicht in atemzügen mißt oder im blut das klopft
ihr ausmaß war diese halde hier · ich kauerte im morgenlicht

regungslos unter einem überhang und wartete
in einer anspannung die nur im ausharren sich erschöpft
glaubte steine gegeneinanderschlagen zu hören ein schnauben
und meinte sie von mir längst schon verscheucht

weil ich den blick dafür verlor sich alles um mich verhärtete
und sah eines davon armlängen vor mir ein horn reiben
an den trümmern · den gelben ring der augen
das fell wie dunkler hafer nein: sand zurückbeugen

das genick und den kopf wegneigen · und hielt still
nach wie vor als könnte man diesen moment mit allem
vergangenen verschränken · dann der nachhall
von hufen im schutt der eine silhouette ausfüllte mit reellem

© Carl Hanser Verlag München Wien 1998 and 2004.

dash upward flank to flank pause nose to the air
and off again a traverse through the glare

heavy beasts whose flaming manes alone
betrayed them against the rock · wind
on my cheek i climbed in the impassable in ravines
boulders broken by frost ground down by sand

and come to rest in that transient balance
whose scale of time supposed a measure
outwith breaths and throbbing blood
its dimension was this scree · i crouched motionless

in the morning light waiting under an overhang
in a tension only perseverance can exhaust
thought i heard stones crashing a snorting and believed
them long scared off by me because i'd lost

my eye for it and around me everything was hardening
and saw it a couple of arms' lengths away
scraping its horn on the ridge · the yellow ring of the eye
its coat like dark oats no: like sand bending back

its neck and turning its head away · and kept as still
as before as if this one moment could interlock
with all things past · then the echo of hooves
in the rubble filling a silhouette with what was real

Translated by Iain Galbraith

Elfriede Jelinek

Clara S.

A Musical Tragedy

Characters

CLARA S.
ROBERT S.
MARIE

GABRIELE D'ANNUNZIO, called COMMANDANTE
LUISA BACCARA

AÉLIS MAZOYER
DONNA MARIA DI GALLESE, Princess of Montenevoso
CARLOTTA BARRA
Two asylum attendants (cops)

In addition a few maidservants, a young prostitute from the village.

Scene of the action: the Vittoriale near Gardone, the villa of D'Annunzio.

Time: 1929, late autumn.

As far as the atmosphere and the costumes are concerned, one could perhaps follow the oil paintings of Tamara de Lempicka.

Part 1

(Formal room, which somehow, however, resembles a dripstone cave. Pictures, draped with mosslike velvet, hang down like stalactites from the ceiling. Everywhere overornate grandeur. Tasteless. In the background a concert grand. At this the child Marie is practicing, intensively and intrusively, some finger and trill exercises by Czerny; she is strapped into a kind of training apparatus (Logier's contraption in which Robert Schumann already had ruined a finger), an apparatus intended to teach a pupil the correct posture for piano playing. A metronome is ticking. After a while Clara, hurriedly and wringing her hands, runs across the stage. Behind her, cheerfully squealing, rushes the plumpish, sensual Luisa Baccara, who however becomes visible a little while after Clara. Luisa is somewhat kitschily Italian, Clara the fleeing German fawn. Luisa catches up to Clara, embraces her. Gasping and anxiously, Clara gives in. Mannered. Exaggerated gestures)

LUISA: I've got you at last, Cara!

CLARA: Clara, not Cara! (*Gasps.*) My inner self is struggling so vehemently against my external self. A woman dedicated to the mind considers the external self unimportant. My heart's about to burst out and fall on the ground.

LUISA: Oh no! I'm sure it won't do that!

CLARA: When she's abroad, a female virtuoso creams off the fame, which she then markets at home. When I say "home," I mean of course Germany, which is where I live. Soon the whole world will be my home.

LUISA: (*kisses her*) It seems to me you're too strongly infected by this hostility towards the body. Soon you will be torn to pieces beneath my hands. I can feel that. The German mind will gradually acquire a taste for it and meticulously tear to pieces any body that appears near it. So what! What I wanted to tell you about my education as an artist was . . .

CLARA: (*interrupts*) Be quiet!

LUISA: You don't want to let me finish speaking because you think only you are an artist, and I'm not! Listen! (*Holds Clara tightly; Clara tries to tear herself away, but Luisa is stronger.*) Just you listen to me! I've always attached importance to being an enfant terrible, whose value lies in towering above the masses, but who in the end puts no obstacles in the way of conforming.

CLARA: You talk and talk . . . A German, however, acts or thinks in silence!

LUISA: Has something killed off your sensuality? It wasn't an accident, I hope!

CLARA: (*pulls the décolletage of her dress together in an exaggerated bashfulness*) My father, that beloved great teacher, and later my husband, Robert, the devil.

(*Luisa giggles exaggeratedly and teasingly.*)

CLARA: (*fiercely*) Don't laugh!

LUISA: (*kisses the reluctant Clara again*) Why call someone a devil today whom yesterday you called a godlike genius? My dear! Look at me! I gladly and freely pass on what the male composer creates. There's no anguish squirming around inside while I do it. Dearest! (*Giggles again*)

CLARA: Your giggling is exaggerated and contrived.

(*Luisa giggles even more loudly; she kisses Clara on the neck.*)

Get away! (*Pushes Luisa away*) My father hammered into me the male concept of genius and my husband took it away again immediately, because he needed it for himself. The power of the censor resides in the head.

LUISA: Why on earth do you want to compose them? So many musical compositions exist already. You could spend the rest of your life rooting around in them like a pig looking for truffles!

(*Luisa pulls away Clara's hand, which has been desperately trying to hold together the décolletage of her dress, and takes liberties. Horrified, Clara leaps up and rushes off, flustered; cheerfully giggling Luisa runs after her. The child practices intrusively.*)

A woman is soft and mostly yielding, a man is hard and presses forward, no matter where it will end. In doing so, he sometimes even produces a composition. A lot more goes into a man than into a woman, that's why he can get more out of himself when it matters. A question of quantity, my sweet.

CLARA: (*breathlessly throws herself into a kitschy embroidered armchair*) Robert, that beast, fantasizes all the time that he's losing his head. On the way to Endenich he remained calm until Cologne; from then on he kept trying to leap from the carriage. All through the Rhineland he kept ripping open the door and tossing his body out into the open. Strong hands had to hold him back.

LUISA: Terrible! Cara! Bella Tedesca!

CLARA: (*exaggerated, almost in tears*) In his head, he says, everthing crowds together and is compressed by a mysterious machine. This dreadful fear of losing your head! Because he knows that his genius lives in there, like the worm in the apple. The worm looks out from time to time and then, alarmed by the world, it withdraws into the shell of one's head and feasts there, eating up the brain.

(*The Commandante enters laboriously, an older man. Clara throws herself into his arms. A friend and a connoisseur!*)

COMMANDANTE: There, there! (*He pats her.*)

CLARA: No! Let me kneel before you! (*She tries to kneel, but he does not let her.*) If you won't let me kneel, then let me at least admire your very noble bearing! It's the result of the fact that although you can't understand the genius of my husband Robert, you nonetheless bow down deeply before him and generously finance his latest work, an unbelievably modern musical creation.

COMMANDANTE: Before you admire my posture, dearest, I'd prefer to have your body! (*He tries to paw her, she pulls herself away.*)

CLARA: You received your money for artistic achievements, now spend it by supporting others! Those in power have never appreciated art. All they know is that you have to pay for it.

COMMANDANTE: The Duce has shown his appreciation for my art. Find somebody else! Now come over here to me! (*Draws her to him*)

CLARA: No! (*Tears herself away*) I'd rather kneel! Let go of me, you . . . you . . . ignorant Italian!

COMMANDANTE: Italian! I've even flown an airplane over Vienna. The whole time I had a capsule with deadly poison on me, just in case something went wrong while I was flying. Back then, that male drive to conquer told me: Fly! The male death wish told me: Die! Art said: Create! The drive to conquer won. I shot forward, unstoppable, through that sticky, waltz-ridden air, scattering leaflets. Greatness lies in absurdity.

CLARA: Wouldn't you perhaps like to take that poison today? (*Pushes him away*) Leave me alone! In me you see embodied artistic genius combined with motherhood. A symbiosis. You should back away from something like that, like backing away from your own inner self, which fortunately you never get to see. Motherhood feeds on artistic genius and vice versa.

COMMANDANTE: Am I now supposed to finance a symphony for your crackbrained natural genius or poison myself?

CLARA: First sponsorship, then a simple, quiet suicide. You'll live on in my Robert! And Robert lives on in himself: what bliss!

(*The Commandante embraces Clara again, attacks her; offended because of the lack of attention, Luisa has withdrawn and half-heartedly reads a book.*)

If you don't show the respect due to a mother, then you should have it for the artist. Back, I say!

COMMANDANTE: I don't care whether you yield to me as a mother or as an artist. By the way, apart from my literary works, I live on, for instance, in my priceless armchairs, padded as they are with original Renaissance chasubles. Besides these I own countless other antiques as well, to preserve our great heritage. I own odes, sculptures, sonnets, and statuettes. Many of them created by more famous masters than your Robert will ever be.

CLARA: Monster! Philistine!

COMMANDANTE: I can speak poetry whenever I like. Right now, for example, I'll start speaking poetry. (*Pulls Clara to him, she puts up a struggle.*) Stop that! I desire in you, in this knowing and desperate woman, she who was broken by the eternal suppression of her female nature, who was destined to succumb to the sudden throes of her sex, who extinguished in nocturnal sensuality the fever that burned in her in the light of the concert stage, that pianist in heat who moves from the delirium of the crowds to the power of the male, that Dionysian creature who crowns, as if in a bacchanalian rite, the mysterious religious service in the act of life!

CLARA: As I hear the talk, you will never catch up to my Robert, let alone overtake him!

COMMANDANTE: As you have seen, it caused me no trouble at all to change over from normal language to the language of poetry.

CLARA: My genuine German composer-husband always has to overcome the greatest artistic obstacles in order to erect a cathedral of music. That's why his work will live on however, while yours must collapse. Especially because as a man and a human being you constantly fail.

COMMANDANTE: As a man I haven't failed for decades! As a human being of course I'm daemonic. To illustrate what I mean by daemonic, I'll just say that beneath my desirous gaze your flesh contracts, in a desirous resistance to a painful shame. My wish strikes you like a moral wound because you know how much bitterness, impurity, lies in this sudden desire. Well?!

CLARA: Wild animal! How I long for the clear and pure translucence of Robert's F-sharp minor sonata.

COMMANDANTE: By the way, I consider you deeply poisoned and corrupted, weighed down by love, experienced in all sensual pleasures, an insatiable temptress. Your notion of the German mountain stream is just a con-job. Trout would suffocate in it.

CLARA: This artist's body of mine, which earlier on even produced its own compositions, when it had time for it, will not be violated by you.

COMMANDANTE: We've got a lot more artist bodies in this house besides yours. For example, here comes a dancer's body pirouetting in right now.

(*Carlotta Barra enters in her training outfit and does exercises at the barre in the background, without paying any attention to the others.*)

Most of all I dislike the body of your husband, this German composer.

CLARA: Because he possesses genius. Genius always goes to extremes, often painful for others. Sometimes it goes a step too far and madness results! Robert knows no bounds. In his desires, as in his demands.

COMMANDANTE: I know that well! I too am such a genius. That's how I know.

CLARA: You're not! You're not!

COMMANDANTE: Yes, I am! Yes, I am!

CLARA: You only know the body of a woman, but not the inner-most essence of art. The artist is a priest and devotes himself solely to the creation of art, to everything else he is deaf. You can't make that claim about yourself.

COMMANDANTE: I am indeed. Above all, I know boundlessness from my own experience. For example in my desires, which are pathological and boundless. The one desire contains the lives of the conquered masses and the intoxication of the unknown par-amours of my various lovers. The other desire contains the vision of orgiastic couplings. So, what have you got to say now?

CLARA: My Robert is the prototype of the chaste artist who lives withdrawn from the world. You are the prototype of the dilet-tante, who is no artist at all! To be sure there are significant cre-ators of art who have a tendency towards an unhealthy extremism, for example, Liszt or the infamous Meyerbeer, but you don't belong to them. Robert, he's the mountain lake or the mountain stream. You, Gabriele, you are the sewer! Your money stinks!

COMMANDANTE: I'm not a sewer at all. I am a successful mixture of cruelty, anger, jealousy, poetry, and pride.

CLARA: Philistine!

COMMANDANTE: (*offended*) Then I'd like to know why you con-tinue to stay here, if I'm such a sewer. Can a woman like you only lie down if the man is a sewer?

CLARA: There's no question of my lying down, Commandante. I'm appealing to your sense of patronage rather than to your sensuality.

COMMANDANTE: What am I supposed to be paying for, dearest? Your Robert's been sitting for weeks on an egg that hasn't even been laid yet. The only thing he can do while sitting there is to look like a genius. I am Ariel, the spirit of the air, incidentally. Do you want Aélis to help you pack? Charles will drive you then. Shall I, as always, have rooms reserved for you at the Palace, precious?

CLARA: (*horrified*) No!! Don't abandon a woman who is yearning!

COMMANDANTE: (*knowingly*) Aha.

CLARA: (*overcoming her reluctance goes to him, gives him childlike kisses on the cheeks*) Let me stay here, please, so that I can sit at your feet, Gabriele!

COMMANDANTE: (*gropes her*) I painfully regret never having had this pianist after a great triumph on stage, still warm from the breath of the audience, covered in sweat, gasping and pale. For example, after the "Hammerklavier" sonata. Or after that sweat-inducing Tchaikovsky concerto. Like this she looks like nothing.

CLARA: (*desperate*) Ariel! (*Throws herself at him like a little girl, tries to embrace him*) You poet-prince of Italy! (*Crying.*) You . . . (*Sobbing*) Priest of your art . . . !

COMMANDANTE: (*practiced, tiredly*) In a flash I see you stretched out before me. Within you, the power torn from the howling of that monster, the audience. Now you are tired and thirst with desire to be taken and shaken to the core. Come, we'll do it straightaway! And afterwards I'll describe what distinguishes a bold conqueror from a similarly bold artist. Basically, nothing.

(*He tries to lead Clara away. Carlotta Barra, who notices this, rushes from the background towards him, jealous that she, as an artist, is not being paid any attention. In front of the Commandante she makes excessively graceful hand movements, fluttering. The Commandante tries to grap her by the breasts, but she gracefully evades him and pirouettes away.*)

CARLOTTA: (*pirouetting away*) More than all other people we dancers are feathers of down. Our bodies are transparent, of light and air. Nothing keeps us on the ground. Sometimes we are less light and air than ecstatic priestesses of our art. (*Pirouettes*) Like now, for example. People search us out like pilgrims searching for a far-off altarpiece.

(*At the door she collides with Luisa, who, nibbling on cookies, comes in again.*)

LUISA: (*softly to Carlotta*) In the long run, if you go on being so obstinate towards him, you're not going to get that engagement at the Paris Opera.

CARLOTTA: (*softly*) The German cow is completely monopolizing him. Before she said that she's a priestess. But then, I'm that already. You expressly said that I could do the nun bit, and now that German woman is doing it without having arranged it with us first. As far as I'm concerned, she can say she's a bird, even a phoenix, if she likes, or a little fawn if she wants.

LUISA: Don't get yourself worked up, Cara. In the long run the best thing will still be to let yourself be fucked.

CARLOTTA: Never! I shall enthrall him with my art.

LUISA: (*skeptically*) Well? You were here first, after all. Stand your ground with the priestess-bit. I'll talk to the German, tell her to say that from now on she's a fawn, and this Robert could well represent a white stag.

(*Both women giggle. Clara and the Commandante, who have been paying attention to the child in the contraption, begin to take notice.*)

CARLOTTA: (*quickly to Luisa*) Speak to him today while you're giving yourself to him. You'll get your thirty percent.

LUISA: Forty!

CARLOTTA: All right then. I have my art after all.

LUISA: (*offended*) I too have my art, it's exactly the same art that you have, only more of course and in another field: pianist. It's agreed! Thirty.

(*Carlotta pirouettes out the door.*)

Ha. Taken in! While I'm giving myself to him, I'll be speaking only about my planned piano recitals in the United States. I'll be leaving in spring, the Commandante has already made the deal for me and provided the subsidy. Till then I'll only have to give myself 120 more times. At the very most!

(*At this moment the Commandante collapses groaning at the piano. Luisa hurries to help him, rings fiercely. Clara corrects her daughter's posture at the piano, plays the mother possessedly.*)

COMMANDANTE: (*groaning*) I am obsessed with beauty: of trees, flowers, dogs, and naturally of women! I couldn't bear it if the woman with whom I was living wasn't beautiful. And I'd find it even harder to bear if there were another woman who was even more beautiful I didn't possess! (*Half chokes*)

(*Aélis rushes up, together with Luisa they put the old man down on a pile of satin cushions, feel his pulse, rub his temples, etc. Mean-*

while the man gropes both women, reaching up under their dresses, etc. The child Marie plays incorrect chords. Clara corrects her.)

COMMANDANTE: (*groaning*) I've had experience living with beautiful women. Something happens when you look into the eyes of a beautiful person: you see an open, honest face. And what is beauty anyway? A goat on a mountain is beautiful, so is the notorious sunset. More important than beauty is . . . (*he groans so much that he has to take a sip of water*) . . . to be loved, to be beautiful in the eyes of a man! (*Coughs, choking, a bit of the water runs out of his mouth. Marie again plays something incorrectly.*)

COMMANDANTE: (*with effort*) Take the child out of that contraption!

(*Aélis hands him a bottle of smelling salts, which he sniffs.*)

CLARA: (*at the piano*) In this condition you can't possibly appreciate the great talent of my daughter!

COMMANDANTE: Get out of that contraption!

CLARA: Haven't you given up the ghost yet? Beast! Monster! You big, strong masculine master, you!

COMMANDANTE: I'll still live to see the whole situation cleared up and your husband finally committed to the asylum. And after that I'll see how his then defenseless wife convulses in a final paroxysm, succumbs in a violent embrace, to find peace at last in a deep, dreamless sleep. (*He recovers appreciably.*)

CLARA: Inhuman oppressor! Before that, Robert will compose his greatest work, a symphony to be precise. He will write it here. Will make your house go down in musical history.

COMMANDANTE: That is unnecessary, because through me it is already in literary history. I am a member of the Olympus of Italian poets. Gabriele D'Annunzio.

CLARA: My husband will be much more immortal than you, Commandante!

COMMANDANTE: No. I'll be more immortal. Beg me not to be so cruel! (*He groans terribly, almost expires.*)

CLARA: Please don't be cruel.

COMMANDANTE: Now ask me not to hurt you! Because there are moments when I don't know myself anymore and think I am a wild animal, a lion perhaps or a bear.

CLARA: (*pressing her daughter to her*) Never! Once, before, he threw his precious wedding ring into the Rhine. Now I want to dedicate my life to Robert.

COMMANDANTE: After considerable reflection, I don't think I will do anything to you now. (*Collapses again totally*)

CLARA: (*pressing her child to her, falling out of her role*) First my Robert will have to suffer this fear of losing his head for a while longer. Of course, that's just a shift from below to above. What he's really afraid of is losing his dick. You see, as the censor becomes weaker, the inhibition collapses. We certainly all have our worries.

COMMANDANTE: (*struggling to his feet*) Would Madam like to see how well-hung I am by comparison? (*He starts to unbutton himself.*)

(*Clara recoils. Aélis stops him, strokes him, at the same time cranes her neck, and looks into the corridor.*)

AÉLIS: Commandante, Carlotta Barra is still waiting outside and she's making a hand-gesture that's supposed to be graceful. You should look at her and get her an engagement at the Paris Opera. Otherwise she'll collapse.

COMMANDANTE: (*coughing*) Is that one I've had already?

AÉLIS: No. One of the infinitesimally few remaining.

COMMANDANTE: She can only give herself to the masses of art aficionados after she has given herself to me. Though there won't be much left over then anyway.

(*Clara and Marie form a mother and child image.*)

The eroticism of German women is world famous. I'll now list the reasons why, first . . .

(*Aélis stops him from detailing the list and turns his head so that he looks at Carlotta, who, not visible to him, performs something on the other side of the door.*)

I can't see around corners. Are the girls here?

AÉLIS: I think so, Ariel, two of them. From Gardone.

COMMANDANTE: Send up the ones you've selected. Wash them first, please!

(*Marie now plays a Clementi sonata to gain his attention.*)

Take the child away, take the contraption away, take the music away! (*He has finally lost his patience.*) Take the child away! (*Roars*)

(*Terrified, Clara tears Marie out of the contraption and presses her fiercely to herself.*)

CLARA: Does that mean you don't appreciate the art of my child and my husband?

COMMANDANTE: I appreciate the emerging female form of your child's body all right, but not her artistic outpourings.

CLARA: (*with dignity, offended, pressing the child to herself*) That's the last straw, Commandante, and you know it. We'll leave now for Cannes, for the Carlton. You can ring us there then, several times a day if you like, to have us come back. But don't be too pushy, because I have to come to terms first with this human and artistic disappointment. My husband, Robert, I'll leave here for the time being. He'll be your guarantee that I'll come back, after the wound has healed. Je vous supplie, au nom de notre clairvoyant amour, ne brusquez pas, ne cassez plus cet admirable demi-poison, élément dans lequel vous m'avez plongée! (*She looks at him expectantly. He does not react, just scrutinizes her through his monocle. Clara offended*) The child, however, I'm taking with me. Not that you should think . . .

COMMANDANTE: (*interrupts*) If I don't give the chauffeur the order, then you'll go nowhere! As far as I know you don't even have enough at the moment for a third class train ticket to Verona.

(*Clara turns away and hides her face in her hands.*)

CLARA: You destroy me completely when you talk like that, Commandante!

COMMANDANTE: My notorious Leda room is waiting for you. Not for long though. Apart from that mon petit prince is waiting too. You know who that is. If not, then read the relevant literature! Shall I show you the state you've put him in with your refusal? (*He grabs at his dick. Clara hides her face again, hysterical.*)

CLARA: Don't! Please, please, don't!

COMMANDANTE: And not to mention a pile of German swill, especially ordered for you. Sauerkraut. If you don't kill me, then this food will do me in once and for all. And then I could offer you my White Lady. (*Taps on the box with the cocaine*)

CLARA: No! I will never let the usual marvelous clarity of my German mind become befogged by a devilish drug.

COMMANDANTE: May I conclude from that, that that's what the intensity looks like which an artist's supposed to need so much in life? Supposedly, one can't separate art from life, because they both should proceed together.

CLARA: My intensity as a German pianist comes solely from a violent dissonance at the beginning of my childhood!

COMMANDANTE: That too goes to make an artist, some suffering casting a shadow over him. Anyway, I am a great writer, and from my inner depths there often bursts forth a wild urge that I cannot tame. And, from the same depths, sometimes, very rarely mind you, there emerges human compassion that is not however as strong as the wild urge. I'm more of a devil than your Robert.

CLARA: No, my Robert is more of one than you. First my father cast a shadow over my life, and now it's overshadowed by problems with a partner. People flee such complications like the plague, an artist feels compelled to seek them out so that they can find expression in his work. That's what's called the depth of a work. In a woman's work it is watered down. The depth disappears with childbirth.

(*She looks pensively into the distance, has released the child who tears herself away, runs to the Commandante and snuggles up to him. The man groans and lets Aélis administer the medicine to him. Aélis motions to the child to press herself against the Commandante, shows her how. Breathing heavily the man rubs himself against Marie. Luisa who has kept herself to the side the whole time and has been spooning up caviar, jealously watches the action and bites into a hibiscus flower.*)

AÉLIS: Luisa Baccara's hatred is making her bite into flowers!

LUISA: (*tries to reach the Commandante, Aélis blocks her way*) All the passion of the night arouses us, throwing one to the other, Commandante!

AÉLIS: It is midday.

(*D'Annunzio moans with pleasure with the little girl. Clara, the mother, stands gracefully at the window and stares—Mignon-*)

*like—into the distance, with undulating hand movements. She does
not notice what her daughter is doing.*)

CLARA: O Germany, Germany, from here it is such a long way to
you, Fatherland. And now I am going to tell you a story from
my rich life.

LUISA: (*spitefully, jealously*) Various people still have the time to
leave the room straightaway, before a German destiny is unfolded. The outpouring of German destinies is particularly
convoluted.

(*D'Annunzio motions to Aélis she should distract Clara from her
daughter, with whom he is cuddling. Aélis understands immediately
and goes over to the window, lays in half-feigned, half-genuine solidarity, her hand on Clara's shoulder, presses her lightly towards
herself.*)

CLARA: (*unhappily, almost crying, exaggeratedly*) This horrible foreign country wears out my natural constitution! Nature! The
night seems pregnant with wonders. The eternal powers reign in
harmony between the earth and the stars.

(*Aélis pats her comfortingly but lightly on the back, looks nonetheless behind her back at Luisa and theatrically rolls her eyes to show
that Clara is getting on her nerves. Luisa reciprocates the gesture
warmly.*)

Ha, nature! The greatest fear of a man is the fear of nature and
the fear of women. But greater still is the fear of his own body.

(*Shrill giggling from the Commandante who presses himself against
the child and rubs himself passionately against her. Clara pays no
attention to him.*)

CLARA: (*while behind her back Aélis shrugs her shoulders and
"speaks" to Luisa, with grimaces*) Those landscapes of horror in
those dead male heads! The darkness in nature as a man sees it
and subsequently represents it artistically! The old bourgeois
dream of the head as the seat of genius. (*She speaks now with
genuine feeling.*) Empty delusion of grandeur! A house with dark
passageways. The heavy burden of the head, he drags it along,
constantly. This mad search for something that has never yet

been written, composed, spoken. Ori . . . gi . . . na . . . li . . . ty! (*Nausea. She chokes. Aélis absentmindedly strokes her head.*) And, in addition, they constantly feel compelled to talk about it, . . . talk . . . talk . . . this yearning, constantly, for the most extreme expression of uniqueness . . . releases energy and the artistic machinery goes round and round . . .

AÉLIS: Calm yourself, dearest! Sooner or later it's going to happen, you know him after all. And—(*whispers*)—he can hardly do it anymore anyway. We've been maintaining the illusion for him for months . . . there are . . . tricks . . .

CLARA: (*screaming*) Tricks!

AÉLIS: Don't scream like that!

CLARA: (*bitterly*) Tricks.

AÉLIS: Well, yes. Or whatever you'd like to call them. If you come to my room after tea, I'll happily show you how . . .

CLARA: (*has not been listening, interrupts her fiercely*) This mania for self-realization. A woman pays for it. (*Exhausted*) An artist's wife pays for it. If she is an artist as well, then one by one her limbs rot away on her living body beneath the artistic production of her husband.

AÉLIS: Now listen to me for a moment! I want to help you! You need the money after all.

CLARA: An artist husband and an artist wife: the blood of the one cannot be separated from the other any more, the one lives in the other, they cannot be torn apart! Either they go together towards some new dawn or they fall, clawed into each other, into a ditch. But by then mostly the woman is already a withered root, while the male artist stands there, still full of sap.

MARIE: (*with the Commandante who is stroking and calming her, bawling*) I want raspberry juice! And then an ice cream with . . . slices of melon on it . . . like yesterday, at supper!

(*The Commandante is murmuring persuasively to her. Clara pays neither of them any attention.*)

AÉLIS: (*to Clara, not without sympathy, but somewhat amused*) Go and lie down, ma chère! Get some rest!

CLARA: No! I have to tell you this, Mademoiselle Mazoyer! I have to separate myself from those soulless piano machines Liszt and Thalberg.

AÉLIS: You are tired, Mrs. Schumann.

CLARA: First I will tell you more about my father, who molded me . . .

(*Screams from various corners of the room:* No! Nothing about Papa! Not again! No! Please, no! etc. *Clara pays no attention to them.*)

CLARA: (*impassioned*) My father was an exporter of pianos. All around, these dead instruments of art. You could hardly wend your way through them. Then there were these male clods who constantly worked away on them! These megalomaniacs! Provincial pianists! And then, every now and then amongst them, there was some shooting star, as they're called in our trade. Rarely. I tell you, Aélis, genius strangles any thought processes of productivity right from the beginning! I was surrounded, at every hour of the day I might add, by Chopin études, Liszt bravura pieces, and by the chronically overvalued Mozart. Only learned to speak when I was five. But my ear was as sharp as a razor. My father wrote my diary himself, while piano-bashers of all ages were feeling me up under my little dress. I couldn't say anything! And surrounding me was this country that incessantly spits out German artists and that is also German itself.

AÉLIS: (*comforting*) It couldn't have been as bad as that.

CLARA: It was! Worse! I insist on my extraordinary fate and my difficult youth like any other artist who has a right to something like that.

AÉLIS: Quel horreur!

COMMANDANTE: (*from the back, with effort, stroking the child*) This impenetrable, lifeless flesh, the solid prison of mankind. How tiring it is to bore your way into it. But now I see her soul, there it is! It reveals itself to me with the eloquence of music. A sensitivity that is delicate and mighty beyond all bounds. I sense that she loves me, not just my body.

CLARA: Only my specialized, finely-honed talent for pressing piano keys, in the right order I might add, always expressed itself outwardly. Anyone who practices can do it. Whoever practices more can do it better.

(*At this moment the Princess of Montenevoso, the wife of the Commandante, drags herself in, looks contemptuously at the group.*)

PRINCESS: I have heard that you are again offending my dignity as your wife while I am beneath your roof.

(*The Commandante leaps up and reverently kisses her hand, pushes Marie to the side.*)

By continually attracting female artists, which I have often . . . which I have often asked you not . . . which I have beseeched you on several occasions to . . .

(*He looks darkly at her, she loses the thread and falls silent.*)

COMMANDANTE: You know, Maria, that I need to have these creatures around me. Only they, these female artists, as you so contemptuously care to describe them, offer me the background before which my poetic vein begins to flow at its most splendid, do you understand? They create in their chaste frailty a flower; I, on the other hand, create the power of marble and the force of lightning and every shadow and every light. Do you understand me?
PRINCESS: Yes, my beloved!
COMMANDANTE: Go now, Maria!
PRINCESS: Gabriel! Ariel!
COMMANDANTE: Go!

(*The Princess drags herself off.*)

PRINCESS: (*in going*) I, of course, could never put up with this if my children were present. I shall write you a long letter from Monte and elaborate further on these ideas.

(*Clara turns around at the moment when the Commandante is turning back again to the child Marie. She notices what is going on, tears herself away from Aélis, who tries to restrain her so as not to disturb the pleasure of the Commandante. She rushes to the Commandante, tears her daughter away with her in Romantic exuberance.*)

CLARA: (*extremely excited*) Je vous supplie, si ce n'est pas de "l'aveugle rancune," expliquons-nous, parlons! Pourquoi ridiculiser les moments qui étaient beaux et spontanés? Je vous parle au nom du "clairvoyant amour"!

(*The child for her part wants to carry on, she tries to get away from her mother's hand, the Commandante grabs at her.*)

MARIE: (*faltering and childlike*) Haven't you noticed . . . dearest Mother . . . that I am already . . . at this relatively early age . . . excellent on my feet . . . but . . . ah . . . I am not yet capable of speaking. But my ear . . . has already . . . just like you when you were a child . . . developed . . . incredibly strongly. But more for . . . musical notes . . . than for language . . . That I should learn to speak . . . is something you . . . have never really bothered about . . . in your desire . . . to make . . . an inspired pianist of me . . . now I am nothing . . . but a pair of hands . . . on which a . . . body hangs.

(*She tries to go back to D'Annunzio. Clara however forces her into an embrace with her; the girl glances, standing on tip-toe, away over her mother's shoulders, back to the Commandante; Aélis and Luisa Baccara flutter around him.*)

CLARA: (*whispers into Marie's ear, frantically*) You'll stay here! One of the all too few pieces I have given birth to, and which is not a complete reject! Nothing but trash! Eight pregnancies, most of them completely in vain. A pity about the effort! One of them gone right away, he hardly lasted out the year: glands! The sons above all! Bad source material. Ludwig insane like his Papa, without the pleasure of relatives visiting him in the asylum. Ferdinand: drug addiction and a relatively quick end. Felix: TB, Julie: TB. You're the miserable remainder, little Marie.
MARIE: Let go, Mama! Let go! (*Tries to get away*)
CLARA: And during my all too frequent pregnancies, when my body swelled up like a pumpkin, I could not perform anywhere, of course. The financial and spiritual loss! Too much to inflict on the discerning music lover. And then all the time the shadow of the inspired father over his brood. His whining while we were traveling, this constant bellyaching because nobody knew him, but everyone knew me. This continual sense of being hurt and sitting around in hotels and inns with the appropriate facial expressions!
MARIE: Don't talk like that . . . about Papa . . . about my dear Daddy!

CLARA: And finally your father's imbecility. Unstoppable. My pregnant belly . . . this excess of nature, which a sensitive man can never bear . . . this well rounded form of femininity . . . all progress sinks before it . . . an artist often has to throw up at the sight of a puffed up abdomen . . . Now he says all the time, something's pulling him into Lake Garda, so that he can drown. He wants to disappear into nature. Earlier, along the Rhine, he had this idea as well. But he is really only afraid of disappearing into me, from whom for years on end, without stop, the fruits of his dick came crawling out. Revolting white larvae, you included, my dear Marie.

(*She gives her little smacks on the head, annoys her. Finally, Marie tears herself away and rushes, squealing and grinning stupidly, back to the Commandante, throws herself onto him, he strokes her lewdly.*)

CLARA: (*offended, looking after her*) The first chapter of the law of art is: Technique as the means. With technique as the end—the whole of art collapses!

(*The Commandante again carrying on intensely with Marie.*)

MARIE: (*fawning to the Commandante*) Afterward, can I . . . go and see the airplane . . . please, please . . . (*Hops around teasingly on his lap*)
COMMANDANTE: Of course, of course, my child. (*Uninterested, and in addition casually*) When you become serious, your mouth, in that pale face of yours, assumes an almost hard contour, as if it were being tormented by thirst, insatiable and created to attract, to take, to hold onto.
MARIE: The . . . beautiful . . . airplane!

(*In the meantime in a corner Luisa Baccara has set the tea table with the servant girls. Yellow roses, etc. She now taps out silent finger exercises on the table cloth, exchanging jealous pianist glances with Clara.*)

LUISA: (*to Clara*) I am the epitome of the Venetian woman pianist, while you stand for the honest but unimaginative representative of the German piano-players' guild. I am sloppy, generous, undisciplined in regard to tempi, but body-oriented and loveable. Simple and robust and afflicted with a dark complexion.

(*Clara stares at her briefly and uncomprehendingly, then she again rushes at the Commandante, who is just kissing Marie, and with the greatest despair, which stands in contrast to the content of her speech, expounds the following to him, while the pompous words of the Commandante are uttered more or less casually.*)

CLARA: Her ear! Her ear! My little Marie's ear can discern many things that others don't notice at all! I developed her slowly into a specialist just as my father for his part developed me magnificently back then. For all the keys she can quickly find the dominant and subdominant and she can modulate as well, whenever and in whatever way she wants!

(*The Commandante, with Clara getting on his nerves, motions to his loyal Aélis, behind Clara's back, that she should get rid of her.*

Aélis takes Clara by the arm and tries to lead her away, gently! Of course Clara resists!)

CLARA: (*hysterically*) It is the sexual side that kills us all. You too, Ariel! This sickness that kills naturally. It ruins even the deepest intimacy between man and wife. My father and Robert agreed on that. The destruction of me as a person happened quickly, by making me into a saint, an ideal figure. A passive presence, remote and harmless. As a result, for the whole time, I have never lived. But to be sure of my complete demise, Robert struck me completely dead with his genius.

AÉLIS: Come, calm yourself! You cannot carry on like that here. After all, you're not in your own home here! Here you only hear cries of that desire that lies close to death. As close as genius is to madness.

LUISA: And for all that she clearly plays the fast movement of the "Moonlight Sonata" too slowly. Like all Germans do, by the way. (*Bites into a peach, the juice runs*) If only one could be a singer. People marvel at a woman a whole lot more when she produces the various notes solely with her body without having to resort to instruments.

AÉLIS: (*kindly to her*) You shouldn't stuff yourself so much, chérie!

LUISA: But unfortunately in this opulent body there resides only an average singing voice at best. (*Continues to eat*)

CLARA: (*impassioned*) I myself was never allowed to compose. Although I wanted to very much. He made me believe that in his shadow I could not even want to do it. Genius wants to begin its journey into abstraction without a woman. A woman is only a bit of bone meal.

(*She tears herself away from Aélis who is comforting her and rushes at the Commandante and her daughter. Aélis wants to stop her. Clara throws herself on the cuddling pair of D'Annunzio and Marie. They fight her off.*)

CLARA: (*effusively*) She is becoming rather pigheaded, my little Marie! And uncontrollable in her desires! An artist is supposed to be humble, that's what my Robert says all the time. Because he has a gift that others don't have, the gift of being talented, says Robert. She even already plays—(*imploringly*)—little concertos, and I could name many of her own little compositional experiments! I, her mother!

(*Again the Commandante rasps asthmatically; in doing so, he involuntarily lets go of the child Marie, who presses childish kisses onto his eyes, snuggles up to him. Aélis leaves Clara and rushes to the man, checks the reflexes of his pupils, fills a syringe which is lying ready and gives it to him in a routine manner. The Commandante soon calms down. Lies still. Clara uses the opportunity to get her hands on her daughter. She lifts the child, who thrashes about, and quickly carries her out.*

Meanwhile, Luisa Baccara has been stuffing herself the whole time jealously and greedily with sweets, now and then she remembers Aélis with telling side-glances. Outside, a whining child's voice (Marie): I want to see the airplane! The airplane! Clara enters again. Clara kneels by the Commandante, feels his pulse, whispers imploringly)

Before you finally die now, Commandante, please, please, support my husband, even if it is only for a year! Please! And my daughter also needs sponsorship, as you have surely seen: her little compositions are for the most part rhythmically correct, the bass line reasonable. At least she does not double the major third as the leading note! Isn't that something? (*As if it were a matter of life or death*) I'll counter now the rumor that my little Marie lost her childhood too early through practicing. On the contrary: she shows feeling! For that, considerable financial expenditure is necessary!

COMMANDANTE: What makes a country famous? Without doubt its famous sons!

CLARA: Sons! Sons! As I was telling you, Gabriele, my sons were in quality even more miserable than the girls, with the exception of Marie. They wanted to compose too of course, the boys, but they never succeeded. Even less than I did. The shadow of their father hung over them like a lot of little axes. They were positively riddled with the metastases of his genius: conglomerations of the most serious illnesses, my sons.

(*Aélis brings in one of the village whores, helps her undress, motions to Clara to go to the piano and play something; Clara however proudly refuses. While the girl settles down with the half-senile poet*)

COMMANDANTE: I represent a gigantic financial and even greater ideological power. Even my prestige with the new people in power is high, it could not be any higher.

(*The girl kisses him.*
Now Luisa, who sees that her chance has come to make her mark, rushes to the piano and cheerfully plays a Rossini overture, "La gazza ladra" perhaps, keeps looking round to see whether she is getting the proper attention.)

CLARA: (*contemptuously*) Sloppy finger control! Wrist too limp. Technique and interpretation lax. Not to mention the choice of program.

COMMANDANTE: (*struggling for air. To the uncomprehending village girl*) Speak! Answer me! Tell me that you could not bear to see the dawn again without me, as I could not without you! Answer me!

(*Aélis motions the girl to say yes, which she does.*)

Maybe right now I'll make you that important son I told you about earlier. Maybe I'll make him now!

CLARA: Being a son means becoming like the father and thereby sealing your own death. Look at my three sons! A conglomeration of mortal suffering! Petrified limbs, little siliceous brains, eyes of quartz, withered heads, dependency of the worst kind.

COMMANDANTE: Later perhaps I could even sire a second son! And then a third! A fourth!

CLARA: From the beginning my maddest son just wanted to compose. He wanted to play every instrument right away, he had to be plucked away from harps, cellos, double basses, tubas, and trumpets. He suckered himself firmly to them like a snail. His mistake was that he thought genius consisted of progressing beyond what is already there. But genius is not supposed to overcome anything, the only thing it can do is put more stillborn babies into shrouds. Everything has existed for ages. Only a woman does not exist and must not exist.

COMMANDANTE: (*delightedly*) It's still going! What did you inject into me this time, Aélis? Phenomenal!

(*Luisa plays the "William Tell" overture.*)

CLARA: (*hysterically*) My God, everything exists already! There's no point trying to prove uniqueness. And nonetheless these composers spit out endless chains of words and music; the more they create, the more they lose their minds. Bubbles of words and notes!

COMMANDANTE: (*jubilating*) Yes! Yes! Now!

CLARA: (*turning to him as if from a dream, but he does not pay her any attention*) Tout passe, tout casse . . . et cette fougue doulour-ouse, si aigre, des derniers jours, passera peut-être, comme tout passe . . .

(*The door is torn open, the child Marie screams defiantly, stamping her foot.*)

MARIE: When can I finally go and see the beautiful airplane? I want to go now!

(*Aélis and a serving girl take the child Marie out again, calming her in an undertone and making promises. Two other serving girls stand around D'Annunzio and the village girl and applaud. The applause is a magical sound, which the two pianists recognize as if in a Pavlovian reflex, they become attentive. Luisa raises herself up halfway from her piano stool, curious, leans forward, bows. At this moment, Clara from behind her maliciously pulls away the stool and sits on it. Straightaway she begins to play Schumann's "Carnaval" or the "Kreisleriana." German school. Not paying any attention to the enraged Luisa, who wants to sit down again and none too gently flops down on the floor.)*

(Offended, Luisa goes to the table and starts stuffing down food again, pours herself champagne, etc.)

CLARA: *(elegiacally, playing)* All the time the annoying public surrounds us, wherever we go, we're never alone in private. We belong to the whole world, and the world belongs to him who takes it for himself. Right after the male genius comes the child genius, but there are even still fewer examples of them. I was once one of them. My father sent me into the pianistic desert. Everywhere these traps set with piano keys! Faced with this terrible aloneness, there was nothing left for me to do but increase further and further the variety and grade of difficulty in my piano playing by myself. *(She breaks off playing with a discord and hides her face in her hands. Quickly reconciled Luisa offers her a slice of melon.)* The thought of artistic fame as my goal in life started early. The world became my element. Apart from that a woman leaves it without a trace. I have even been compared with the child of an elf!

(Carlotta pirouettes in as if on cue. Performs ballet exercises, waves about with her arms)

CARLOTTA: As I hear, people are talking here about the essence of art. I too belong to this art and would like to make a statement about it now!

LUISA: I have delighted thousands with my wonderful piano playing, and those who could not hear me in person were able to hear me on the radio.

CARLOTTA: I express art exclusively with the help of the body, which means I can twist and turn every millimeter of myself in the most improbable ways. I am, you might say, the incarnation of art itself. Let me show you that more precisely! *(Dances)*

LUISA: Many who were permitted to hear me on the radio sent me a letter about it.

CARLOTTA: I received many more letters than you! They were the letters of thousands of ballet fans. Sometimes a rôle was even tailor-made for me.

LUISA: Thousands of times piano pieces were expressly dedicated to me! Personally created for me! Often at the sight of me a piano fanatic was gripped by a frenzy that took control of him. As soon as a piano music enthusiast saw me, desire took hold of him like tigers' claws around the throat. Luisa, Luisa, Luisa, he cried out then.

CARLOTTA: With me the ballet connoisseur cried out: Carlotta! Carlotta! Carlotta!

CLARA: (*has not been listening*) Luisa . . . listen . . . it is a dark, heavy burden when mental debility seizes an artist husband. Do you understand? We've come here to present to the Commandante with his incredible fortune this madness as genius. (*Startled, she falls silent.*)

COMMANDANTE: Yet again a woman is crying out for me. It is this woman here, I hear. (*Crawls towards Clara. Clings to her and drags her by the legs down to him; she cannot hold herself and falls over D'Annunzio.*)

AÉLIS: (*commentating*) Yes, yes. No one can resist him and no one has ever resisted him.

LUISA: (*giggling*) He is completely insatiable in his desires. In his physical cravings he can only be compared with your Goethe!

CARLOTTA: (*practicing ballet and giggling*) "He once told me—(in order to excite me!)—how Goethe when he had no woman handy, rather than waste time looking for one, would jerk himself off under his desk so as to be able to get back to work immediately."[1]

CLARA: Our prince of poets! (*Struggles with the Commandante*)

COMMANDANTE: (*panting*) And as far as quality is concerned, I am, as a prince of poets, his complete equal. Now look at me at last, chiara, carissima, with the eyes of a loving woman. Look! Go on! Look at me now with as much desire and imperiousness as possible. As if you were just at this moment sure of possessing that elixir of love that will bind me to you once and for all.

---

[1] In English in the original German text.

CLARA: (*pushes him away and scrambles to her feet*) Aha. So you also want to be a prince of poets. Ariel. Gabriele D'Annunzio! And us women in soundproof, lifeless holes in the ground.

COMMANDANTE: Answer me! Answer me with a *YES!*

CLARA: (*scornfully*) The role of the passive, remote saint is often assigned to us as well. As I've already said, I am more the elf-child. Sometimes also called for short the angel-child. Sitting at the piano and thinking up songs. And as she strokes the piano's keys, in magic circles there appear and flee, one person upon another, one scene upon the next, an aged erlking, a serene Mignon, a valiant knight in his armor of light, a nun on her knees in her prayer's ecstasy. The people who heard it, they roared and raged, as if they were offering a singer praise. The angel-child though in great dismay, then lightly homeward wends her way. Did you get that bit about the nun, Luisa, my love?

LUISA: Better that one about the singer. Personally I always got more applause than Patti, Melba, and Malibran combined.

COMMANDANTE: (*coughing*) Probably a woman is more like nothingness. Nothingness! One cannot really touch her. Better to stare at a naked flame for hours than work one's way into a woman. A woman, you see, has an insatiable craving, which a man can never satisfy. The result: fear! Therefore, one must turn a woman into something repulsive, possibly even something putrefying, so that it makes you sick. (*He vomits loudly into a bowl, which Aélis has quickly held out to him.*) And just the thought of it has made me throw up. From revulsion. Sometimes a woman is also a grave, much more often a sort of butcher or even a cook. (*Retches again*)

LUISA: (*hurrying to him*) My beloved Commandante! Gabriel! Ariel! Ariosto!

CLARA: (*disgusted*) My father, the piano salesman I'm constantly talking about, once said in company a cheeky snowflake had flown onto his arm, and look! That snowflake was me! But to a man who can say something as tasteless as that about the butcher, I can't tell him about the snowflake. (*Plays "Carnaval" again*)

COMMANDANTE: Sublime moment of no return! Even before the soul is aware of it, the hands are already making their grasping movements. They're enjoying the flesh that they have attracted.

CLARA: Gabriele, listen. I'm telling only you this because I trust you! Since the outbreak of his madness, my husband Robert speaks only of his extraordinary products, but he is not producing anything at all anymore! His madness seems to me and to him the reason why he cannot generate any delicate creations of sound any more.

(*Luisa feeds the Commandante tenderly and teasingly, bills and coos childishly with him as if with a little child, playing tickling and teasing games etc. Disgusted, Clara plays Schumann.*)

COMMANDANTE: (*to the pleasantly surprised Luisa Baccara*) Louise, ma chère! Je reçois votre lettre qui me déchire trop doucement. Le malentendu se prolonge. Je vous attendais tandis que vous m'attendiez. Venez!

(*Groaning, he crawls to his feet supporting himself on Luisa. She continues to support him and, looking with triumph at Clara and Aélis and the practicing Carlotta, she leads him off. Commandante from off-stage: J'attends, j'espère! Je veux!*)

AÉLIS: (*to Clara, dryly*) Well, the tour to America seems to be in the bag! (*To the serving girl*) "Clean up the mess, please!"[2]
CLARA: (*despondent*) Aélis, you've got to help me!
AÉLIS: Oh, yes?
CLARA: I can't pay for me, for Robert, the child, and the attendants, not even for a single night in a cheap rooming house if I have to leave here. Even in the off-season!
AÉLIS: (*sympathetically and in solidarity*) Has it been so long since you've had any income then, my dear?
CLARA: What do you think an asylum like that costs. In the end I had to take him out of it. The Commandante is our last hope. (*Ardently*) Do you think he heard that about the snow flake before or not? Should I perhaps tell him that I'm at the crossroads between child and girl?
AÉLIS: Don't exaggerate!
CLARA: Honestly, I'm not exaggerating. That story about denying the body doesn't carry much weight with him. Should I rather say that a woman is a silent, but rotting hole?

---

[2] In English in the original German text.

AÉLIS: Don't say that. He already threw up before when he heard that. You shouldn't choose such unappetizing comparisons. Is that supposed to be typically German?

CLARA: The German loves his excrement more than any other race, just look at the typical German toilet! I need the money!

AÉLIS: (*with sympathy*) "I could advise you to find a way to please him in the nude, because he is especially curious about your physical characteristics. But I'm sure you will tell me now how timid you are in his presence and say that as soon as you stop your piano playing you become almost ugly, like a post."[3]

(*Desperately Clara hits her fist against her head.*)

Just look around you! Do you think a man like that will fall for the art bit?

(*She points to the architectural monstrosities around everywhere.*)

CLARA: I still think the longer I resist him, which he's not used to, the more precious I'll become to him.

AÉLIS: Maybe, maybe not. The day before yesterday he suggested I should fuck him one of these nights, outside your room, moaning loudly, and finally crying out, just to arouse your jealousy, but at the same time your fear, that you might have no value for him at all.

CLARA: Should I pretend I'm going to leave?

AÉLIS: It may work, then again it may not.

CLARA: Later at dinner I will in any case—(*sobbing*)—speak of the enormous pain of the act of production and the desire for the product. (*Crying*) I will describe the man-devouring landslides of my Papa and my husband. Always connected to money, that shit of the dead.

AÉLIS: (*with sympathy*) . . . which at this moment you so desperately need, my dear.

(*Shrugging her shoulders, she exits snipping off a few withered blossoms from a plant. Since she no longer has to keep control of herself, Clara now slumps, with all signs of despair, at the piano, plays a few bars of Schumann.*)

---

[3] In English in the original German text.

CLARA: (*seriously, not hysterically*) They kept on and on at Robert for so long for the musical ideas to come out of his head, until it finally burst. This horrible love of abstractions! This total abstraction, music! Everything that comes out of the body, a child for example, everything is for a man a source of revulsion. At the same time he constantly encourages a woman to bear children, to stop her producing her own art. He does not want to see any competition grow up. (*She plays.*) The only thing that comes out of a man's body is every now and then a lethal ulcer or a suppurating tumor you can pierce. These cerebral giants! They work against their bodies. These inhibitions that lead to the final mortal illness of the head! They deny the body, push it onto the woman, and the creative head explodes. (*She plays Schumann.*)

(*The curtain falls.*)

Part 2

(*Dining room. Just as cluttered as the salon. From the ceiling hangs either a big model of an airplane or a part of an airplane (the latter, however, in its natural size). Large, sumptuously set table with all sorts of extravagance and flowers. The characters from before sit around the table in great disorder, continually change places, eat in a very unappetizing way, throw bones on the floor, etc.*

Choreography!

The Commandante, who in Part 1 wore a brocade dressing gown, now wears a Fascist uniform with shining riding boots, along with a riding crop. At a children's table to the side sits the mad composer Robert S. with two asylum attendants who must appear really dumb and who look after him roughly. Cops. Shaved heads. White laboratory coats.

Clara again leaps up and hurries to the window, gracefully leans out, shades her eyes with her hands.)

CLARA: (*impassioned*) My arms are bared to the neck and perfect in their form. From them you can easily gather that I was once a blossom onto which a late cold frost fell. This frost is that madness, which in an artist you can call maturity.

ROBERT: (*equally impassioned, but with flickering eyes*) Wonderful suffering! Marvelous wounds! (*He giggles.*) Afflictions of the ear! Angels! Taking away from me now completely the writing of symphonies. With everything that goes with it! Fine! Still more hallucinations! Angels sometimes relieved by devils. This wonderful illness of the head. It takes up my whole existence so that I can't find any room in it any more. Today I'll throw our ring into Lake Garda for the third time. This time I hope no one will bring it back again. The ring became superfluous once the wife overtook the husband, slipped while she was doing it. (*Giggles*) Pains in the head!

(*Attendant force-feeds him.*)

COMMANDANTE: (*bites Luisa on the neck*) The most beautiful symphony for me is the sound of a motor. Sometimes in a land that is less affected by a Mama's molly-coddling than our Italy, a man gets the idea that he has to up and away, wife and child cling to him and say, stay in here and down here, but he pushes them away, painstakingly services his flying machine, and rises up and away. That's what happened with Charles Lindbergh, who crossed the Atlantic. He knew: I have to get over there now and cross and cross and cross.

ROBERT: (*gives a shrill giggle. An attendant hits him on the hand with a spoon because he is about to tip the whole saltshaker onto his food*) In my exaltation I am inclined to confuse the ideal with life, fulfillment with that which we hope for! But no matter what comparison I make, my little Clara has to be the loser. Especially in regards to the common comparison with the ideal.

(*Clara leaps at him, buries her head in his lap, the attendants push her away like a piece of wood because she is disturbing the feeding procedure.*)

CLARA: (*nonetheless impassioned*) My sacred heart of Jesus! My magician of music! Think positively, so that you'll get better! These painful meetings with the growth in your brain kill all the joy of the present for you. You could fill up this time, for instance, with composing.

(*Robert giggles childishly.*)

ROBERT: Choirs of angels! Suddenly choirs of devils! Then very pretty melodies.

CLARA: (*to the Commandante*) Listen, Gabriele, he's composing all the time! He's his old self again, your artist colleague. Soon the symphony will appear in print.

COMMANDANTE: A man strives for conquests. He conquers either a foreign territory, as far away as possible, a woman or a corridor in the air. The deluded masses applaud him. The masses are body-oriented like a woman. One can take possession of them whenever one chooses. Only yesterday I saw a huge mass of young bodies in athletic clothes. Black gym shorts and white tops. Very pretty. Tasteful. They were swinging clubs. Wonderful.

LUISA: (*to Aélis who is keeping a watch on the table*) Have you read that book by him? Where page after page their bodies convulse, while some sort of juice runs down them, because they're moving so suddenly. Mostly pomegranate juice. It stains their rustling clothing. And then a body trembles passionately, and someone sinks down into a stream that's either boiling or freezing. And after it's gone on like that for ten pages or so the woman says: I am leaving with the others now. I'll meet you in an hour at the fence of the Gradenigo garden or at this or that cypress, which we will have to agree on. (*She giggles.*)

(*Aélis threatens Luisa playfully and puts something more onto her plate. Whenever the Commandante looks at her, Carlotta makes graceful arm and hand movements, but he pays her no attention.*)

ROBERT: Genius lies down like a heavy delusion on the pistons of my artistic machinery. Now there's a note coming! Listen! (*Quavering, he sings a note.*) Don't you hear anything?

CLARA: (*enthusiastically*) Yes. My dearest, now you have it! You've already made a start. Go on!

COMMANDANTE: I don't hear anything.

(*The women parody Clara, draw each other's attention to notes that cannot be heard, laugh silently, press their hands to their mouths, writhe with silent laughter.*)

ROBERT: Unfortunately I've got a production block, sorry. For the moment it is stuck in the tumor in my head that will have to grow and explode first. Ouch, this pain in my head! (*Takes hold of his head*) I'm going to scream out loud. (*Does so*)

COMMANDANTE: (*is clearly losing his patience. Takes an orange from the fruit basket. To the child Marie*) If you find the orange and eat it up where you find it without using your hands, then you'll get one of those jewelry pieces Roman society is justifiably so famous for throughout the world.

(*With a squeal of delight Marie leaps up, the Commandante hides the orange somewhere under the table cloth on his own person, Marie crawls without hesitating under the table and attends to it during this sequence. Clara does not notice anything of this.*)

PRINCESS: (*who has been quiet the whole time, holding herself aloof*) You do this under the gaze of your wife, Gabriele, even though your recently drug-addicted son is not here. Don't do it!

COMMANDANTE: But I will do it, I am doing it! Now more than ever!

(*Carlotta makes ridiculously graceful movements.*)

ROBERT: (*becoming lively*) Purple wounds, playing into violet. The head can always convince itself of its own strength. Great ideas! In a woman they just appear as bubbles of air. Often fetuses. Now even a shadow of a great deed. Bodily illnesses piled one on top of the other. Disgusting nature! Here, as in Germany, a woman is extremely dangerous. Dis . . . gusting representations of nature.

CLARA: A musical idea, not a poetic one. Robert! Music! Some money-making creativity for the piano and violin. Get on with it! Your material conditions just have to take on a completely different complexion.

ROBERT: (*rationally, taking the spoon away from the attendant and eating relatively respectably by himself*) None of those music-loving females, who crowded in on me with their bodies, worm-ridden with their enthusiasm, was in any way able to bind me to her permanently. Besides which their letters teemed with stylistic and grammatical mistakes. They were never the women I was supposed to take them for.

CLARA: (*tries to kiss him, he turns his head away*) Say that thing about the angel child, Robert! The Commandante wants to hear it again!

COMMANDANTE: Not at all. Definitely not. What I want to hear is the familiar droning of airplane engines. (*Moans loudly. Marie is doing something under the table.*)

ROBERT: My skull! My fontanel! Nature is dreadful! It causes this pain in my head. And in the meantime angels look after the progress of my art.

COMMANDANTE: (*to Aélis. Moaning briefly he places the child's head in a different position*) In the past we invited the most beautiful women in society to bite into fruit. And then the bitten fruit was auctioned off for a lot of money, for an orphanage or a maternity home. The mouths of men roughly widened the tiny bite wounds in the apple. Money was even requested for being allowed to drink from the cupped hands of beautiful women. The highest amounts were offered to Countess Scerni to wipe her hands dry on a blond beard. Once I received from Countess Luconi, I don't know for what price, a Havana cigar that she had earlier held in her armpit.

CLARA: (*disgusted*) Oh, ugh! Ugh! Ugh!

(*Aélis laughs, twittering coquettishly; Luisa joins in, tries to wipe her hands on the Commandante, but he gives her a whack. Carlotta dances again.*)

Where have you put my daughter?

COMMANDANTE: Yes, wherever have I put your daughter Marie? Yes, where? Do you know, Aélis?

AÉLIS: No, no idea.

(*A hubbub of women's voices: No! Where is she? Yes, where is she? etc.*)

COMMANDANTE: (*to Clara*) "Wonder what you are doing alone in your bed, all alone with your legs spread! I'm waiting for your soulful kisses you told me about, the way you liked to be kissed under the armpits and so on."[4]

---

[4] In English in the original German text.

CLARA: The mother animal is going to scream loudly: Marie, Marie! (*Screams. Marie under the table, half-choking in the clothes*)

MARIE: Here I am, mother.

(*With a scream of rage Carla hurls herself under the table and drags her somewhat disheveled daughter from under it by the legs, her pants can be seen, the Commandante is quite delighted.*)

CLARA: (*impassioned*) Pay for . . . the symphony! Recognize . . . the tune!

COMMANDANTE: (*to Clara*) Your Robert won't be creating anything with his shattered senses! And even if he were to create, then he would have to flee the larger audience like that deadly disease that finally caught up with him. My dream, as the poet Gabriele D'Annunzio, is to be a unique specimen, devoted to the unique woman, giving up every benefice except love. The true connoisseur of my art cannot be whoever buys my books, but whoever loves me. The laurel wreath only serves to attract the myrtle.

CLARA: (*despairing, Robert giggles happily*) But fame! The world!

COMMANDANTE: Comes only after death as every pupil knows. Consequently not enjoyed during lifetime. Unfortunately, unfortunately.

CLARA: But our pecuniary situation!

COMMANDANTE: Can be improved decisively in no time by surrendering your body, dearest.

CLARA: (*sobs loudly*) But a body like that is only enough for fourteen days at the most!

COMMANDANTE: Yes, yes. Art lasts longer, I have to admit that.

MARIE: Is that the airplane? (*Marie goes to the huge airplane fuselage and fingers it curiously.*)

COMMANDANTE: Get away from that airplane right now. It has to be protected from damage. It's not for children's hands. Women too, unconscious as they are, can never bear the element of automatism, of being moved automatically. Only a man is made to be a machine in a machine and therefore to speed across the water in a motorboat or to rise up into the air.

(*Surprised and enthusiastic exclamations from the women around the stage.*)

Robert suddenly, for inexplicable reasons, extremely lively. A moment of clarity. He grabs the heads of his two attendants and cracks them together so that they both remain, dazed and groggy, sitting in their chairs. Carlotta waves her arms about. No one pays her any attention. Luisa quietly and piggishly gulps down food, then smears the Commandante's face with chocolate so that it looks like shit, giggles drunkenly. The Commandante distractedly kneads Luisa's body without letting the German artist couple out of his sight.)

ROBERT: *(rationally)* When you were explaining about the machine, Colonel, it suddenly occurred to me how incapable my wife Clara has always been of independently composing music. Of producing the magic of art. She cannot even comprehend the border between sanity and madness. I cross this border every day as if it were the most natural thing in the world, back and forth, back and forth. The secret of madness has to remain alien to her. Because madness is silent. Yet not even against her artistic impotence was she able to take decisive steps. No way of working it off. No sport in forests, no senseless running through park landscapes. Even today she still does not understand that the very thought of a product of genius has to peter out in a ludicrous seedling box of unconnected notes. *(Laughs good-humoredly, but rationally)* The only effect of her attempts at composition was the gradual dying off of her female sexual attraction for me. *(He pats the two growling heads beside him good-naturedly.)*

CLARA: *(coldly)* Whoever thinks of me, thinks of me not as a brother thinks of his sister or a boyfriend of his girlfiend, but as a pilgrim thinks of some far-off altarpiece.

(Immediately Robert cracks up again, he throws himself naughtily to the floor and bites into the rug; the attendants, still somewhat dazed, look after him. Robert screeches shrilly on the floor. Those eating at the table leap up to enjoy the spectacle. The Commandante again lures the child Marie to him, by holding something up in the air, she jumps up high to get it, he holds it higher and higher; eventually, Aélis takes the child under her arms and raises her so that she can grasp the object. With cries of joy she looks at it and smothers the Commandante, who whispers something into her ear, with kisses. The child laughs happily. She is kissed and stroked. Again Luisa leaps up in jealousy and tries to get between them.

Aélis, however, skillfully pushes a big blue grape into her mouth so that, groaning and almost choking, Luisa falls back again into her chair.)

ROBERT: (*screeching*) I am an enfant terrible. A word I just heard for the first time! Now I know exactly what it is. (*Sings a few bars of an operetta melody*)

LUISA: (*has finally swallowed the grape, in rage*) That's what *I* am! That's what *I* am, this enfant! I have explained in detail why.

ROBERT: (*childishly*) No, *I* am, no *I* am! The first time when I was almost certain I was to lose my mind, Clara was just turning from a child into a young woman. The doctor said: Find yourself a wife, she'll cure you straightaway. I found Ernestine von F., my first sensible betrothed, but I cast her out later in favor of Clara, the hyena-virtuoso. (*Giggles shrilly*) Since I have known her, I have been planning and making drafts nonstop for completely new compositions; now I'm going to sing at last the beginning of my new symphony!

(*He sings the first bars of a well-known, light-classic piece from the international concert scene that everybody knows: the "Blue Danube Waltz" or Beethoven's Fifth, for example. The choice is entirely up to the director. But nothing by Schumann, of course.)*

LUISA: (*bursting out laughing*) But it seems to me, Master, that this bold, modern work already exists!

(*Robert sings more and more impassionedly, laughter at the table, those present fall screeching over each other. Clara is being driven to distraction, stamps with her foot, tugs at Robert, no success.)*

ROBERT: (*while singing, briefly interrupting this*) The mechanism is overwound! Here again I've found another masterless sound that I pick out of the air. Now it's still my own private property, soon it will be the property of the general public: it consists of a few thousand concertgoers, though that means in the whole world. (*Sings. Breathlessly stopping*) Scabies, mange, sepsis, pus, secretion . . . pile of shit! (*Sings impassionedly*) The composer wafts away, the singer sings the high note. (*Sings it*)

CARLOTTA: Didn't anyone see the arm movement I just made?

CLARA: (*screaming*) My magnificent Robert . . . into an asylum! No!

COMMANDANTE: (*absentmindedly, looking down on Robert*) There are of course some sports that keep a person on the ground where he can, at best, practice at the greatest of speeds. But the air is the real element, though only as long as just a few can rise up into it.

CLARA: I have been sacrificed in the sacred place of your genius, Robert!

(*As Clara becomes quieter and colder, the Commandante turns away from her and towards the other women, takes lilberties with them, feeds them.*

Clara quietly to Robert, who splashes things around in the dining room, splatters the attendants' faces with ice cream and is smacked for doing so.)

This ghastly marriage to you! Every time I went to the piano and wanted to compose, I found the apparatus already occupied: by you!

(*Provokingly Robert sings the catchy tune from before.*)

Playing the piano was my way of earning a living, mostly our only one! Now I have to rely on my flesh and bones!

COMMANDANTE: (*casually to the others*) "The cold weather and the ride in the Mas have given me a terrible hunger but especially a great desire to chiavare."[5] (*Turning his back to the audience, exposing himself to Aélis—the child is still sitting on his back—he tries to reach the airplane from this position, to start it. To Aélis*) "Can't you see what a state the little prince is in? I hope this horrible German woman will leave soon! All the people at the station have rushed up to me, some yelling "Prince," others "Excellency," and the German woman has been dumbfounded."[6]

(*Aélis claps; this is the signal for Luisa who, unsteady and rather drunk, goes to the piano and in an unsteady tempo plays the same catchy tune that Robert has been humming.*)

---

[5] In English in the original German text; the word 'chiavare' is used in Italian in the original.

[6] In English in the original German text.

ROBERT: (*roaring*) Une tigresse! Lioness! For whom I've been long-ingly waiting my whole life! A companion who would be my equal! Bravo, bravissimo! (*Leaps at Luisa, the attendants hold him with difficulty.*) My ear! My wonderful ear! How absolutely clear! Coming over me is a spiritual bond with a female mind! Hourrah! How clearly I can hear it!

(*The asylum attendants are half-dragged along with him.*)

Nobody else hears it, understands it! My ears cover my body like antennae. Tactile hairs. My sensuality is awoken by genuinely real art. There it is! Cilia! You there! Hurrah! Do you compose without hands? My ear completely suppresses my thoughts, how beautiful! I am a breathing mountain. Mount Olympus, in fact. I can hear the movement of the drafts of air, loudly, pounding around like giant herds of machinery! You there! Hey!

CLARA: (*despairing*) When a woman's abilities develop beyond the norms of time, the result is a monstrosity. She is an offense against the proprietary rights of him in whose service the she-animal must put herself. A woman's mind is just there—(*in extreme agitation*)—for the creation of new dishes and taking out the trash. (*Collapses in exhaustion*)

ROBERT: (*jubilant*) Yes! Play that transition once again, you wonderful woman, you!

CLARA: I was not even allowed to use the second piano we got later to practice on, so that I wouldn't disturb him while he was creating!

COMMANDANTE: (*watching the driveling Robert with enjoyment*) But what if, for example, I too were to lose my mental powers. The slow decay of the mind can happen unconsciously as well. An artist who is struck in his mental powers need have no aware-ness of his own mental debility, just as the mentally ill person—(*points like a ringmaster at Robert*)—has no awareness of his own insanity. Panic-stricken fright!

(*Cry of great delight. Aélis lets herself sink backwards, smiles, violent movement from the Commandante. Marie almost falls down off him, desperately holds on tightly, squeals in annoyance. Robert falls around the neck of one of the attendants, kisses him ecstatically all over, gently; the man is totally bewildered, fights him off, but Robert develops immense strength. D'Annunzio has now tidied himself up, hops around with the child Marie and follows, as if in a theater, the events that are coming to a head between Clara and Robert.)*

ROBERT: *(tenderly to the attendant, who is warding him off)* Dearest fellow, I compose so hard every day, be nice! Mostly my ear works against it and ruins everything again. But not today! Listen! Here you can hear one fruit of my work. *(Loudly and madly he sings the catchy tune from before, accompanied by Luisa at the piano. The Venetian laughs resoundingly while playing: a good joke.)* Little by little the ear destroys—*(sings)*— composed material that is already finished. *(Sings)* What remains—*(sings)*—is insanely complicated and very modern! A musical torso! *(Sings. After a while he falls silent, exhausted.)*

(Pause. Outside the windows the sound of boot steps. Parade. Pause. Then from outside the Giovinezza can be heard. Those present fall silent, the Commandante stands at attention.)

CLARA: *(waves hectically with newspaper pages)* Let me read my reviews and those of Robert.

COMMANDANTE: Silence!

CLARA: *(is hissed into silence, occupies herself excitedly with the newspapers)* Here . . . listen . . . read it yourself! *(Reads aloud)* 'I tell you and I'll write it at any time in my new music journal that in your . . . he means in *my*, the swine! . . . piano concert first of all a young phoenix wings its way skywards. White yearning roses and pearling lily calyxes. Within them a radiant girl's face. Boats boldly over the ways . . . and *ONLY A MASTER'S HAND AT THE HELM IS LACKING, FOR IT, SO VICTORIOUSLY AND QUICKLY TO . . .*'

(At this moment there is a strident attack of laughter from Robert. Clara stands stiff and enraptured. The child Marie breaks the silence with her crying.)

MARIE: Papa, I am scared! There are so many noises! Papa! *(To the Commandante)* Does the beautiful airplane also fly, Uncle?

(She is calmed immediately. Luisia drunkenly plays the catchy tune. Robert conducts along. Impassioned. Clara furious and jealous)

ROBERT: This . . . lady here—(*he means Luisa*)—is wonderful. She has never trashed me. She is a good woman! Plays my thoughts even before they have been thought out! Those notes of originality come shooting out of me at supersonic speed, she catches them in the air. Bravo!

(*Clara heaves violently.*)

My ear! This torture of the ears! Penetrating into all my bodily orifices. A mastering of the ear won't succeed. Ear eats thoughts. A head, that's what I am, totally. (*Giggles, spits out spinach*)

CLARA: (*in despair*) Your great F-sharp Minor Sonata is nothing but a cry of the heart unto me that I am not allowed to respond to. I respond to the cry through my art!

(*About to go to the piano to play the F-sharp minor sonata, but Luisa is already sitting there grinning spitefully. Clara pulls her off the stool. Luisa falls down and cries. Clara sits down and plays Schumann, which makes the composer terribly angry. He tries to throw himself on her but is kept firmly in check by his attendants.*)

(*plays sobbing*) By means of carefully placed childbirths you torpedoed my modest progress again and again. You did not review my Piano Concerto Op. 7 in your journal! Instead of that you sang the praises of that Sterndale-Bennett! And yet all the time my music was like a sheep bleating only unto you, my beloved! And a good pianist has an intrinsic creativity! Is creative!

(*Little Marie rubs herself backwards and forwards against the neck of the Commandante so long until they both fall down. The women hurry over to help, calling out in doing so: Are you hurt, Commandante? For God's sake! etc. Only Carlotta continues waving her arms movements as before, a pile of bodies on the floor. Clara: F-sharp Minor Sonata of Schumann ecstatically, Robert becomes white-hot with rage.*)

ROBERT: Stop! Away! Away with this trash, intended for foreigners, composed by foreigners! Junk Dilettantism! Bad quality! Unoriginal! Spitting out horror! Fear of losing potency! The result of a puritanical gearbox in the head.

(*Vomits loudly on the middle of the table. The Commandante creeps disgusted, shocked, and bewildered to Clara, whimpers.*)

COMMANDANTE: "Just look, darling, at my torment and my emotion . . . May I kiss you under the armpits! Please?"[7]

CLARA: (*triumphantly plays Schumann*) In faithfulness unwavering! Do you hear it? Do you hear how beautifully I play it: your F-sharp Minor Sonata?

ROBERT: (*has torn himself away, rushes at Clara again*) Infernal music! The one from before! Play the new work! The one the other lady played!

CLARA: But this supposedly new work from before already exists, Robert!!! This is your F-sharp Minor Sonata!

ROBERT: (*shrilly*) You beast! Devil! In this trashy music I miss that boundlessness I always have within myself! Give the woman the myrtle wrath!

CLARA: (*plays*) But Robert . . . this was composed by you back then, an original piece, exactly like this . . . do you want to see the music? Robert, the music! Breitkopf and Härtel, Leipzig. Black on white! "Sonata in F-sharp minor" by Schumann, Robert.

ROBERT: (*white-hot with rage*) You bitch! Woman! Falsifier! Killer of the artist's product! Killer of the spirit! Murderess of potency! (*Weeps*) The musical heritage a heavy burden. Don't you see— (*suddenly quiet and in despair*)—Clara, how my thoughts are always moving on? The mechanics for this lie in those thoughts themselves! I can't do anything to stop it! Nothing! (*Shakes Clara insistently, who desperately plays on*)

MARIE: (*from a distance*) Let Mama go, Papa! Let go!

CLARA: (*with difficulty*) Help!

ROBERT: Stop it! (*Throws himself at her*) Enough! Enough, child!!

CLARA: (*calmly*) When you call me child, that sounds nice, but when you think of me as a child, then I will step forward and say: you are wrong!

ROBERT: (*formulating with difficulty, pulls Clara from the stool*) I want to hear my composition again, the one that the beautiful lady played before so perfectly in tempo and dynamics! Not this pile of musical trash! It is probably one of your own lousy products! Ugh! Ugh! That's disgusting!

CLARA: Robert! What I am playing here was composed by you. Your F-sharp Minor Sonata!

---

[7] In English in the original German text.

ROBERT: (*now wrestles with her. The others form a silent circle around them. The attendants do not intervene, stand nevertheless at the ready.*) A pretty house, not far from town, blissfully and quietly living with you! You would of course cultivate your art. (*Groans, because Clara is beginning to strangle him.*) But not so much for everyone and because of earning a living, as for a few select people, especially for me! And for the sake of our happiness! (*Groans more strongly*)

CLARA: (*groaning with the effort*) Tell me this one thing: Why do you avoid every opportunity of mentioning me in your journal? (*Chokes him more and more violently*)

ROBERT: (*already half suffocated*) That from before . . . my head . . . ouch! . . . Ouch, ouch, that hurts! . . . Pain in the head . . . Artistic achievement lies beyond a woman . . . for only natural achievements of the body count for her . . . for the very reason . . . a woman . . . is . . . pure nature. (*Dies, strangled by Clara*)

CLARA: (*getting up exhausted*) Skilled, powerful fingers well trained with discipline are also good for something. Before that, it just went deeply into the art of knitting, stitching, and sewing.

(*Examines her fingers, does a few finger exercises to make them supple again. The rest of the characters stand around in deathly silence.*)

CLARA: (*with difficulty*) The world of the male genius is the landscape of death. The cemetery.

(*Curtain falls slowly.*)

Epilogue

(*The same room as in Part 1. Only this time at one of the high windows there is erected a sort of alpine garden (imitation of the Zugspitze), made of stone blocks. On it, high up, there is a summit cross. The whole thing should be as high as possible. On the mountain there grows gentian, rhododendron, and edelweiss. Perhaps a clear brook made of plastic could run over it. At the foot of the mountain Clara is sitting with Robert's head in her lap; she has strangled him. But no Catholic pietà atmosphere! She is wearing a dirndl. The two*) *asylum attendants watch her from some distance. They wear: knickerbockers, white knee-high socks, and brown shirts. The other characters lounge around in a loose grouping. They are wearing fashionable ski clothes, very chic and exclusive, ski caps and pullovers. Only the Commandante has kept his uniform on. And Aélis has also not changed. Against the walls lean skis. Incidentally, on the top of the mountain lies a little snow. The light shines in such a way that it illuminates the mountaintop and the cross on it in a radiant and somewhat supernatural light. The whole thing is of course a little corny!)*

CLARA: (*to Robert's head*) Above all, I am amazed at your mind, at all that is new in the "Kreisleriana" for instance. Also at your great F-sharp Minor Sonata, whose authorship you so callously denied a moment ago. Actually, you know, I am sometimes terrified of you, is it really true that this is what became of your husband?

COMMANDANTE: (*shaking his head*) For the first time I find myself now before one of those rare female feelings that light up the gray and changeable sky of human love affairs like a beautiful and terrible streak of lightning. (*Lightning flashes over the alpine garden.*) It does not bother me.

CLARA: Sometimes I get the idea that I could not satisfy you, but you could love me always for that reason! Now at least I understand everything and your music, that's enough to make me happy. (*Kisses the head*)

(*Another lightning flash on the alpine garden, soft rumbling of thunder, still very muffled*)

LUISA: (*to Aélis*) My sleeping car leaves in half an hour and still no sign of the police.

AÉLIS: Patience, dearest! We are somewhat remote, and today there is another parade.

CLARA: A completely new feeling is coming over me, a feeling that I summoned up myself. What an artist experiences, he converts right away into a work. He experiences everything more deeply than the nonartist.

CARLOTTA: (*doing ski exercises*) All the time I can hear those weak little beaks pecking from outside, those who have never gone to a concert or a play in their lives. Sometimes they softly screech out. Puny birds!

LUISA: (*chewing*) Loneliness is also often the price of fame.

CARLOTTA: Those birds I spoke of, outside, would gladly be lonely if only they were famous!

(*Both of them giggle.*)

PRINCESS: Please, show some respect for the dead, ladies.

(*Lightning. Clara smothers the head with kisses. Sheet lightning in the sky, soft thunder*)

CLARA: (*suddenly crying out*) Robert, I will get you the edelweiss from up there! From the steep mountaintop. (*She starts to climb the alpine garden, small stones start rolling down.*) But I do not want to frighten the timid wildlife, not the chamois, and not the even more timid ibex.

(*Those standing around are disconcerted. Clara climbs, a light wind has arisen and blows through the room, the gentle power of nature can be sensed.*)

Do say something, Robert! While you were alive, you only piled up stillbirths in the sand, perhaps your death has freed your musical language from madness. Now I have no fear of female nonconformity any more and at this moment I am climbing a phallic symbol. And you can't do anything to stop me! (*She climbs.*)

(*Now and then a gust of wind, doors spring open, but still restrained.*)

CLARA: (*fighting with the mountain*) A man depicts things, a woman is depicted. I did nothing but depict your masterpiece on the piano. (*Pants. Reaches the edelweiss, the wind becomes stronger.*) A man froths over with potency. A woman only froths within herself. Clothes detergent, hopelessly encased in the machine.

(*She has the edelweiss, comes down with it, sliding in a shower of stones, puts the flower into Robert's mouth like a small green branch into the mouth of a shot deer.*)

I am half-sick with joy, this time at your wondrous "Fantasie"! (*The roaring of the wind gets louder. In the room things start to move.*) When I think of it, I always go hot and cold. But tell me what sort of spirit you have so that I can try to copy it. Once I am completely united with you, then I will not think of composing any more! I'd be a fool! (*Howling wind. She kisses Robert.*) You could only write your "Novelettes" because you touched such lips as mine! I always had a strange fear of showing you my compositions, I was always ashamed. Even of my Idyll in A-flat major. (*She suddenly pushes the corpse away from herself, pants.*)

COMMANDANTE: (*disgusted, to his wife, the Princess*) I only acknowledge Beethoven, that almost supernatural master. Only yesterday, I remember exactly, she played the two Sonata-Fantasies Op. 27 perfectly. What a pianist! One of the "Fantasies," the one dedicated to Julia Guicciardi, expresses hopeless renunciation, it tells of waking up after a dream that has been dreamt for far too long. The other, in the first bars of the Andante, points directly to a sense of peace after the storm; then, hesitatingly, there springs from the allegro vivace of the conclusion a new courage, almost a passion.

CARLOTTA: (*kissing Luisa*) Listen, little Louisa! Do you hear, now they are hitting against the walls outside again! Do you hear their beaks? Thousands! Millions! Piano pupils hunch themselves without letup over their instrument, radios bark, connoisseurs talk about completely imperceptible, faint differences. The one hears a nuance, the next hears the same nuance, but totally differently. The third hears a distinction. It tears their head open.

(*Lightning flashes, thunder growls, the snow on the mountain is lit up. A few withered leaves blow through the room. Marie becomes afraid and flees to Clara. Clara pushes her away roughly with the result that the child falls down. Crying, she lets herself be comforted by Aélis.*)

CLARA: (*shaking Robert's body*) Robert! Listen! You said that my beautiful composition was not allowed to be called an "Idyll." You insisted on "Notturno," even "Nostalgia" or "A Maiden's Nostalgia" you found fitting. You wouldn't even let my little work have the name I had chosen! What's more, it was more a waltz than a notturno. (*Subdued*) Forgive me, Robert, I only meant . . . And then you changed it completely. Changed it. Surely you will forgive me when I say that after your changes I did not like it as much any more. And forgive me that you didn't like it. (*Shakes the body forcefully, the attendants approach.*)

Robert, your love makes me endlessly happy! (*Shakes him*) One thought troubles me from time to time: whether I will be able to bind you to me. I strive, as far as I can, to unite the housewife with the artist! It is hard.

(*Leaves swirl through the room, fog surges up, in the distance a yodeler, the wind howls more loudly.*)

I would also like to produce pieces of music myself; people forget a pianist! But it can't be. No woman has ever been able to do it, so why should I? No! That would be arrogance. I want to be the bride of your heart, nothing else!

(*She sinks over him, evidently something rustles in his breast-pocket, she notices it, takes out a piece of paper, smoothes it, reads it.*)

Oh, one last greeting of love from you! Thank you! Your obedient Clara and wife. (*She drops the paper heedlessly.*) But to put this song into music, I can't do it even if you want me to. It is not laziness. No, to do that you need a mind, which I don't have.

(*She goes to the piano and begins to play the catchy tune that had already become Robert's undoing. Her playing intensifies as she goes along, becomes quicker and ever quicker, intensifies. Parallel to this the storm atmosphere in the room becomes stronger, romantically wild, storm, thunder rumbling, lightning. After a while it becomes quieter and snow starts to fall down on the mountain cross. Like in a glass ball with a Madonna that you turn upside down so that it snows.*)

AÉLIS: (*putting down a tray and screaming over the noise*) "He told me"—(*points to Clara*)—"he had succeeded in getting her to take a little cocaine and that the effect had been excellent, because right away she entered into a kind of unconscious state! He immediately took advantage of it to look at all her body. He kissed her all over and he also rubbed his you-know-what on her stout arm, like a village barber whetting the razor."[8]

(*Laughs loudly. The piano playing intensifies. Clara begins to gasp.*)

CLARA: The universe of music is a landscape of death. White deserts, ice, frozen rivers, streams, lakes! Immense plates of arctic ice, transparent right down to the bottom, no tracks of the predatory polar bear. Only geometrically arranged coldness. Frost lines as straight as a die. Deathly quiet. You can press your ten fingers against it for hours, and the ice will show no sign of a print.

(*She moves her lips more loudly, but plays so loudly that nothing else can be understood. All watch her attentively. What will break first, the piano or her? Finally, after a mad intensification of the music, Clara sinks from the stool. At this moment absolute silence. Only the snow falls down thickly onto the beautifully illuminated summit cross. Silence.*

An attendant approaches hesitatingly, followed by the second attendant, picks the piece of paper up from the floor and reads it falteringly and illiterately. It is noticeable that he has a cleft palate. While he reads falteringly, the second attendant takes the opportunity to kick the two dead people maliciously, and in a way that the others do not see, in the ribs or elsewhere with his mountain boots.)

ATTENDANT: Green, green is . . . the jasmine tree . . . when at night reposing . . . then the . . . sunbeams . . . tenderly . . . kiss it to . . . unclosing . . . and 'tis waked . . . to snowy white . . . "What befell . . . me in . . . the night?" . . . Thus it . . . is when flowers . . . dream in . . . springtide's . . . bowers.[9]

(*Snow flutters down silently. Curtain falls.*)

For the musical tragedy *Clara S.* quotes etc. were woven into the text from the following works:

---

[8] In English in the original German text.

[9] The text used here is that of a poem by Friedrich Rückert, set to music by Robert Schumann as Op. 27, N°. 4. The translation of this poem, *Jasminenstrauch* (*The Jasmine Tree*), is taken from the English performing version by Frederic Field Bullard, first published in 1903 by the Oliver Ditson Company.

Clara Schumann: *Diaries, letters*
Robert Schumann: *Letters*
Gabriele D'Annunzio: from the novels
Tamara de Lempicka and Gabriel D'Annunzio: *Correspondence*
Aélis Mazoyer: *Diaries*
Ria Andres: *Am Ende angekommen*

Translated by Ken Moulden

Originally published under the title *Clara S. Musikalische Tragödie* by Prometh Verlag, Köln. Taken from: *Theaterstücke,* copyright © 1992/2000 by Rowohlt Taschenbuch Verlag GmbH, Reinbek by Hamburg.

Thomas Bernhard

Is It a Comedy? Is It a Tragedy?

After not having visited the theater for weeks, yesterday I planned to go to the theater, but two hours before the start of the perform-ance, during my scientific labor and so in my study—I'm not en-tirely sure, whether in the foreground or the background of medical matters that I must finally conclude, less for the sake of my parents than for my overexerted head—I wondered whether I should not after all refrain from the theater visit.

I haven't been to the theater for eight or ten weeks, I told myself, and I know why I haven't gone to the theater. I despise the theater. I hate the actors. Theater is just a perfidious impertinence, an im-pertinent perfidy. And I should suddenly go to the theater again? To a play? What is that?

You know that the theater is an obscenity, I told myself, and you will write the study about the theater that you have in mind, a study of the theater that will be a slap in the face of theater once and for all. What the theater *is*, what the actors *are*, the authors of the pieces, the directors, etc. . . . .

More and more I was dominated by the theater, less and less by pathology, frustrated in my attempt to ignore the theater, to assault pathology. Frustrated! Frustrated!

I got dressed and went out onto the street.

The theater is only a half-hour walk for me. In that half-hour it became clear to me that I *cannot* go to the theater, that a visit to the theater, to a theatrical performance is forbidden me once and for all.

When you have written your study of the theater, I thought, then it will be time, then you will again be permitted to go to the theater, so that you can see that your treatise is *correct*!

It just bothered me that things ever got to the point where I bought myself a theater ticket—I *bought* the theater ticket, I didn't receive it as a *gift*—and that I tortured myself for two days in the belief that I would go to the theater, watch a theater performance, the actors, and behind all those actors smell a wretched, stinking director (Herr T.H.!), etc. . . . but above all, that I had *changed clothes* for the theater. You *changed* for the theater, I thought.

The theater study, one day the theater study! A person can describe well what he hates, I thought. In five, possibly in seven sections with the title *Theater—Theater*? my study will be finished in a short time. (When it is finished, you will burn it because it doesn't make sense to publish it, you will read it through and burn it. Publication is ridiculous! *Unavailing purpose*!) First section, THE ACTORS, second section, THE ACTORS IN THE ACTORS, third section, THE ACTORS IN THE ACTORS OF THE ACTORS, etc. . . . fourth section, STAGE EXCESSES, etc. . . . last section: SO, WHAT IS THEATER?

With these thoughts I arrived at the Volksgarten.

I sat down on a bench next to the Meierei, although sitting down on a Volksgarten bench at this season of the year can be *fatal*, and I watched with an effort, with pleasure, with enormous concentration *who and how* one goes into the theater.

I am satisfied *not* going in.

But, I think, you should go in, and in consideration of your poverty, sell your ticket, *go on*, I tell myself, and while I am thinking that, I take the greatest pleasure in mangling my theater ticket between the thumb and forefinger of my right hand, mangling the theater.

First, I tell myself, there are more and more people going into the theater, then fewer and fewer. Finally, no one will go into the theater anymore.

The performance has begun, I think, and I get up and walk a short way in the direction of midtown. I'm cold. I haven't eaten anything and, it occurs to me, I haven't spoken to a single soul for more than a week, when suddenly I am spoken to: A man has spoken to me. I hear a man asking me what time it is, and I hear myself exclaim "Eight o'clock." "It is eight o'clock," I say. "The play has begun."

Now I turn around and see the man.

The man is tall and thin.

Besides this man, no one is in the Volksgarten, I think.

Immediately, I think that I have nothing to lose.

But saying the sentence: "*I have nothing to lose!*" and saying it *out loud*, seems senseless to me, and I do not say the sentence, although I have the greatest desire to say the sentence.

He has lost his watch, the man says.

"Since I lost my watch, I am forced to talk to people from time to time."

He laughed.

"If I had not lost my watch, I wouldn't have spoken to you," he said, "spoken to *anybody*."

Most interesting to him, said the man, was the observation that, how—after I had told him that it was eight o'clock—he now knew that it *is* eight o'clock and that today for eleven hours without interruption—"without an interruption," he said—he had walked in one thought, "not back and forth," he said, but "always straight ahead, and as I now see," he said, "in a circle. Crazy, isn't it?"

I saw that the man had on women's slippers, and the man saw that I had seen that he had on women's slippers.

"Yes," he said, "now you may get ideas."

"I," I said quickly, to divert myself and the man from his women's slippers, "I planned to visit the theater, but right in front of the theater, I turned heel and didn't go in the theater."

"I have been in this theater very often," said the man—he had introduced himself, but I had immediately forgotten his name, I don't remember names—"someday for the last time like every man some day goes to the theater for the last time, don't laugh," said the man. "There's a last time for everything, don't laugh."

"Oh," he said, "what's playing today? No-no," he said quickly, "don't tell me what's playing . . ."

He went into the Volksgarten every day, said the man, "Since the start of the season I have gone into the Volksgarten about this time, so that here, from this corner, from the Meierei wall, you know, I can watch the theater-goers. Remarkable people," he said.

"Of course, one ought to know what's playing today," he said, "but don't *you* tell me what's playing today. For me it is extremely interesting *not* to know for once what's playing. Is it a comedy? Is it a tragedy?" he asked and said at once, "No-no, don't say *what it is*. Don't say it."

The man is fifty, or he is fifty-five, I think.

He made the suggestion that we walk in the direction of the Parliament.

"Let's walk up to the Parliament," he said, "and back again. It is remarkably quiet when the performance has begun. I *love* this theater . . ."

He walked very fast, and it was almost unendurable to me to watch him. The thought that the man had on women's slippers caused me to be ill.

"I walk the same number of steps here every day," he said, "that is, in these shoes I walk from the Meierei to the Parliament, to the Volksgarten fence, exactly three hundred and twenty-eight steps. In the *buckled* shoes I walk three hundred and ten. And to the Swiss Wing—he meant the Swiss Wing of the Palace—I walk exactly four hundred and fourteen steps with *these* shoes, three hundred and twenty-nine with the *buckled* shoes! Women's shoes, you might think, and it may be repulsive to you, I know," said the man.

"But I walk on the street only in darkness. The fact that every evening at this time, always a half-hour before the start of the performance, I walk into the Volksgarten is based, as you can imagine, on something shocking. That something now lies twenty-two years in the past. And it's very closely connected with women's slippers. An incident," he says, "an incident. It's the same feeling as back then: The curtain's just gone up in the theater, the actors begin to act, out here the lack of people . . . Let's walk," says the man, after we're back at the Meierei, "to the Swiss Wing now."

A madman? I thought, as we walked to the Swiss Wing, next to one another. The man said: "The world is totally, thoroughly legal, as you perhaps don't know. The world is just one monstrous system of laws. The world is a penitentiary!"

He said: "It's been exactly forty-eight days since I last met a human being here in the Volksgarten at this hour. And I asked *that* man, too, what time it was. And that man, too, told me that it was eight o'clock. Remarkably, I always ask what time it is at eight o'clock. That man, too, walked with me up to the front of the Parliament and up to the front of the Swiss Wing. By the way," said the man, "and this is the truth, I didn't lose my watch. I never lose my watch. Here, see, is my watch," and he held his wrist in front of my face so that I could see his watch.

"A trick!" he said, "but to continue: The man whom I met forty-eight days ago was a man your age. Like you, taciturn; like you, at first *un*decided, then resolved to walk with me. A natural sciences student," said the man. "And I told *him*, too, that something shocking, an incident, that lay long in the past, was the reason that I stop by here in the Volksgarten every evening. In women's slippers. Identical reaction," said the man, and:

"By the way, I never have seen a policeman. For several days the police have avoided the Volksgarten and are concentrating on the Stadtpark, and I know why . . ."

"Now it really would be interesting," he said, "to know whether, in the very instant that we are approaching the Swiss Wing, in the theater a comedy or a tragedy is being played . . . This is the first time that I don't know what's playing. But *you* mustn't tell me . . . No, don't say it! It wouldn't be hard," he said, "while I'm studying *you*, concentrating totally on *you*, occupying myself exclusively with *you*, to figure out whether at this moment in the theater a comedy or a tragedy is playing. Yes," he said, "gradually my study of your person would explain everything that's happening in the theater and everything that's happening outside the theater, everything in the world, that after all is connected to you completely at any time. Ultimately, someday, the moment could really appear when, through my most intensive study of you, I'd know everything about you . . ."

When we had arrived in front of the wall of the Swiss Wing, he said: "Here, on this spot, the young man whom I met forty-eight days ago took his leave of me. You want to know *by what means*? Watch out! Oh!" he said, "*you're* not taking your leave then? You're *not* saying goodnight? Yes," he said, "then let's walk from the Swiss Wing back to where we came from. Where did we come from anyway? Oh yes, from the Meierei. The remarkable thing about people is that they constantly confuse themselves with other people. So," he said, "you wanted to go to today's performance.

Although, as you say, you hate the theater. *Hate* the theater? I *love* it . . ."

Now I realized that the man also had a ladies' hat on his head. I had not noticed that the whole time.

The coat, too, that he had on was a ladies' coat, a ladies' winter coat.

He actually has nothing but women's clothing on, I thought.

"In the summer," he said, "I don't go to the Volksgarten. No theater is playing then either. But always when the theater is playing, I go to the Volksgarten, because when the theater is playing, nobody but me goes into the Volksgarten anymore because the Volksgarten is much too cold then. Single young men come into the Volksgarten and, as you know, I address them immediately and invite them to walk along, up in front of the Parliament, up in front of the Swiss Wing . . . and always back from the Swiss Wing and from the Meierei. . . . But up to now, and this just occurs to me, not a soul," he said, "has walked *twice* with me up to the front of the Parliament and *twice* to the Swiss Wing and so back to the Meierei *four times*. We've now walked *twice* to the Parliament and *twice* to the Swiss Wing and back again," he said, "that's enough. If you like," he said, "accompany me a piece toward home. Not a single soul has ever accompanied me from here a piece toward home."

He lived in the Twentieth District.

He was *housed* in the apartment of his parents, who six weeks ago had died ("Suicide, young man, suicide!").

"We have to cross the Danube Canal," he said. I was interested in the man, and I had the urge to accompany him as long as possible.

"At the Danube Canal you must go back," he said. "You may not accompany me farther than to the Danube Canal. Until we have arrived at the Danube Canal, don't ask *why*!"

Behind the Rossau Barracks, a hundred meters from the bridge that leads over into the Twentieth District, the man stopped and looking down into the canal water said suddenly, "Here, on this spot."

He turned around to me and repeated: "On this spot."

And he said: "I pushed her in quick as a flash. The clothes I have on are *her* clothes."

Then he gave me a sign that meant: *Be gone!*

He wanted to be alone.

"Go!" he commanded.

I didn't leave at once.

I let him have his say: "Twenty-two years and eight months ago," he said.

"And if you think it's pleasant in prison, you're wrong! The whole world is one single system of laws. The whole world is a penitentiary. And this evening, I tell you, in that theater over there, whether you believe it or not, a comedy is playing. *Really* a comedy."

Translated by A. Leslie Willson

Barbara Frischmuth

The Waters of Love

She was a survivor. She could still recall the times when she would brush against the others when they all wheeled about together. Could recall the uncontrollable greediness in wanting to snap up the biggest piece for herself, recall the wild chases they had to toughen themselves up, and the love play during which they threatened to murder each other. She could also still believe in the safety and security offered by another body, but she herself preferred to be the provider of that sort of security. Not only did she traverse all that space with her body; she also could afford to offer some space within her own body. And although she had ingested so many things, she hardly knew who she was.

She didn't have a name of her own and had no name for the Higher Being she was dependent on—after all, it was the Higher Being that was providing the manna. It was perfectly clear to her that she had gobbled up all the others, but that lay in her nature and had little to do with her person.

To say that she was constantly bumping up against the boundaries of her world was simply a figure of speech. In reality she glided along very close to the glass wall without ever touching it, except to nibble at the deposits that kept forming there.

She knew that something was out there, even though her perception of it was blurred. The lips of the Higher Being made irregular movements, as if they were constantly releasing the moans and groans of the prayers that all living creatures were expelling into IT. ITS mode of locomotion was the same as that of all mammals. It

was obvious that the Higher Being, whenever IT manifested IT-
SELF, chose to appear in the form of someone in authority. She recognized this fact without rancor although she did feel a twinge of
regret. One was, after all, a thing created, and one had to put up
with it. Any further reflection on the matter was excluded by virtue
of that tight bond of dependence.

He was still suffering from the pangs of separation. He hadn't forgotten the nest he came from or its physical warmth or the feeling
of claws, of teeth. But there was a pain that far exceeded the pain
of separation: the pain of longing for the primordial landscape, for
the broad reaches of his ancestral home, for that which was truly
his. It was the desert in his head, that desert which had molded his
way of thinking and which triggered the painful longing for the ancient homeland that had given him his name.

The Higher Being allowed him close approach. He occasionally
climbed up on IT, and the search for physical warmth almost
caused him to overcome his natural feeling of revulsion toward
hairless skin. The smell had, at first, nearly knocked him
unconscious.

He was permitted a modicum of freedom, and he got over the
feeling of agoraphobia; he soon risked crossing the empty area in
the middle of the larger space instead of working his way along the
joints and cracks; he raced through any number of tunnels and past
hissing, moving but lifeless objects; he hid behind dead, heavily
branched trees, scaled the slopes of rugged canyons, and gnawed on
little houses, even biting the door off one of them. This was something he had never been able to do in his own quarters.

The Higher Being saw this and raised up a roar, expelling air
rhythmically and with all ITS might. As soon as the little hissing
containers stopped moving, he looked into them because they had
something tasty in them. He thanked the Higher Being by propping
himself up on his powerful tail and folding his paws around the
tasty morsel.

One day the Higher Being stood up while he was still on IT. He
usually jumped off on such occasions, but this time he kept still and
raised up his eyes to gaze on Higher Things. The landscape was
transformed. Shining upland plateaus covered with sparkling containers filled with vegetation; flat rectangles, edible, like wood, were

piled up on outstretched fibers that roughened up the smooth plane of the surface.

Blinded, he paused for a moment, then curiosity swept over him like a hawk. In the thrill of his dawning awareness he calculated where it was best to land—and jumped. The Higher Being didn't make the slightest effort to lay a finger on him; a noise had diverted ITS attention, and he wasn't even aware of ITS presence any longer.

With bated breath he sat in the shadow of a pile of something that smelled so dry that he had to sneeze. In his excitement he whetted his teeth on it for a while. Flakes came up, black on white, in among the lids.

All of a sudden, his eyes caught sight of the same primal image that he had in his mind's eye; it was in a nearby container standing next to one of the piles. Sand was shimmering in it, whitish, yellowish, brownish . . . and was shaped in gently curving dunes; small rocks were scattered among them, big enough to hide behind. He felt completely overwhelmed, and his heart was all aquiver.

So that's what the desert looked like. He had suspected it, had always suspected it.

As the sole survivor she was thankful for anything that was worth looking at. She also liked to put on a show. She knew all about the elegance of her fanlike movements and how expressive her eyes were, unmarred as they were by fluttering eyelids.

As she slowly focused on him, she felt a shiver go right down her spine, right through the cartilage. Her longing had conjured him up out of the depths of space, although she didn't know what shape he would actually appear in. As far as his size was concerned, it was enough that it corresponded to the world of her desire . . . Oh yes, his eyes were small, and every now and then something flopped over them, but she was the one their gaze was directed at. That alone was enough to excite her beyond all measure. She had been by herself for so long that she didn't even bother to nibble at that scruffy old aquatic plant any more, although she did still rub herself up against it.

This magnificent creature had been sent to liberate her from her loneliness. She needed only to entice it, make eyes at it, lure it toward herself by looking at it. She was all worked up and kept moving back and forth, always keeping him in sight with one of her eyes. And her gaze was enticing, enticing . . .

A creature was floating up and down over the marvelous desert. Apparently, it was such a good jumper that once it had taken off from the ground, it could keep itself up by slight, elastic muscular movements. He found this remarkable, but then again, he had seen many things that were remarkable. His breathing was calm again now, and he could take a chance on scurrying over to get as close as possible to the sand. He hurtled around the outside of the container, looking for a little door, but he couldn't find one. He thought hard, very hard, harder than he had ever thought about anything in his whole life and concluded that the door must be up on the top because there always has to be a door somewhere.

He was very sad that he couldn't smell the sand, although his nose was so close to it, but he would, all right, he would. . .

A crumb from the pile was still stuck between his teeth, the pile he had been chomping away at in his excitement earlier. And suddenly he knew what to do. Enthused by this, his very own idea, he overdid it and could have fallen off too soon, but he finally made it up there. The creature above the marvelous desert who could jump so well had eyes like craters, and he, for his part, was not immune to vertigo. The smell—or so it seemed to him—was a little like the one that greeted him at the very beginning of his life. Fascinated, he hesitated for a moment on this, his own personal stairway to paradise, but merely looking at something that promised to be his primal homeland was not enough: he wanted to feel it, with his feet, his nose, his belly.

She knew that she would soon have him exactly where she wanted. How could he of all creatures resist her when she was making eyes at him like this? She could almost sense how she was going to rub herself up against him. He looked like the kind someone could really rub up against. All she had to do was to swim up and down a few more times and show him her glistening, pastel-colored, unprotected flank, let him sample the whole length of her, so to speak . . .

He already sensed the nearness of the desert so strongly that it made him sneeze again. Something in him registered a short, shrill warning, but that kind of banal intuition could no longer get through to him. The image in his head corresponded too precisely with the image before his eyes. He folded his paws together and jumped.

The boy who owned all this howled with rage and disappointment before going to bed after he'd picked a fish scarred with toothmarks and a drowned jerboa out of his aquarium. Since it was too late to bury them in the yard, he put them in the refrigerator, so he could give them a decent burial the next day. And he decided to dump the entire contents of the aquarium into the hole after them. It really wasn't worth keeping the oxygen pump going just for that one scruffy old aquatic plant.

Translated by Gerald Chapple and James B. Lawson

© DIMENSION² 4.2 (1997): 243–251.

Norbert Gstrein

The Honorary Consul—Excerpt

The Honorary Consul's accomplishments are not undisputed, but it is an undisputed fact that during his lifetime he was a man of action. The prosperity that our village experienced is practically synonymous with his name. As alderman and chairman of the tourist office, he had been responsible for changing the former farmers' village into a "showcase for international tourism" (at least that was his favorite quote), and it would be excessive to list all the offices he held throughout his career; after all, he was captain of the fire brigade, chairman of the mountain rescue and ski club, and he's even supposed to have been a sexton for a few months. The accounts, that much is certain, were rather sizable, and he had the reputation of being a freedom fighter for a long time, even if that was just a figment of the imagination: tourism as religious warfare, a crazy notion unique in its own way.

We were all surprised that, in the very year when talk of a crisis could no longer be ignored, a bus stopped in front of our friend's house on a weekend after the winter season, and he himself greeted the arrivals, journalists from Hamburg, Munich, and Frankfurt, all men, as it turned out. We were surprised when, on the evening of the same day another bus arrived, a bus with only women, some extraordinary beauties among them. When they got out and, without looking back, disappeared in the Post Hotel as well, rumors developed, and we were no longer surprised. "The Honorary Consul knows his business," we said, once we had regained our composure. "You've got to hand it to him."

That was on a Friday; not one of the journalists nor any of the ladies could be seen in the village, and it was of no use that we kept walking past the Post Hotel; the curtains were drawn, the window shutters half closed, and on the main door hung a sign that said "Private Party. The Tourist Office." Not even on Saturday, the following day, did we get to see them. Instead, we were able to observe a photographer and his assistant around noon as they were taking pictures for a calendar; pictures of the stable and the barn of our only farmer who was still alive (it took them a long time to find the proper angle between the hotels); of the altar's cross, which they had dragged out of the church together with the priest and propped up on the edge of a dirt road in the forest; of an old man who was leaning up against the wooden tile front of the grocery store—pictures of glistening, sun-drenched rows of icicles; of snow fields covered with flowers; and of the shiny asphalt of the street, wet with melting snow. And after they had also taken pictures of each other, they disappeared behind closed doors. In the afternoon and in the evening, till long into the night, music could be heard from inside, and we needed little more than the imagination of philanderers to figure out from what we were excluded. Sunday came, and we watched in the morning as they, apparently exhausted, all got onto the two busses and left, and if anything was still capable of amazing us, we simply marveled at the fact that our friend had even tried to keep this whole thing a secret.

A few weeks later, he showed us the articles that had appeared in the travel magazines; they sounded like hymns of an island of the blessed, an oasis of peace; they talked of a place where time stood still, usually with the very same heading, "All say hello, everyone knows everyone else, everybody is happy to be back again," and we sat in the sun on the terrace of the Café Tyrol, lit the cigars he had distributed, and read the nonsense. We knew it brought us guests, it brought us money, and we could calmly open the daily newspaper and begin our reading as usual with the insolvencies, the settlement suits, and the filings of bankruptcy. "Cheers!" we said, "cheers! Mr. Honorary Consul," (we were formal with him for fun) and raised our glasses. "We are proud of you."

We overlooked the absurdities, which occurred again and again. It didn't interest us whether his business practices were proper, whether all that talk about fraud, official misconduct, and embez-

zlement of public funds was true or not. We knew that the waitresses, the chamber maids, and sometimes even the kitchen help in
his hotel were not safe from him, but we didn't think anything of it
as long as he didn't violate the principles of a man of honor and
didn't force anyone into anything. Even what he did to his wife,
whether he truly kept her locked up to get her to stop drinking,
whether he meant her well or whether he feared a scandal, didn't
matter to us. We spoke in terms of mere peccadillo, and when accu-
sations grew stronger and he defended himself, we didn't pay attention to what he said; we paid attention to how he said it, whether
it was in the gibberish of a local politician or whether he had remained a human being.

The changes in him, which—with hindsight—we saw as the beginning of the end, began over a year before his death, and if we ignored them at first, it was only because we were experiencing
attacks on tourists at that time, and our village was filled with journalists for days. For the first time, it wasn't about the usual trifles,
insults, damage to cars, and similar things, but physical attacks,
and we surmised that if we didn't do something immediately, then
the damage could no longer be repaired. "The Honorary Consul,"
we agreed, "should make a public statement."

We wanted to get our friend to deliver an appeasing speech on
Christmas eve before midnight mass in church, but he refused, and
when on the following weekend guests were leaving everywhere
early, we saw him sitting in the sun in front of his hotel and looking
on. "This is nothing yet," he prophesied. "Soon it will end in
bloodshed."

After this, he was nowhere to be seen until New Year's Eve. The
few advances that we dared usually failed; either his wife would not
let us past the door, or he let it be understood himself that he
wanted to be alone. At Easter, we heard that he was in the clinic
because of his heart troubles, so they said, but they also said it was
treatment for an addiction, and we knew both were possible and
didn't investigate any further. We had stopped worrying about him
when he came back and initially pretended as if nothing had
changed. Nevertheless, he had changed—and substantially; he
seemed in a way transparent, something we had never known about
him, debilitated although he still had his beer belly and his hot

head, that thick head, which glowed red with the smallest of exertions, but his panting was no longer the panting of a daredevil who seemed to be beside himself with vigor. That system of a human being, which he was, was no longer under excess pressure; it no longer cooked, no longer bubbled in him; it led to no explosions. He wasn't the bully of earlier days; he had become calmer, even if it seemed to be a calmness that he had not chosen, a forced calmness, a standstill that could unravel itself from one second to the next. We indeed were getting the impression he might be under the influence of medication when he, for the first time, appeared in our midst again and silently hugged us one after another and didn't let go for a long time, and so we also tried to explain why he suddenly got sentimental, but it was an explanation which we didn't believe in.

The boozing alone couldn't be it. If he was a drunkard, then we were all drunkards, and we didn't even consider a notion of that sort. (We didn't live badly.) The amount of alcohol that he was able to down in his best days was, before and after his absence, considered average, not more and not less, and certainly no reason to look at him askance. His drinking was possibly more thorough now, just as if he wanted to inspire his own courage by drinking, and then it was the kind of courage of those who had resigned, or he was giving the impression of doing some kind of work by drinking. There had never been any aggression on his part, and there wasn't going to be any in the future either; he only became more reserved, more motionless, more inaccessible for questions and sat there as if nothing around him mattered. The jokes, with which he always got the waitresses to laugh, suddenly fell flat, and what did come across wasn't entertaining, just awkward, as if the distance between him and them had become insurmountable. When he had consumed too much, he took on the air of a soldier, and on occasion he would take on the stiff posture of a cavalry man while sitting on his stool, or it could happen that on his way home he would fall into a dilapidated goosestep while carrying the walking stick that he had gotten for himself like a rifle across his chest. At times we were able to hear how he commanded his own human being, often enough interrupted by hiccups that usually plagued him in such situations, again and again an "excuse me," and how he disappeared in the darkness with his "left right, left right."

We had started to call him "Sir." Because no matter what he did, he did it with class. We watched him in the morning when he crept up the gravel road in his four-wheel drive to that tavern belonging to some fortune seeker, apparently, to some foreigner; it had been opened up in no man's land, and when he came down again before sunset, we noticed how fast he drove, the dust soaring up many feet behind him, and that the noise of the engine swept in shock waves over the valley, and, as he came closer, that he was dressed up to the hilt and that he indeed was carrying on a conversation with his dog who was sitting next to him and whose head was nodding continuously from all the bouncing. We had our misgivings, like everyone in the village, and whenever he went hunting and with that very rifle, which before him his father and his father's father had already used, disappeared in the forest, we waited for a shot, of which we'd know, wherever it came from, it was not a shot at an animal. Then he jumped in a drunken fit from one of the cable suspension lines that were used for transporting goods—from several feet high, out of the open box, which had carried him on some weekends up to his mountain hut for supervisory purposes, and we gave him up for lost, even if he appeared again with a neck collar and both arms in a cast after a few days in the hospital. "The Honorary Consul isn't going to live much longer."

At that time he had already resigned from all of his appointed offices. On his sixtieth birthday in the early summer, he appeared publicly for the last time, and there was only a small number of people who had assembled in front of the fire station to hear the speeches. Then it quickly got quiet around him, and the rumors that still existed were like the rumors about a dead person, a mixture of condemnation and legends, or they were in reference to his state of health. "The Honorary Consul has had a heart attack," people said; "he must have cancer," and when that did not suffice, one spoke of debts that amounted to millions as if it were the worst disease imaginable: "This is his death."

We didn't know what was really wrong with him, but when we went to visit him one evening and were unexpectedly admitted, we were astonished at how much value he placed on the remark that it wasn't all his fault. The story that he told us regarding this was somewhat melodramatic, and we didn't pay much attention when he began talking at length about his wife and his two daughters.

The following day we barely remembered any of it, although we had, of course, noticed how important it was to him to make a confession, and if a cry for help was at the bottom of this, it wasn't noticed because we had expected the craziest things from him but surely not that.

Translated by Harald Becker

© DIMENSION² 3.1 (1996): 45–53.
© 1995 by Suhrkamp Verlag.

Elfriede Jelinek

Children of the Dead—
Prologue and Epilogue

Prologue

The country needs a great amount of space higher up so that its blessed spirits can move properly above the waters. At some locations it reaches over ten thousand feet. So much nature has been used on this country that for its part, perhaps to repay its debt to nature, it has always handled its people rather frivolously; hardly have they taken the bait, and it has already tossed them aside. This country's great dead, to name only a few of them, are Karl Schubert, Franz Mozart, Otto Hayden, Fritz Eugen, Zita Zitter, Maria Theresiana, in addition to what its military academies in the new district of Vienna produced up until 1918, in Stalingrad in 1943, and the other few odd million crushed individuals. A locus of deals and counterdeals, therefore; and to these wheelings and dealings there belongs tourism of the sort where people, instead of being worn out and tossed aside, return newer and better than when they had left, still get less for themselves because their budget is used up. It was worth it, though. Many people, unfortunately, have fallen to their deaths in the process. We are here (and feel our being there strongly!) in an Austrian village—more exactly, at its outermost edges, which the mountain seems to have pocketed. It is rather on the periphery of tourism, almost undeveloped. Only older people and large families with many children travel here because there is very little in the way of sports or entertainment. But there is good air and deep woods. And beautiful mountains that are around 6700 feet high; and few are even higher. The region, however, does not fully belong to the high region of the Alps. Hiking trails, a small local train, brooks, a clear river; but if the technicians open the dam gates too quickly, then the trout suffocate in the mud, float belly up by the hundreds—glittering squadrons who have just crossed over their pitching and swaying road—around by the bridge, and drive away the hikers who want to cross over to the inn that is built into the cliff and can only be reached by climbing up a kind of chicken ladder, an almost impassable path.

Several of the guests have signed up for an excursion today. They want to see the wild alpine region with its lakes and view the little castle of the archduke from the House of Hapsburg who way back then had married the daughter of the postmaster of Aussee and thereupon, like a mole, dug up the countryside—besides the daughters on the earth, there also had to be, for the sons, some iron left beneath the earth that could be processed into huge quantities of plowshares or cannons, both coexisting in harmony as usual. The earth gave the ore, and the owners of the forges from the Mürz valley and the owners of the iron from Vienna gave to the earth the country's pliable children, fodder for the cannons, in return. In this region it is thus possible to see quite a lot if one is interested in the history of the archdukes of ore. Fresh cold air. The minivan that had been ordered on time stops in front of the inn, which is part of a farm and a bed-and-breakfast. Six people have signed up for the tour. Two of them, a married couple from the Ruhr area in Germany, are dawdling about in the entrance, asking each other about forgotten items and the planned destination for lunch (included in the price); after a while, a single woman from Halle in former East Germany joins them; they all chat a bit—will the weather hold, will their clothing be suitable, will they manage to have a tour guided by one of the descendents of the archduke? Will they be able to admire the famous speedwell thistle in the garden that was personally planted by the archduke himself in honor of his beloved postmaster's daughter? The Chrysler Voyager that wants to collect the tourist group shoves its snub nose across the parking lot; it has already gotten the scent of its live prey. It has the power over who will be delivered at the destination and in what condition; it has wild horses under its hood. The driver is already slightly inebriated, but that doesn't matter to him because everybody here is a little drunk all the time; it is the local custom, after all. And the local masters all compete against each other with their excretions every evening in front of the inn. At eight in the morning not even those who participate in the preliminary rounds are playing; they are sleeping, leaden from the previous evening. When the three passengers have claimed the best seats, ready to be launched onto the water-gray rural highway that—from left and right, from above and below—is almost crushed by succulent green, the other four people arrive. Wait. That's one too many. Doesn't matter. We'll squeeze in closer together. On vacation one happily expects things of oneself that at home one would not tolerate. One of them, a young man, did not sign up but would like to come along anyway. Then again others— obviously, mother and daughter, the daughter not as young as she once was—certainly will not want to miss out or be separated. Besides that, the old woman absolutely wants to sit up front. That is not possible. But it works out that everyone can squeeze into the car. We're none of us all that fat, joke the passengers who are happy to have company. In the air lies a mysterious sense that the day would yet become pleasant and that people want to learn something in order to happily, indeed, all too happily, be convinced of belonging to this world.

Quite some time has now passed; the sun has climbed a bit and is now, approaching noon, catching its breath; but the car, it rolls; now it is even climbing high up a mountain road, higher and ever higher spiraling up the switchbacks. It appears to be quite warm outside. People on bicycles display their bodies. The ribbon of road a light gray, living passage of time. The mountain panorama unfolds here, at the so-called Lower Alpl, in all its splendor; the names of the peaks are all mentioned; they are almost drowning in all the sunshine; the motor purrs reassuringly. They are now approaching the highest point, the peak of this ancient pass, and at the other end we have to descend back down again. The summer storms that raged with particular violence here—they have torn parts of the road down into the river. Lovely red-white-red plastic tape is strung over and over at the edge of the road between stakes where the asphalt has broken off. Caution! Automobiles as well as other traffic on road! Where earlier there had been a nice and solid shoulder and one was always able to pull over just in time whenever a larger car approached from the opposite direction, there is now a sheer drop-off, a jagged wound at the sides of the road. One need not insert anything into it, no spear, in order to see that the wound is real. Over and over signs posting extreme speed limits; a snail's pace is in order here. A voice from Halle on the river Saale demands, in peculiar German, that this commandment be upheld; the woman was itching with old obedience, but in this country we in principle just do not comply so exactly to the order by the authorities that depend on us and want to spoil all our fun. Here the authorities are still something that in principle must be fought. So, we'll just take it at forty mph; what could possibly happen. I'll tell you: By coincidence, a tour bus, unfortunately, happens to want to cross over exactly the same stretch of road. Bad luck. This gigantic appearance disguised by colorful sheet metal with advertisements is clearly the stronger one here. The monstrous storm that a month ago had bitten a piece out of the roadside and spit it into the creek is now being served an unexpected dessert that is not much more enjoyable. Only a bit of garnish is missing. But wait, we'll make a further delivery: the bloody cardigan, for example, is just the touch; the shoe that has been torn off there, yes, a little asymmetric; the other one is missing; it is still on a dirty, twisted foot. And what is the minivan suddenly doing down there, turned over on its back like a thoughtless bug by a huge kick, all four legs outstretched in a helpless freewheel, idling. Here lie four people who have been ejected, not wearing seatbelts, of course. And now they are bright and colorful splotches of cream or whipped cream sprinkled on the steep meadow's edge that, together with the pieces of broken roadway that have not all been cleared away yet, merges with the creek, still swollen with floodwaters. One, two uprooted trees in the midst of it all; that, however, was caused by the floods. A twisted young man, two twisted women, an old woman, screaming, screaming like a sinner before the tabernacle—hurry hurry!—so that she can get in a few more shrill noises before this streetvending of people is closed. The torsos are snapped at an angle, the arms thrown up as though a deep joy had taken hold of them. Cool mountain air brushes past. The wheels are still spinning. The driver is pinned and is stuck behind the steering wheel that has crushed his rib cage; fluid is running from his mouth. He will certainly not be able to drink it any more; he has been dragged away from his liquor discounter, the bottle of his life half full in his hand; still he seems to want to oppose the control of a higher power. Getting out of the bus above, people go their ways, also screaming and crying, trying to climb down to the meadow that is cheerfully colored with splotches of humanity. Tall spruce trees are towering. Birds call out because of the disturbance but are not in the least impressed. The bus driver mumbles something to himself; he is sitting on the running board of the dangerous colossus that has been entrusted to him. The aromatic mountain climate is in any case more robust here. The driver is, as are his passengers, Dutch, and he no longer understands the mountains, nor the world, nor the defeated people here, this race who considered itself to be master of its nature and who cannot even master its own cars. Some have been felled; a clearing has opened up; the trees gladly make way for the light to illuminate all of this like a floodlight. Residents of the plain are ready to help and clamber, like rolling stones, across the mountain slope. From above, from the huge balcony, the veranda of the tourist café, they throw down even more human wreckage that has survived for the time being and that is so sorry for the victims that it will hinder the rescue efforts. Everyone wears colorful vacation clothing until the evening approaches. Then they pull on the cardigans. Like a playful dog, woolly and impertinent, nature jumps around its guests, encircles them, whirls them through the air without catching them because some other little flying twig is more tempting; moodily, nature touches this and that with her paws, lets it go again without any consideration for the fact that this playmate is completely crushed, torn to shreds by her. She sniffs at the pieces, cries her song into the light until night falls, and then she cries another song from deep within her throat. Nature! Her clumsy jumps take in large areas; large areas are also taken up by the bulldozers that are already approaching. Such human-sized dolls that are scattered about here are a continual delight, the limbs spread wide, the mouths no longer uttering words. Branches are broken off; leaves already begin wilting on them. Springing up tall in the warmth of midday are the piles of humanity, decoration for the countryside from which the country lives; they are extending up the slope, all the way to the restaurant, and they even intrude inside where those who continue on alive are bustling about and saving what is theirs from

the garbage pile; they have been spared and can now exhaust themselves on the jogging trail. Dark woods at the end; after all, it was
only the edge that was trampled over by the last storm like stitches
are pulled out of a hem; soon construction crews will stitch it up
again and take us up also in the event that we dare to race away
over it at something more than twenty miles per hour. Let's proceed
on foot, into the high-lying forest! The sun shines a light in our face;
we believe the brightness before us to be a mirror and hit our head
violently against the rock that we are ourselves. Thus we plunge
down into the high-lying valley; the dogs bark; something seizes us
by the scruff of our neck, but it is not the dogs, for this time they
want to assure us of that.

Epilogue

People leaf to their heart's content through the book of their life;
sometimes they try quickly to conclude an unfinished chapter, but
usually they do not succeed. They then often feel tempted to immediately begin a new chapter without having finished the old one
first. This mistake is one I will not make. At some point it must end,
says a certain politician; and then, hesitantly, measuring off a time
delay of two hours for the sake of decency, another one says exactly
the same thing, but differently. Two hours is also what this gentleman will wait, then it will definitely be the end. But those whose
end it is are not asked. What moves me, toward an end that is now
so far back, to still want to piece something onto it so that I can, at
least, with my fingertips, reach it? Who will still want to put on this
dress? Many would like to, but then it does not fit them. Perhaps I
have really made the hem too long? Nobody is tall enough to be
able to fit into this dress. This shoe that is lying there, bloody,
should also kindly be put on by somebody else!

    As great as the damages are that flooding can cause, the most
unimaginable devastation, however, is caused by mudflow catastrophes. Entire towns sink in mud and rock debris through and
through; their houses are swept away, and their cultures utterly destroyed. Many towns in the mountains have been buried so deeply
by mudslides that the ground floor has become the cellar because,
after the flooding mud, it was just not possible to remove all the de-
posited material. This is why, for example, since the great Schmit-
tenbach catastrophe of 1737, visitors have had to step down several

steps into the parish church in Zell am See while, prior to that, the town square was on level ground with the church. Or in 1567 the narrow Seidlwinkel creek near Rauris overran its banks after a storm, flooded the town of Luggau with a terrible mudslide, destroyed thirty homes, and caused one hundred people to suffocate in the mud.

We can thus be happy as we look into the mirror that we are not among the dead in this country this time, which is clearly indicated by the fact that we can look into our faces in the mirror and not onto pure nothingness.

The bed-and-breakfast Alpine Rose, in so-called Tyrol in Styria (this is actually not a town but rather a place, a collection of a few isolated cottages and a larger estate that, remodeled, has been used for a long time now almost exclusively as a bed-and-breakfast), and all the people, animals, and personnel that had been staying at the bed-and-breakfast were first picked up, then pushed aside a bit, and finally engulfed and completely buried by a mudslide that had broken out of the narrow ditch that had been built to contain the torrent. That really puts the crowning touch on this year of catastrophes. First the floods, the damage to the roadways (the repair work has not even been halfway completed; everywhere small contingents of troops are standing around in their yellow protective clothing, raking, pouring, smoothing, adding onto idontknowwhat; and already new projects have to be planned: all volunteer fire departments and quite a few engineering units of the Austrian armed forces are in constant deployment. Please tune in to our special nightly report at six!), the wind damage, the cracked bridge piers, and now we can all drape dark cloths over ourselves because the death toll is not coming down. The mudslide had dissolved into individual streams, spreading out like a fan. This caused its velocity to decrease. The solid material then stayed put, indeed, right on top of the Alpine Rose bed-and-breakfast, which is now located within the mass of rock debris, but at a completely different location than where it had originally been built. Picked up and pushed aside. Fortunately, the valley becomes wider at this point so that the mudslide gently ran itself out. If it had become lodged in the lower reaches of the ditch—as happened once many years ago when the torrent still flowed through its original bed (at that time five farmsteads, including the entire inventory of their dead, had to be abandoned forever)—then due to the mass of the mud pushing from behind, it could have resulted in much heavier mudslides and greater devastation; indeed, then the entire town of K. would even have been at risk!

The cleanup operations drew on for quite a few days; the hope of finally still encountering anybody alive had to be given up early, however. Right now the provincial governor is vowing to the director of disaster prevention and control on live television, still very much influenced by the impression of what has just happened, never again to build homes where nature does not want them. Fortunately, this impression will quickly pass. Against better knowledge, in order not to hurt tourism, the rumor was spread among the public that there still might be people found alive in the rubble. The heavy equipment—bulldozers, dredgers, the shovels—advanced for days many steps down into the restricted area, day and night. A stairway into the depths where there has to be a house—bend down and do your job! There, a shattered beam! and here! the shredded right hand of a person! We continue to dig; the metal shovels burrow ahead and come across a sign: hair. Human hair. It is dug up. Everyone is sleeping. But: there is simply too much hair here for the estimated number of mudslide victims. Please, now is not the time to think it over for a long while; we must press forward to those who have nothing to say to us! The faces of the young engineers and of the old bucks on the road construction crew become more and more serious. Hair. Hair. And there as well: hair! Occasionally, someone presses it briefly like a hand, lets it run through his fingers like a rope: Will it lead us perhaps into that eternity that we have always wanted to see? They become more and more persistent, are silent for longer and longer periods. The workers give each other strange looks and, almost embarrassed, decline the sausages with mustard and bread that they are being offered. Nature has won in a certain sense, but perhaps we can get something out of her victory; the hair of about two hundred people has already been found, although only a fraction of this number could have been staying here, and that would be not as much as the air breathed by somebody whom we did not even know, sorry! The leader of the deployment team goes into his improvised office in a hastily hammered-together barrack, writes something down, and then comes back outside. He offers an explanation that does not explain. He declares a news blackout, to which, however, we will not be held. We don't believe him, even if he has not said a thing. The disaster expert, who has just not made a statement either, will be publicly commended tomorrow, but his facial expression will be elsewhere.

The young military recruits are suddenly and all too quickly pulled from the job. Now older, more experienced workers attend to this task. The region has been blocked off over a large area. I do not know any more.

A secret report that, therefore, even I have not read, allegedly states the least of the peculiarities (what would have been the really serious ones?) about this strange rescue work is supposed to have consisted in the fact that in the buried house a huge number of dead people were found who, according to the unanimous judgment of the pathologists, had to have been dead for a long, some of them for a very long time, when they were buried by the liquid mud. Now, now—one should not say anything rash. This just does not happen. After all, this bed-and-breakfast was not a cemetery for the nameless! Gentlemen from the city suddenly became available and, in their parkas and sturdy shoes, climbed about in the dirt, debris, and rubble. They soon enjoyed this activity. But what they then stated to the public sounded rather lame. Such people are not happy to say that they have nothing to say. And yet none of them has forgotten what he saw.

One more comment on the sidelines, where we tame ones live and where we keep even tamer ones (hopefully!) at home as our companions: Stop, what's on that sign? This region is doggone and all? No, it says, this region is our one and all. So: About twenty five miles away from where the catastrophe happened, at the regional hospital of that region's capital Mürzzuschlag, at the same time that large areas of the Styria were buried in a landslide, fifty-three-year-old Karin F. succumbed to the serious injuries she had suffered as a result of a serious accident between a bus full of Dutch vacationers and a minivan at the Styrian side of the Lower Alpl. The mother of the deceased, who originally had not suffered any major injury from the accident, was staying at the time of the natural disaster at the Alpine Rose bed-and-breakfast and, therefore, is counted as one of the victims of the terrible suspicions. The Dutch travelers, in the meantime, were able to begin their journey home on a replacement bus.

Translated by Louise E. Stoehr

© Dimension² 5.3 (1992): 439–453.
Taken from: *Die Kinder Toten,* Copyright © 1995 by Rowohlt Verlag GmbH, Reinbek bei Hamburg.

Gert Jonke

Thunderbolts of Cloth

Good Day! Thank you very much indeed for the accommodating willingness on your part to give me such a friendly reception. You must be the managing director—wait, no, the administrator, nono, pardon me, of course, the owner of this cloth warehouse, aren't you. Tell me, is everything always in order here? Nono, don't be alarmed, I'm not from occupational health and safety and certainly not from the labor union. This is then your largest storage warehouse for cloth? Magnificent. Congratulations. Admirable, this striking similarity to the heavenly equipment rooms of our largest and most distinguished opera houses! Yesyes, these at first unimaginable collections of bolts of cloth, stacked up on top of and next to each other; these accumulated mounds, entire provinces of material folding upward into real hill formations in one single—and often within—the most confined room that is soon ever more stuffed, soon entirely stuffed with the many rag piles that are slowly but surely spreading out—dangerous—you know, their inevitable expansion due, particularly in the summer heat, to the additional fluffing of dust particles and their no longer preventable propagation on account of the most revolting fuzzy concubinages of ever-matted velour and its resultant furiously wool-hampering hordes of amphibian bastards—goaded by the neural paths of silk threads that, gone wild, run through everything, unwind in maddening speed, and scream at a pitch that pierces through everything—if such a room, even in whizzing shots of felt, slowly overflows from every crack and gap with the frayed rests and epileptic fits of textiles, bundled toward the exit gates and gone completely insane, then, yes then—often from one second to the next—a so-called *dust explosion* inevitably takes place, understand? You really didn't know that, nono, it's nothing felty soft or fluffy; instead, as good as nothing is left from the affected building! Did you know that?! But as one can see, there is really hardly the slightest cause here at your place for concern about this; everything is neatly laid out in an absolutely well-mannered order, quite peacefully on your countless shelves. Something similar, however, that we assume to have taken place with more frequency lately and that, recently on a visit to another cloth warehouse, I personally had the opportunity to experience: how every one of the cloth bales stacked one upon another simultaneously began to unroll itself—at first, we thought it was some sort of invisible accomplice—but no, it was the bolts of cloth themselves, all of them gone mad, that rolled themselves out of their shelves, extending their colorful banners into pathways, until their countless lengths chased through the room and unleashed a terrific whirling cloth hurricane, and only because the salesmen remained steadfast and were able to keep all of the doors locked tight, was the cloth unable to escape into the city before the textile storm, finally exhausted, settled into one gigantic rag pile in front of the main entrance. Tell me, hasn't something even remotely similar happened to you inside here, or don't you believe that such a thing could possibly happen to you here?! No?! You're actually shaking your head!? About me or about what I was able to tell you? Just watch out!

Oh no, there! Just look, and there and there and there too, yes yes, now there no doubt just as soon! Here, the mischievously gleaming poplin! And over there, the furiously laughing linen! And already right next to it, angrily shining damask! And there, already furiously glittering brocade! And over there, the imbecilic grin of the completely idiotic loden cloth. Now we're in a fine mess. And how it all unrolls quick as wildfire!

Real thunderbolts of cloth.

Just look over there, the necks of some of your employees downright wrapped round by cloth nooses ever tightening their hold, the bodies of your salesmen dragged to the portal of your warehouse and crushed together, so as to force the people either to open the door or otherwise to be strangled . . . !

Open! Opened! Finally, some fresher air.

Everything empty. What is now most likely happening out there in the city; for the time being, I don't even want to think about it. But, then, didn't I warn you?

Where are you anyway?

Simply gone.

Just simply disappeared.

Translated by Louise E. Stoehr

© DIMENSION² 4.2 (1997): 267–269.

Michael Köhlmeier

Telemachus—Excerpt

We have digressed far off the subject. Four years later: Telemachus is sitting in his father's study, his legs up, his hands folded on his stomach, his head somewhat at a slant. How should he look back at his morning and realize that it was a failure! How can he claim to know that? What is being judged here? Should evidence be offered for three, four hours? Did that tiny length of time achieve its last goal by noon already? Will the time of real life be treated here like the broadcast time of a TV show? Are we on a quiz show or what! And if it's so that, only at the second of death, accountability is made for all the seconds that preceded? Perhaps, it will turn out for a person that two billion seconds of failure were necessary in order to make a glorious triumph of the last one, the second of death? That thus, after this confusion of improbabilities that constitutes life, death was the one true goal that was always declared, though not accepted. *Finis autem viae hominis est mors sua.* That the last second, the last battle, the last fight . . . Are we really digressing? Anyone who bears a name that states that it's the last thing that counts, no matter what that will be, can surely not be troubled by the appearance of two, three, four hours. Truth is a way of seeing, not a result. No, Telemachus was now not preparing his speech, either. He relied on his good fortune. Being lucky, you see, is the best plan. Growing beyond oneself is a question of opportunity. But opportunity is a ripening force that cannot be acquired with impatience. One's inner attitude is decisive here. *Act as though you were lucky!*

Now it'll be time, said Telemachus to himself. He locked the door to his father's study behind him, put the key in his pocket. He called the dogs to his side, the male to his right, the female to his left. He walked to the people's assembly slowly and with a dignified posture, his chin elevated, his shoulders square, his hair swept back from his brow and temples. He didn't cut across the grass but walked close past the terrace where the men, probably again about twenty, spent their time like gossipers—sat on the railing, their elbows propped on their thighs, or lounged on the cushion-covered wicker furniture, flopped onto chaises or leaning against columns. They were small figures, even seen from close up, provided with tobacco, glasses, and snacks. They received only a quick glance from the corners of his eyes, the son of the man on whose property they were gnawing. They didn't dare to send after him even one of their customary remarks, for they were afraid of the dogs and, at most, grumbled out of crooked mouths because the animals were not in their kennel as they usually were at this time; they didn't know either what those men wanted who were standing there in front under the oaks. And they got up out of their wicker chairs and chaises, and looked at the son of Odysseus as he approached the men down along the avenue, the dogs at his side. And those handsome men, uninvited men, the suitors of his mother were astonished because he was so beautiful and of divine grace. For that's what Athena wanted, who watched over the scene, spread over sky and earth, intermixed with the elements.

Who were the men over there in front under the oaks, and how many were there?—How many? Not very many. Sadly, that must be said. It would be hard to talk about a people's assembly. Even divine determination could not change that. What was here was at most the idea of a people's assembly—but the idea, anyway. Since ideas actually, as was decided after countless hours of thinking, are the forms of a universal living together, it can doubtless be deduced logically that the numerically smallest community stands also for its essence, thus, for community itself . . . In this or a similar manner, Pallas Athena would argue with herself. For admittedly she, too, had counted on a different gathering of the people, and now she had to improvise and take into consideration anew divinely collegial assistance to put her plans through.—And so it happened: Whatever doleful picture this crowd might offer, Athena, who was also intermixed with the air that Telemachus breathed, gave the young warrior on that afternoon such courage and such confidence—blind and divine, both of them, reasonable and fine-grained as the sand of Mnemosyne—that nothing was able to rattle him, not even the sight of this run-down, angry, valiant, tottering mob . . .

There is, first of all, Aegyptus, the hero bent with age. We mention him first because he will be the first to begin to speak. He can no longer extend his fingers, which had all his life gripped the handles of tools—he had carved out patterns for a living. Since the day he was told that his work was no longer required, his fingers have remained bent. His grip is as firm as it ever was, but when he starts to pick up an object, he must clamp it in his bent claws—or someone else must do it for him. So his hands had become like a toy Play Mobil figure, into whose hollow little hands one can press various objects with a light click. Before that, his hands had been chapped, hard and dark in the creases of skin, for they had been used incessantly; they had been dry and warm. But then, when they were no longer used for work, dampness had formed in their fists—indeed, like between wood and lacquer—the clenched palms had sweated from not being used, and the sweat had washed them clean and made them soft, and they had become pale like the wee hands of court ladies. One of his sons, Antiphus by name, had joined Odysseus before Troy. Aegyptus has been waiting to this day for him, the oldest, who had always been his favorite. (Being considerate of the father, we want to reveal only in parentheses: He waits in vain. Antiphus came to a gruesome end, devoured by a one-eyed monster, between whose teeth his remains hung for another day.) Aegyptus says: "Men, listen to me now! Listen to what I have to tell you!"

And from the rear, he is immediately interrupted: "Come, come, come!"

He turns around—he cannot just twist his neck around any more, he has to maneuver his whole body—looks, recognizes, and hisses: "Now him! My goodness! Phemius, why did you invite him?" And waves around the thing in his hand—we forgot to mention that Aegyptus brought along a weapon, a bicycle pump, and he waves it around in the air—and against whom?

Against Peisenor, who is also called the Crier. He now stands behind him and agitates. Had Aegyptus not noticed him previously at all? Can be that he did. But he acted as though he didn't notice him.

"Come, come, come," Peisenor says further in a husky voice; he hardly has a voice, the Crier. And he, too, turns now against the bard: "Phemius, you should have told me that he would turn up here. I don't want to waste my time!" A short, broad, once hard-hitting hulk of a man is he, with an ax-handle head on which everything is extended to the same degree: neck, lower jaw, temples, brow, perfectly straight and half a head high, no back of the head, hardly any ears, taken altogether a smoothly lathed globe on white-shirted shoulders, only his thick-lensed glasses stand out, behind which his aged eyes swim in pink tears.

"Not with him, I can't!" he screeches, means Aegyptus, but grabs for Phemius' face because he can't guess, because of near, far, retinal, and cataract sightedness, who is who and how far away he stands from him. His overalls are smudged and his hands, too, up to the elbows and higher. Actually, he had just been in the process of greasing the wagon axles when Phemius beckoned him to the fence, and then he had crept away, for his own people were not supposed to know anything. He had a horse whip stuck in his boot; it's possibly good for scaring off lizards but also, just possibly, the only useful thing that his descendants had left him.

"If you can't with me, then just go back home," Aegyptus rails at him.

"Come, come, come," he hears yet again.

And Aegyptus: "Do you have just three words in your fat belly?"

And Peisenor: "Come, come, come!"

"Once in eighty years a different word from you! Once! Just once!"

"What do you want to hear, then, you dried-up prune, ha?"

"See, see, see! He can do it!"

And they pay no attention at all to Odysseus' son, they're so busy with mutual shouting and mimicking and enumerations of dignified nonsense—Peisenor, the Crier, and Aegyptus, the hero. And they pay no attention to the dogs, who are trained for angry words and let their throats growl. If every kick in a dog's hind end made a foot a millimeter shorter, then hero and crier would not be there at all, that's how often in their lives they kicked at curs.

"Don't bother with those two," says Phemius to Telemachus and puts an arm around his shoulders. "All old men argue. Battos, for example, would have come, too, but then he didn't want to because I'm here. He hates me. He says. He lent me his old truck, but he doesn't want to have anything to do with me. He doesn't hate me. I tell you. I just get on his nerves; he's spent a lot of time sitting, and that makes you contentious. And here," Phemius makes an introduction to the people's assembly, "this one here is old Loosh."

Loosh is someone who nods and laughs and points his finger. Suit, hat, and shoes worn crooked, shabby, stale, all one and the same, interchangeable. A face, mixed altogether out of scabs, threads of spittle, and bags under his eyes. He has his pant pockets full of rocks, some quite sharp-edged ones among them, a slingshot stuck in his belt. He has put his handkerchief under his hat against the heat. He has small, clever eyes that are bedded in his spoiled face like little pieces of mica.

"Loosh," Phemius cries out, "Loosh, Loosh, he's the son of Odysseus!"

"Sure, sure," says Loosh and jingles his pant pocket and wags his finger, as though he had caught someone doing something mischievous.

And there, too, is Michael: bowlegged and a behind twice as broad as his shoulders. Still sharp. Where is he then? Ah, there. Now here, now there. And gone again. Hardly glimpsed, then out of sight. Hey! Already after someone again! A weasel, that old man. Eighty seven. You have to sniff him out. Gives off a rustic, sour smell, that man. He has brought along a rake. A rake with an over-long handle. Who knows what kind of things he plans to rake over to him with it. And then the wordless old man who stands right next to the oak, thin, withered, feeble, tall, and bent over at the top, with a stubbly face, who holds a pistol in his hand—he has clamped the barrel under his armpit . . .

"Who's that?" asks Telemachus. "They've all forgotten his name," says Phemius, "but everyone knows him, me too, and we don't want to be impolite enough to ask him his name. He was the youngest at home. None of his relatives is alive anymore. He's probably over ninety. The pistol doesn't mean anything."

"Can he hear me?"

"I just don't know exactly. Can be that we've forgotten his name because he can't talk anymore."

Is that everybody?—Yes.—The whole people's assembly?—Yes. They came here on Batto's truck. Phemius drove it; the men sat in the back on the truck bed—an old vehicle, three-wheeler, just one seat in front in the cab, only two gears and one for reverse. Now the thing is standing in the shade of the first oak, sunken on its shock absorbers, and its radiator's making a face as though it smelled something foul.—By the way: Phemius is armed, too—no, not with his banjo, with a cudgel that could also pass as an old man's cane.

And there—look!—there comes someone else! The people's assembly wasn't complete, after all! A thin horse is approaching; a tiny rider sits on it, looks like a blue chocolate-bar wrapper that was wadded up on the saddle. Now he leaps off, lands like a fly. Is shrunk to just over a yard, the manikin, wears a blue uniform and a blue, broad-rimmed hat with gold braid on the rim.

"That's Halitherses, the seer," whispers Phemius respectfully. "There's a lot of songs about him"

"Am I too late?" asks the seer. His small face is broad and dark like an old crab apple. From his chin to the tip of his nose is hardly room for two thumbs. In between, his mouth is a rip; there've been no lips there for a long time. Halitherses is at least a hundred years old. "I've come to hear the son of Odysseus," he says with a strange voice. Takes his hat off, scratches his mown skull.

The men bow to him. The discord between Aegyptus, the hero, and Peisenor, the crier, is buried. The dogs bark short and clear. The horse trots behind the house to drink his fill from the water trough—with the seer on their side, no plan can go bad.

"Speak," he says to Telemachus. He says nothing else.

"Yes, speak," says Aegyptus, too. "We'll listen to you!"

"Anyone who can will listen to you," says Phemius. "And whoever can no longer hear will read in your mouth and your eyes what you say."

So now the time had come for Telemachus' speech. Neither a lectern nor a microphone were there, no journalists, no neutral observers, no cameras. Before him stood only the people, his people, his army—there weren't many soldiers, but together they filled a good half a millennium with experience . . .

"Men," that's how he should begin his speech, the general, the beloved son of Odysseus. That's what was written in Athena's film script. Slightly bent over, he waited—for what?—still held his dogs fast by their collars. They had their mouths open, and their red tongues hung to the side over their teeth; their legs twitched nervously, and their eyes moved from one to another. Phemius took the dogs off his hands. The general was supposed to have his hands free while speaking. Perhaps, he intended to become violent, which depending on circumstances would sweep away not only the people but also all the other higher creatures . . . Phemius hummed a low tone—"a-oohoo"—that sometimes without any recognizable rhythm he raised with "ai-hid" to the blue note and left it hanging there limply. That calmed down the dogs.

And so now Telemachus opened his mouth to speak—his hands free, his heart swollen with wild fury—that is, he cleared his throat, took a deep breath. Because he turned his back to the house, he did not notice that the men against whom, on the advice of the goddess, he had raised this valiant army, had stepped from the terrace and slowly came nearer, though stopping within earshot. For the dogs in Phemius' hands turned their heads toward them, and their open, panting maws, next to divinely blind courage and divinely blind confidence, were Telemachus' most dangerous and—after critical consideration, admittedly—only weapons . . .

Why was he still hesitating? Everything was prepared, set into motion by Pallas Athena . . . or was the miserable reality before his eyes too harsh so that it showed even through the sand that Pallas Athena had strewn into his eyes, that it even penetrated the boards of deception that Pallas Athena had nailed to his brow?

Translated by A. Leslie Willson

Kalypso—Excerpt

It was the first time that he heard her voice. She had a wonderfully sonorous alto voice, as gentle and mild on his ear as thistle oil for his throat. She repeated her name, slipped closer to his cot, introduced herself to him, and at the same time took his shriveled-up fingers into her hands, tenderly touching the tips with her thumbs. She didn't say, "My name is . . ." She simply said her name so that one would think it was just some word—in case one didn't know it was a name.

"What is that?" he asked. His voice was nothing more than a soundless whisper.

She repeated. And repeated. And said her name over and over again. "Kalypso, Kalypso, Kalypso."

She was amazed by the happiness the sound of this word created. Its second vowel bounced out of her mouth with a cheerful and giddy flip of her tongue, just in time before the consonant immediately following closed her lips. Was it that she had never before articulated her name? Had no one ever asked her about it? Had she never, in her life, heard her name pronounced? Had she never been called by anyone? Who had given her this name? Who names creatures like her, anyway?

We move through misty terrain because we must never forget when approaching the most beautiful woman that she is a nymph. In the poem, she is even called a goddess. Her divinity is emphasized by a certain quality, namely by *deinos*: which means *tremendous, large*, as well as *awe-inspiring, honorable, dignified*, but also *terrifying, horrible, dangerous*. Her father, so we hear, was the Titan Atlas. Who was her mother? We are told in another legend that she, who in that legend is also called "the one who awakens desire," was one of the three thousand daughters of Okeanos and Tethis. This ancient brother-and-sister pair, like Mnemosyne, was begotten of the heaven and the earth, of Uranos and Gaia. Kalypso, the brother-sister-child of memory? Elsewhere it is written that she and several of her sisters had not been able to stand the rough nature of the sea. They had been transformed into streams and were poured onto different islands—Kalypso onto Ogygia. There she, thanks to her loveliness beyond form, would change into exactly the kind of creature a foreign visitor most desires as he sets foot onto the island. If the visitor were an albatross, she would become a female albatross; if he were a swimming bull, she would become a cow; if he were a mallard, she a duck; and if he were a man, she a woman . . .

"Is Kalypso your name?" asked Odysseus.

She nodded, shrugged her shoulders, and withdrew into the shadows of the candles again.

He couldn't speak anymore that day. He fell asleep. Did he dream? Nothing clear, nothing that hurt him, nothing that caused misery.

It happened on the following day, or even a day later, that he covered himself with his sheet when Kalypso wanted to rub his body down with oil. It wasn't necessary any more, he said. Besides, he was ashamed because he was so ugly and she was the most beautiful woman he had ever seen.

He was the most beautiful man, she said.

He contradicted her; we know this. Why should he have to be the most beautiful, anyway, as long as he lived! She put her hands on him, caressing the sheet. He contemplated her face, her hair, her arms. Everything was perfect beauty and perfect life, and his lust for her was aroused. He didn't think anything about her was supposed to be not exactly right or, at least, exaggerated or missing just so that I can feel generous and forgiving or, at least, pretend to be forgiving. Did he also not want to disturb this beauty in the least bit? No, what he was wishing for was not a trace less of paradise. He did not think, "What am I doing here?" For he considered himself a man who had barely escaped death, and she—who was the first bit of life he saw before his eyes after he had emerged from the darkest darkness—she had to be the most beloved, the most reverently beloved, at least, for a day, until he again became accustomed to dear life in sunlight—he flirted with her.

"Kalypso is your name?" he asked.

She nodded.

"I thought I had dreamed this name," he said. "Would you like to know my name?"

She nodded again. He said his name. She repeated it after him: "Odysseus."

"Your name is more beautiful," he said.

She repeated his name, and said she thought it was just as beautiful.

But he said her name was also mysterious unlike his. "Kalypso, Kalypso, Kalypso." While he was saying the name with different stresses and modulations, he thought about what charming things could be associated with it. "Kalypso," he said, "Kalypso, you with the nimble hands, with lips so full yet not too full, lips that are red but never turn into a shade of blue or brown, as is often the case with heavily red lips." Because he sensed he was about to sink down to the place where Hades' gates were so close, he kept talking; he linked word to word and spun himself a web that kept him in the light. "Kalypso," he said, and a trace of panic colored his voice, "Kalypso, you with the graceful nose whose nostrils flare in delicate openings that are like the shapes of tiny pear imprints, a form the word 'nostril' cannot adequately describe. Kalypso, your brows are arched like the line of a swan's closed wings. And your eyes are beauty in and of themselves . . ."

Right at this point, his eyes fell closed. Hypnos, the god of sleep and son of the night, whose soft repose is spread out near the gates of Hades, approached in flight. He came alone this time, without anyone from his countless number of sons, the dreams; and he gave to the sufferer a long, deep, merciful rest. Kalypso could not satisfy the hunger of her heart. She bent down over the sleeping man, strewed his skin with kisses, and giggled a little about it. She was filled with joy.

Kalypso Goes Shopping

Kalypso then hurried into town. She had not dressed up, had neither done her hair nor put on the black and red dress. She had not put on make-up nor paid attention to her graceful walk. Never before had she been to town during the day, but she thought little about it. She took the bus, bit her lips with anxiety, and spied through the window for a store that might carry white linen clothes. He had been wearing nothing but a shirt and pants when she found him. The shirt and pants were tattered. As the sun dried them, it became apparent that they could not be used for anything but dust rags because the salt water had ruined the fabric. Kalypso was filled with the thought to do something nice for her man. Already, she referred to him in that manner. New clothes, the same clothes, only new, that's what she had set her mind to. She was full of sobbing, racing impatience.

At the main train station, she got off. She checked the schedule for when the next bus would go back. In a hurry, she then mingled with the hurriedly walking people. She allowed herself to be carried through the station lobby by the stream of people. On an escalator, she dove with them into an underpass where flowers with great calyxes were for sale under electric lights. That's where she detached herself from the crowd of depressed people and ran up the next staircase back into the sunlight. She was full of sobbing, racing impatience.

A girl sat on the stairs, where a ray of sunlight ran diagonally across her forehead; she stretched out her desertlike hand, which was grimy with black dirt; her fingers grappled greedily. "Give me the coins." Judged by the color of her voice, the girl was still very young. Her mouth was covered with sand and beautifully arched. The lower lip was chapped in the middle, forming a vertical wound. "Those are heavy for you, anyway."

Kalypso gave the girl what she wanted. And while she emptied the clinking contents of her purse, her hands were shaking.

"Hey, wait," said the girl, "you're a beauty; you should also be kissed by good luck. Take me out for something! At least for coffee. I'll tell you stories for a brandy and a coffee."

Kalypso only shook her head and went on.

She entered a department store on the ground floor, where they sold jewelry and asked one of the cashiers for the department with white linen clothes, if such a thing existed. Meanwhile, she impatiently drummed the laminated coin dish with her fingertips. She was referred to the fourth floor. That's where the sporting goods were. That's where she should try. She squeezed herself onto an escalator again, this time between short-necked female customers, who all looked up as if expecting salvation. It made her stomach turn that everything around her had such a strong odor of perfume. She thought the smell was on her fingers, so she spat on them and wiped her hands clean on her chest. She passed the others in an impolite manner and, while still on the escalator, motioned to the sports department salesperson that she was in a hurry.

It was cool in there. The music was turned down so that only the hissing of the drums could be heard. She bought a pair of pants and a shirt that looked similar to the worn-out ones—white and loose. She had brought the worn-out ones as samples. The salesperson understood immediately, also saw her hurry, and was at her service without small talk, without casting strange glances at her beautiful body, and without embarrassment before her unimaginable magnificence.

She hadn't had time to wonder about the salesman's calmness. Between soccer balls in baskets and tennis rackets hanging on lattice wire racks, she held the clothes to her body. When the salesman pursed his lips and shook his head as if giving advice, she quickly said that the shirt and pants were for someone else. However, she wanted them to go with her looks too. She also grabbed a pair of linen shoes, hastily estimating the size. She had the things wrapped up and didn't even wait for the salesman to snap the push buttons on the nylon sack.

She also got some cigarettes, a few packs of different brands: light ones, strong ones, some with filters, some without. He had asked for cigarettes but then hadn't told her what kind he wanted. Later, she had forgotten to ask him. She looked at the wristwatch of a man who was waiting at the stoplight, and she saw she had another whole twenty minutes until the bus would leave.

He might want to read something, she thought, when he lies there awake and recovering. That's when he will to want to read something light. She stepped into a bookstore. But then she remembered his eyes, which were kind of milky around the edges already, and she thought that reading might be too strenuous for him.

A saleswoman approached her. She had a pointed chin, a happy and crooked mouth, and her hair dyed henna-red. She was petit and fragile; one eye was floating a little to the outside, and that even looked nice. "Can I help you?" she asked.

Kalypso said that she had a patient at home who was in the middle of recovering from a disease. And, at first, she had thought that he might want to read something light, but now she felt that reading might be too strenuous for him anyway.

"I think so, too," said the bookseller and smiled impishly. "Buy him a comic book. When people are sick, they like looking at pictures. They really like watching TV best. But TV isn't good when you are sick. And then comic books are similar to TV, except they don't strain the eyes so badly."

While she spoke, she walked over to a rotating shelf. She had a bouncing step, and her heel hardly touched the floor. Kalypso followed her.

The henna-redhead spoke softly, and one had to stay close to her if one wanted to hear her. "Here," she said and pulled out a comic. "The hero is a little boy with a stuffed tiger to play with. He plays with the tiger and imagines it were real. I know what you think. You think it is for kids. You're right, but then again you're not. I don't know if your patient is a kid."

"He's not," said Kalypso.

"Makes no difference, actually that is even better. It's too sophisticated for kids. But for a sick man who is smart, it is ideal."

"He is smart," said Kalypso.

"And is he also someone who likes stories?"

"He is."

The henna-redhead with the pointy face rolled her good eye and said, "Wasn't it just so nice when we were kids and got sick and then healthy again and looked at picture books. And, now that we are adults and get sick and healthy again, we like remembering it. And that's good. We do get well a little bit faster—perhaps not measurably but still—by looking at a picture book. Reading in general is sophisticated, and so is looking at pictures. And being sick is sophisticated as well, at least, if you are about to get well again." She opened the comic book. "The boy, like I said, is named Calvin, and his tiger is named Hobbes. But there are stories without the tiger, as well. Here, for example. Read, please. That's just about how the other stories are."

She turned the comic and handed it to Kalypso. "I'll be right back," she said and turned her attention to another customer.

Kalypso looked at the open page of the comic. On the top right, it showed a man in a dark blue sweater sitting on the stairs of his house. Everything was framed with frayed black ink. Calvin, the boy, whose head was rosy red and twice as big as his body, steps out of the house and walks up to his dad in the second picture. And his bubble says, *How come old photographs are always black and white? Didn't they have color film back then?*

The father holds a green coffee mug in his hand, has one leg crossed over the other; and forever, until the end of the comic, until its consumption through time, Calvin's father is going to sit in this picture like that and say: *Sure they did. In fact, those old photographs are in color. It's just the world was black and white then.*

Really? asks Calvin in the next picture. His question will stretch until the end of the world and will remain unanswered in the world of this little picture. His hair will be yellow peaks framed in black forever.

The world didn't turn color until sometime in the 1930s, says the father. *And it was pretty grainy color for a while, too.*

That's really weird, says Calvin.

Well, truth is stranger than fiction, says the father and drinks out of his green mug, but still his thirst will never be quenched. In the same picture, Calvin stretches out his arms with the four-fingered hands. Above his open bean-sized mouth hovers the heavy bubble with its white spike: *But why are old paintings in color? If the world was black and white, wouldn't the artists have painted it that way?*

The father in a new picture: *Not necessarily. A lot of the great artists were insane.*

Calvin's face, reduced to a gaping mouth, filling an entire picture: *But . . . but how could they have painted in color anyway? Wouldn't their paints have to have been shades of gray then?*

The father: *Of course, but they turned colors like everything else did in the 30s.* Now the father puts his arm around his son—no, that wasn't said right: the father has put his arm around his son— that's how to say it. When did he do that? Is the history of that motion not recorded anywhere? Has it been forgotten because it wasn't worth telling?

In the last picture in this story's world, the father sits next to his son. Calvin asks, *So why didn't old black-and-white photos turn color too?*

Because they were color pictures of a black-and-white world, answers the father.

"Sophisticated, huh," says the saleswoman. It was only then that Kalypso noticed that she was standing next to her again.

Kalypso bought it and went back to the train station. She crossed the lobby and waited by the bus stop. She had not even spent an hour in the city, but she had bought him clothes, cigarettes, and a comic book. She was proud of herself.

Then, on the way home, the sky was like she had never seen it before. Grayish white clouds, thin like empty boards of a freestanding bookshelf, floated on top of one another and multiplied the horizon. It seemed to her as if she were at home on each one of these plains, as if she were expected everywhere. Her heart had been pounding in her throat with joy, and she knew that she would never forget this trip home from the town.

Translated by Kathryn Ott and Björn Freitag

Peter Rosei

Case Pending—Excerpt

The long-awaited banquet at President Gruber's is taking place this evening. An invitation to this banquet is a big honor. It is important to know that Gruber is the most outstanding and certainly the most influential attorney on the Supreme Judicial Board. For many years he has presided as Chair of the commission, which is made up of the best legal minds in our system, and because of his extraordinary accomplishments in all areas of the law, he is well-respected not only by the Ministry but even beyond our borders. Countless foreign universities have awarded him honorary doctorates. He is often called on as a consultant in international disputes, most recently on an extremely difficult problem of the demarcation of territorial waters. His opinions are not always accepted without contradiction, as is often the case in matters such as this; however, they are always cited with utmost respect in all learned journals.

It has been two weeks since the day I received the invitation to the banquet, and I am still very anxious. My agitation, instead of decreasing, has gotten more and more pronounced, more and more unbearable. In the last few days, I have hardly dared to let the invitation, a beautiful, longish deckle-edged note card, out of my hands for fear it could be stolen. From the very first moment, this invitation seemed to be something that could change or decide my life. I have taken out the invitation at least a hundred times during the last two weeks. By searching for some little peculiarity, for instance, an unevenness in the print or a particular shape of a letter in my name that had been written in by hand, I have tried to clarify the significance and possible consequences that this invitation could have for me. As great as my happiness had been when I first received it, it had now slowly changed into fear. I am not even sure that the initial joy had not all along been simply fear in another form. In my hands the invitation card had become more and more a kind of playing card, an unknown card in an unknown game, a card of which I didn't know the value or whether it meant victory or defeat.

During times of despair, indeed, for nights on end, I stared at the invitation, turned it back and forth in my hand, and stared at it again, thought about not going to the banquet and excusing myself on account of a sudden illness. But then I would immediately reproach myself bitterly for my cowardice, my lethargy, my vacillating. I told myself, "You have to catch the ball they threw your way. They certainly won't throw you another one."—Who knows, I thought, perhaps you are dramatizing everything unnecessarily. Perhaps your name was put on the list of invitees by mistake, and somewhere a secretary who doesn't know you—and doesn't know who is hiding behind the name of Malej—made out the invitation in ignorance and sent it to you. Perhaps the doorkeeper will discover the error this evening and politely, but firmly, turn you away. But perhaps people will think that you secured the invitation deviously, perhaps through bribery or forgery, and will threaten you with the police or a disciplinary action. Perhaps . . .

As I look at the clothes that I had made especially for this evening and that are laid out in front of me, I am thinking, as I sometimes do, that it would have been better if I had never received the invitation. Then I wouldn't have had all kinds of hopes about the evening and also wouldn't have had to be afraid. Everything would have been the way it always was, the way I have always considered it necessary for my particular lot since I had never seen or experienced anything else.

I am a legal records clerk, a small bureaucrat, and I do my job. My accomplishments are not small, but they are hardly outstanding. People like President Gruber have always been as far out of reach to me as the sun from the earth.

And then I get this invitation! It's white as snow with its text sharply etched in antique lettering in the middle of which the name MALEJ is neatly inscribed in blue-black ink.

Without a thought I used to pass by the wide, beautifully curved outdoor staircase that leads to the offices of the highest officials and entered the ministry through that narrow side entrance that opens into the offices of the subordinate clerks like me, but since the day I got the invitation, I have become painfully conscious of my situation. Everyday when I am sent to deliver an urgent document to the main office that I am assigned to as a clerk, I come into the big, bright room of the head of the section, Ministerialrat Seidl. The large windows in his office open onto the Heldenplatz. Seidl is the highest of my immediate superiors, but in comparison to President Gruber, he is nothing. Even when I have nothing more to do than place the file I just copied on the sidetable immediately next to the door, I have enough time between my bow upon entering and bow upon leaving to notice very clearly the practically inexpressible difference between this room and its lord and me and my completely windowless office. And although there are eight of us in the office, it measures barely fifteen square meters.—During the last few days, I have often thought how light and roomy the office of the president must be. After concluding these thoughts, I again and again looked at the fact of my invitation.

First, always the same questions: WHY, HOW COME, FOR WHAT REASON? Then always the same answers that aren't really answers, that all begin with the word PERHAPS and end with a question mark—how I tortured myself during the last few days with this game of question and answer. Perhaps you were invited simply for the amusement of the guests, as a kind of entertainment, for a late-night laugh?

Soon everything will have passed. In a few hours, I will know for sure. At any rate, I have done everything I can to prove myself worthy of the invitation. I had a tuxedo made by the best tailor in town and paid for it out of my savings. For a long time I didn't even dare to step into the shop. I was never as aware of my own wretchedness that had become as comfortable to me as my own skin as when I stood in front of that shop with its gleaming marble facade and brass-plated door. Or, indeed, when I stood in front of its uniformed doorman, who was apparently drunk and wanted to throw me out immediately—probably because he thought I was a beggar. My response to the tailor's French greeting and the incomprehensible jokes that the assistants taking my measurements according to his orders made was a mutter that I was barely conscious of. The mere visit to the tailor's had demanded of me the utmost self-control; actually, it would be more honest if I said: self-deception. Now that I had lying in front of me the tuxedo, the fine shirt, the proper bowtie, the black shoes, the top hat, and all of the accessories necessary for a man of the world, my efforts to get them don't seem so bad. Vanity does its part to make self-deception complete. As I walk back and forth in the room, I practice my bows and how, with a nonchalant gesture, I let the lady go first, how I offer my arm to a lady, and by the softest pressure lead her in this or that direction, etc.—I cannot dance. I'll have to watch the dancing—I believe social dancing to be an anachronism in our time. Dancing is passé; that's what I could say, that's what I will say, that's how cleverly I will disguise my inadequacy.

Again questions beginning with PERHAPS arise. Perhaps this invitation means I'll get a promotion at the ministry or at least I may look forward to it in the future? Perhaps it is a kind of prelude to my career? Perhaps I'll just get a pretend promotion only to be immediately demoted and be made the laughing stock of the officials?

After all, I am a person too. Why should I be the butt of such terrible jokes?—It is true I am only a clerk, I come from modest surroundings, and from the standpoint of the ladies and gentlemen invited to the banquet, I come from the gutter. Yes, I come from the gutter.

But who could notice that? My clothing is absolutely no different from that of the others, my face is clean-shaven, my hair is not too long or too short; I won't say anything unless I am spoken to; and, surely, I won't be spoken to very much since I don't know anyone there. My face is pleasant if not attractive. My hands are well cared for, my gate is balanced and deliberate.—In the short span of two weeks, I have actually succeeded in taking on the behavior of a well-trained monkey. On the one hand, I am repulsive to myself; on the other hand, I am proud of myself. In two short weeks I have made, at least at first glance, the perfect gentleman out of myself. Every little thing in my appearance, my demeanor has been thought through carefully. When things don't come naturally, they must be thought out and calculated. I must admit that the difficulties of this have almost become too much for me. Without knowing it, I entered a labyrinth with my decision to go to the banquet. For example, the pride I felt earlier, while looking at my dress clothes, has now long vanished since I have put them on. But I am not obligated, not even now, to actually attend the banquet. No one is forcing me. I kept my invitation and all my preparations secret from everyone, that is, from my colleagues, for I don't know anyone else. At first, it was because I didn't want to have to share my pleasure with anyone. I would walk through the corridors of the ministry with a halo of glory visible only to me—my gate would be slower than usual so as to do justice to my new dignity. Later I became ashamed of my secretive preparations. I felt like a traitor.

And now the true blessing of keeping it quiet is revealed: I am safe from the ridicule of my colleagues. There is no connection between any of the gentlemen invited to the banquet and the class of officials to which my colleagues belong—"You too belong to this class. You are still a member of this class. It's true that you have been invited," I say as I stand before my wretched mirror in which I can see only my face, not even my entire head. "It's true you were invited, but even so, you belong to the class of scum." I look at my fingernails. The bit of dirt I discover under the nail of my right index finger seems to me to be the proof of the correctness of my self-evaluation.

Over there on my night table are the newspapers. All of the papers of the capital have already reported in great detail about the banquet and the personalities who will be attending. I can cite practically by heart the articles that are written in a slimy, self-serving tone. During the evenings of the last few days, I read them again and again. While reading them, I was proud to be among the invited. As I lay on the bed—my sublet room is furnished with only that night table, a basin made of white enameled iron, a dresser, a table, and an easy chair—I tried to imagine the splendor of the coming evening. At that point I usually saw in my mind's eye a lot of waiters scurrying back and forth over the gleaming marble or parquet floors. Half waking, half dreaming, I imagined the glow of a chandelier. I never got beyond those platitudes. MARVELOUS, again and again, I pronounced this word that the reporters used so often. MARVELOUS, INTOXICATING, ENCHANTING. For example, I tried to imagine the ENCHANTING WIFE OF THE HOFRAT . . . I have spent hours filling in the details of ridiculous imaginary pictures like that.

Translated by Ruth Gross

Out of the Future—Excerpt

A surprise was waiting for him in his office. It had been confirmed that the deceased persons were indeed Doria Allman—and her daughters, Blanche and Nancy. But, oddly enough, there was nothing missing from the apartment, not money nor any other item of value. This meant it was unlikely that whoever did it was just some thieving drifter. It's possible that the perpetrator turned the place upside down just to throw off any investigation.

This Nancy worked as a doctor, had worked as a doctor, in one of the transition camps. Of course, as a doctor, she had access to all sorts of poison. However, the one-way needles that he had found in a trash can—they were washed out clean, and one could not ascertain what the contents had been.

The Allmans had been killed by lethal injection. That much was clear.

"So, what do you think," Plokow said as Ries looked in before leaving, "do we get down to business tomorrow?!"

"First, there has to be another tomorrow, my dear colleague," Ries replied as he carefully shut the door. That was his way of joking.

He, Ries, went down the long, half-dark corridor, picked up his briefcase in the office; it lay ready for him, mostly empty, then he took the express elevator to the exit. As he walked out of the building, he took a deep breath. Judging by the expression on his broad face, one might think this was a great evening, a tepid summer evening in the making. However, everything was like always; the lamps out in front and the beams from the street lights shone down; the temperature the same, neither cold nor warm; six o'clock, the streets were crammed with people.

The first thing Ries did was to go find one of those fast-food places, the kind that only pretends to be different, by changing the packaging and other little details. Hungry, he ate a shish kebab sandwich, French fries, and he drank a beer out of a plastic cup. The beer did not have much alcohol, no head, didn't foam at all. He sat quite comfortably on his plastic stool, made to imitate wood, his feet stretched out in front of his little table; he had set his briefcase down on the next stool. He stared into the expansive room, thinking about nothing in particular; the room's floor was cluttered with tossed food packaging. People were standing in two rows up at the mirrored front—First, Ries's fingers fished the tomato slice and the salad leaves out of his sandwich and dropped them into his mouth. Then, with giant bites, he slowly chewed on his bun. The beer tasted a little sour. There was beer on tap in the German Club, a Bavarian recipe. Now, that beer tasted good! For a moment, he felt like going to the club. Felt like really knocking back his share. Combined with this new stuff—what was it called?—one was clear-headed the next day. And, besides, maybe a few traces of alcohol might get the old brain working even sharper? Ries grinned.

The crowd streamed down the street as thickly as before. Ries had left the fast-food place and drifted, briefcase in arm, with the flow. The laughing, the calls and mutterings, the traffic noise, all this inspired him in a good way. At a street corner, he stopped and thought it over one more time, to go or not to go to the club. There were these waitresses there, and—oh, well. And there were broad-shouldered bar tenders in green, traditional costumes with those little hats; all of them were ready and willing for a little cash. And a piece of roast, "Jägerbraten," with those big dumplings! That was his favorite. Ries just liked the club in general. Of course, he thought some of them took their "Germanism" a little too far: steel helmets with cow horns on them, and those peppy, happy songs to which they would jump about slapping their shoe soles. All that was just plain dumb! As he recalled the yodeling so many of them practiced, he decided not to go to the club, after all.

He crossed one of the large squares. Everything was empty and lonely. There were, though, drifters camped out in dark corners; they had cooking fires going. The flames licked upward to the dull sky. Lights were shining in the offices of the ministry, whose buildings encompassed the square like protective walls. Ries walked down a street, turned right, then left, and landed, as if by chance, in an area of town where the sidewalks are full of whores. Blonde, light red, fox red, black: willing flesh stood everywhere, you just had to serve yourself.

But Ries could tell right away that his uneasiness was greater than the particular enjoyment that one of these creatures—Clones every one—could afford him. He tried seeking diversion in a peep show for a while.

He rode the subway out to the West Belt, to the last station. At the edge of the elite section of town, there is no way through. The station was lit up but seemed abandoned. Ries walked along the desolate street on the edge to the noble area, and he looked toward its distant, glimmering lights. The hills there really did look like, well, like crowns, adorned with diamonds and glistening jewels reveling in their own shine: What were they singing, those lights? It was a sound void of words, of meaning, and yet it shot through bone and marrow; it broke Ries's heart.

From a somewhat elevated position he, briefcase in arm, looked back at the city. It sprawled out in a pale, diffuse shimmer of brightness.

He wandered on through the sleepy streets, the empty streets, streets excited every night from the hustle and bustle of the city, until after many a twist and turn, he finally reached his own neighborhood sometime around morning.

Nancy: That part of it had not given Plokow any rest, and so he took a helicopter out to Camp 23, where Nancy Allman had worked. Who knows, maybe there was a clue to be found? Perhaps, she had mixed up the lethal dose there?

First came the grid-shaped residential areas, then the industries in their flat buildings with high stacks, and then, kilometer after kilometer of vegetable plantations, with black plastic tarps spread out to protect against extreme sun. These were the fields where all those drifters interned at Camp 23 worked.

This gulag of camps was quite practical. After all, the people there had a roof over their heads, food, and medical care. The gulag was vast, that much Plokow did know. They must have had some horrendous problems in the East for everything to be so messed up here. One had heard a lot—in the media: about plans for growth, innovation, about colonization; but he, Plokow, had never really listened to any of it. What did he care? It was a matter for management; those people up there got good money to deal with stuff like that. You never found out what was really going on, anyway, what it was all for. And maybe no one knew.

"I'm setting her down," said the pilot. "You'll just jump on out, so I can take off again right away!"

Right—he didn't want to be on the ground any longer than he had to. As Plokow hiked over to the headquarters building, a bunch of cloned children were waiting for him. Rocks in hand, they stood staring from some distance at him with mistrustful, hate-filled eyes. The ground was covered with gravel, here and there a stinging nettle.

"Allow me to introduce you: Commissioner Plokow from the City Police—and this is Dr. Novak; he is in charge of our medical division!" The camp director was a small man with skin scarred by acne and with indefinable Mongol-like eyes; it was he who introduced them. Cigarette butts swam in a tin can on the table. Relatively speaking, the barracks was comfortably furnished, even a small library—though, as Plokow noticed with semi-amusement, consisting mainly of detective novels.

On the way to the barracks containing the clinic, the doctor complained about the miserable working conditions. Plokow shut him up by asking whether he was another one of those bleeding hearts. If there was anything Plokow couldn't stand, it was this hypocritical sympathy with the Clones. They were just standardized material. As best as humanly possible, they were created resistant to fear, care, and pain. They lived bountiful, productive lives! The doctor changed his tone immediately and gushed praise on the achievements of the gulag: "Look around, our group here is very healthy! No sexually transmitted diseases, no Aids. And we have a plentiful crop of new ones—know what I mean. They all fit the standards, our little ones; they'll be first-class citizens! They'll look back on Camp 23 with fond memories."

The doctor walked beside him, slightly tilted forward; he looked pale and large in his lab coat—like a ghost.

They went down a hall with a darkly oiled wooden floor; the last door: a white standard door—"Allman worked in there," explained the doctor. Plokow indicated that the doctor should wait for him.

Plokow was quickly finished in the room. Its walls were lined with white medical machines. Two windows opened to a windswept assembly yard, now empty. In the background was a row of barracks.

The desk stood in the middle of the room. Nancy Allman had examined her patients on the chair there, behind the desk; it was a simple revolving chair.

On the shelf over the wash table was a pair of pearl earclips, hers, probably.

In the desk: nothing. Plokow thumbed through her notes on different cases. Here and there a name was underlined in red: Chertkov. Ugudar. Solomin—it would take forever to track down all those names. Plokow turned off the neon light. The doctor was waiting in the hallway; he self-consciously cleared his throat; he had probably been listening at the door.

"Why did Allman work here with you people?"

"She wasn't assigned to us—maybe out of idealism." Plokow wasn't one for word games.

The doctor accompanied him to the assembly yard; through the neon light emitted from the light poles, the sky looked dark gray; and tiny, far away, the stars showed themselves in it. The wind was extremely strong out here in the open, and the doctor almost had to shout his explanations, although he stayed close to Plokow: to the left the Normative Adjustment barracks for the children conceived conventionally; then the Clone Boxes, where they produced and cared for children according to the wishes of different companies; and, finally, living quarters for the adults. Everything was kept in good condition: television, central heating, containers of bliss.

"We take our mission here very seriously," said the doctor as they entered the barracks. "Our society needs healthy, athletic people—and no other kind."

The work day had concluded, and the beds were full. Some lay still, eyes open, a bliss-needle sticking in the arm. Others were busy happily screwing each other, in part supported in their efforts by select chemicals. Heaven knows, they didn't let themselves be disturbed by visitors, at most, they would smile and wave the visitors over—a couple of arms shot up as Plokow and the doctor walked between the bunks.

"What do those people want?"

"They are volunteering to take the Injection. They don't want to live anymore. It's their right, you know."

"Of course," said Plokow. He thought about Nancy Allman. This had not exactly been a dream job.

Translated by Scott G. Williams

© DIMENSION² 1.1 (1994): 119–127 (for *Case Pending*) and DIMENSION² 3.1 (1996): 105–113 (for *Out of the Future*).

Michael Scharang

The Last Judgment of Michelangelo Spatz—Excerpt

I opened my eyes. Through the window I saw houses I had never seen before, which led me to conclude that I was dreaming again. Oh yes, I had seen these houses before, but never while it was dark. Now I understood that I was not in Vienna but in New York, and not at Maria's house but at my apartment.

I needed to get up, but it was not as usual the urge to urinate that compelled me, but rather the opposite: thirst. My throat was dry as dust. The papers said this was the driest September in 110 years. Daytime temperatures were above 86 degrees Fahrenheit. And now, so it seemed to me—and my thirst confirmed this—now it was not much cooler.

I turned on the light and sat down at the desk. As I saw by the big wall clock hanging above the desk—for when you sat at the desk, you were looking at a wall, which I found very agreeable—it was 10 p.m. I had been asleep for five hours.

Next to the telephone was a box with a blinking red light. I examined it; it was an answering machine. I pushed a button and heard Maria's voice. She was back, would go on to Boston with the dog. She thanked me for taking care of the dog and said she was glad I would stay in New York for a while. She told me she was surprised I had gone apartment hunting so quickly. I should have waited and asked her. She would get in touch as soon as she was back.

I listened to the message again. I could not detect any joy in Maria's words about my staying in New York longer than she had planned and renting an apartment for this purpose. I did not want to jump to conclusions. Should Maria hold it against me that I did not wait for her at her house, then she would just tell me so next week.

Unlike me, Maria would say what was on her mind, and while I could not do that with her, she could say to me: You should have asked me. My explanation for this was that, when we were fourteen, she had taught me about love, and she had remained the one who instructs and I the one who needs to be instructed.

It was not midnight yet when I collapsed on the futon again dead tired. I had arrived in New York a few days before, and now, stretched out on the mattress, I felt as though in all this time I had never had a second's rest, not even in my sleep. I wondered if the sensation of breathing in a city had been true.

At that moment, I thought the opposite was the case: The city had taken the breath out of me. In addition, the apartment seemed to have cracked my limbs. Fortunately, I need not savor this impression to its fullest extent, as I fell asleep.

The next morning my beginning as a writer in the new apartment turned out promising. After sleeping for ten hours and building up my strength, the latter of which was signaled by my erect member and by my body's pleasure in extending arms and legs until they trembled with the effort, I wrote down on a slip of paper a list of some items to buy at the supermarket in front of my house.

Because of my financial situation, I prepared for home cooking, encouraged by the well-equipped kitchen, in particular, the gas stove and refrigerator. These were two mighty pieces of equipment whose every part was so massive that, were these appliances quickly supplied with wheels, they could, in a pinch, also serve as combat vehicles in a war; and the refrigerator door handle, in addition, as a roadblock; the dials on the stove, as compass bowls; and the oven, as a field kitchen.

I entered the supermarket and saw in front of me a young man sitting in a shopping cart, weeping bitterly. The people were passing by him. I stood near the entrance and in people's way. So I took a step sideways toward the large glass panel, through which daylight entered the store but had no chance of holding its own against the brighter neon light.

I could not go on. I would have been prepared to accept that an African American sat in a shopping cart crying. However, that the people not merely walked by him but purposely ignored him, that I could not accept.

In Vienna you can watch at every street corner how people concentrate all their efforts on not simply not paying attention to others but ignoring them in such a way that the victim feels put down. In New York, it seemed to me, you also paid no attention to other persons, yet not in order to hurt their feelings but—on the contrary—to protect them, to avoid violating their physical space any more than you had to in a big city. Nowhere but in New York, according to my apparently rash opinion, was the individual well tolerated precisely because the others did not pay attention—out of kindness, not out of malevolence.

And now this incident in the supermarket: I kept standing there bewildered, watching people turning away from the weeping young man. Perhaps, I thought, I haven't been in New York long enough. If I had been here longer, I might not even notice that a young man was sitting in a shopping cart crying. Or, perhaps, I thought—and the thought frightened me—perhaps, I am not up to this town.

I decided to speak to the young man. I gathered up all my courage and stood near the shopping cart in which he sat. To my relief the man stopped crying. I asked if I could help him. He said yes.— Should I help you climb out of the shopping cart? —No. You can only help me by buying a lot of stuff, no matter what. It has to be a large amount. Toilet paper rolls. Potatoes. Giant-sized bottles of spring water. Those things are always needed and don't cost very much. At the cash register you ask that all the stuff be delivered. By me! You tell the woman at the cash register, I want this man to deliver my stuff. In order for everyone to see this, you hold out your arm and point at me.

I did as told, loading a sack of potatoes into my shopping cart, plus a pack of twelve toilet paper rolls, and five plastic bottles with a gallon of spring water each; this pretty much filled up the cart. Then there were fruit, vegetables, and yogurt—things I thought of while considering what to eat that weekend. I did not consult the actual list that was in my pant pocket. I would come back to it during my next purchase.

At the cash register I asked to have my purchases delivered, in fact, by this gentleman. I pointed at the man in the grocery cart. The lady at the cash register nodded approvingly, as though my wish coincided with hers, and shouted: Bob! He jumped out of the cart and was at the cash register in just two steps. He took up his work. This included placing the items in plastic bags as soon as they had gone through the hands of the checkout clerk. He did this with so much care that I recognized that here someone was not merely doing an unskilled job as best he could but expertly carrying out his trade.

Fruit and vegetables were not tossed into the bag together, one on top of the other, as I would have done it, but placed next to each other carefully so that no damage from one to the other could possibly occur. And when the man put the items in a shopping cart, the heavy water bottles, of course, went at the bottom, and then the potatoes. On top of that, however, not the vegetables and fruit, but the toilet paper; perhaps, I thought, so that it might not wrinkle. The manner in which he handled the items was remarkable too: Every motion was precise, just the way a drama teacher would demonstrate how the part of a grocery deliveryman ought to be played.

The young man wheeled the shopping cart out of the supermarket. Once outside, I immediately joined him in order to pump him for information. However, he asked me to walk ahead of him, as real customers would do. He would answer my questions at the house.

So at my apartment, I invited him to be seated. There was no coffee, no tea, no beer, no wine, no mineral water, only the spring water in the giant bottles. I filled two glasses with water. He said his name was Bob. I already knew that. I told him my first name and, out of habit, my last name. Bob asked for ice cubes in the water. There was a freezer shelf but no ice cubes.

Bob had followed me into the kitchen; he reached for two empty metal trays, in which there were cube-like grids, taking them from the freezer shelf. He said that the trays should be filled with tap water and set in the freezer. And he did so. That's how ice cubes were produced, he said. In the United States these were a basic food, and in the future I might remember this for the sake of my guests.

One could tell I had been here only a short time. New York must seem strange to a nomad like me.

Did you say, nomad? I asked. One could see that I was from Mongolia, the young man answered. He said he had read a few things about that country. And when in addition to my first name, I had given the name of my tribe a while before, he remembered also having read about a Mongolian tribe by that name.

You are right, I said, sometimes I find things strange in New York, for instance, when I see someone sitting in a grocery cart and crying in a supermarket.

Waving, Bob signaled his disapproval. Well, his case was not remarkable—one just had to put on the right show, then life would go on. His show didn't go down badly: I was not the only one who had responded; in fact, a few hours before, even a native, a New York man, had gone along with the show.

I did not understand what he meant. He saw this by my face and came up with an explanation for my lack of comprehension: Nomads, he said, don't have TV. However, you can only understand my problem if you understand about TV.

My brother, he continued, recently put on a huge show. A week ago he declared himself to be a murderer. On principle, he made his statements only in front of TV cameras. America talked of him for days. So it wasn't long until TV approached me too. Soon I was the big discovery.

My brother, the evil black man; and I, the good one. The country was happy. At last, it could again be said that prejudices against blacks did not exist. One of the brothers is a murderer, the whites announced on TV and in the papers; but look at the other, the younger one: He works in New York City as a grocery deliveryman, and he is hard working and popular.

They filmed me at work; they interviewed and photographed me; and all the people who came to the supermarket wanted to have only me as their grocery deliveryman. I jokingly said that I was booked up, that I only had a few hours left at night; then they came at night so that I had to work around the clock. Never before had I earned so much on this job. The people were happy to pay twice as much. A week later I might have charged four times as much.

That was the case until yesterday. Then my brother insisted, again on TV, that he had faked it, that he was no murderer, but had wanted to show how readily whites are happy to believe blacks capable of the most absurd atrocities. Finally, he ceremoniously announced where the victim, whom he supposedly had brutally murdered, was living. The girl was found unharmed.

My brother's story ran under a new title: African American Dupes Public; he fooled us, that deceitful swine.

Then they came to me in the supermarket with their cameras. The story about me now was: This is the brother of that deceitful swine; he probably was in on this. From that moment I was finished. Nobody wanted me to deliver groceries.

That was yesterday. I ran to the TV broadcasting company and screamed: There is a new victim in this case—me. They could see that. And they hunted all over the country for another case like it. They did not find any. But with only one single case you can't put on a talk show.

But why am I telling you this, Bob said; you have no idea of the importance of TV. TV has become part of life, the stage for life. At least, beyond Mongolia. Suppose one or two people with my same fate had been found, one or two women or men with a sister or brother who falsely accused himself or herself of murder; then, my life could continue on TV by being compared with other, similar life stories.

I would sit in a TV studio with my companions in misfortune, with an audience around us, and would tell my troubles: that the customers in the supermarket where I work no longer want my services, in fact, don't even look at me any longer.

After that, said the young man and sipped at his glass of water just as I did, after that, one companion in distress after the other would talk. One would, for instance, say to me, Don't get all pissed off about something like that. My brother—that was ten years ago—confessed to four murders. Oh, how people felt sorry for me for having such a brother: me, an insignificant but well-behaved and decent man.

That was in Seattle, my companion in misfortune would say; I was working in a tire shop, and the whole town wanted me to change their tires. The proprietor doubled my wages and then tripled them, just so I wouldn't quit and open my own shop. It would have been a gold mine—but not for long. They tried to find my brother's four murder victims and didn't find any. Then I knew: This asshole isn't capable of killing even one person.

Finally, he confessed that he was not a murderer. This meant I was finished, the man from Seattle would have said. They avoided not just me but the whole workshop; the owner fired me, and I had no other choice than leaving Seattle. That's why I live in New York now. That's what, if he existed, my companion in misfortune would say, the young man said, and the TV audience would think that I did not deserve the same ill treatment as the man from Seattle.

However, because this man does not exist and there cannot be a talk show about me, I have to start at the bottom as an individual case without help from the media, and put on my own show at the supermarket.

I thank you, Bob said, for paying attention to me. The two of us have to keep on working together; people need to see that in spite of my jerk of a brother, I'm a sought-after deliveryman.

Just tell me when to come to the supermarket, I answered. I had an ulterior motive in saying this: I wanted to find out more details about his brother.

Bob told me that his brother claimed to have eaten his niece. TV had also uncovered the tragic story of another brother, whom the police shot dead by mistake.

That's exactly what I saw on TV the day I arrived, I shouted. Now I'm also getting to know the third brother. That can't be mere coincidence.

Bob laughed. He said, every other sentence you hear in New York is: that can't be mere coincidence, the reason being that this city is made up of nothing but coincidences.

You are right, I said and felt sheepish. Just tell me one thing: What was the coincidence that led your brother to accuse himself of murder?

Bob laughed once more. That was no coincidence, he said. My brother saw no way out and, in fact, did not have a way out. That's why this maneuver. He also thought he needed to invent a rationale: He wanted to confront the whites with their racism.

But that, Bob shouted, is a rationale that has no basis whatsoever. Racism! Those times, the times of lamentation and of hope, are over. There is no black in the United States any longer who looks to the whites for anything. The whites don't even get blamed any longer.

They suffer horribly from this. And my brother soothes this suffering and makes himself popular with the whites by accusing them of racism.

Translated by Ingrid Lansford

© DIMENSION² 6.1 (2002): 137–147.
Originally published under the title *Das Jüngste Gerichte des Michelangelo Spatz*, copyright © 1998 by Rowohlt Verlag GmbH, Reinbek bei Hamburg.

Joseph Zoderer

The Turtle Festival—Excerpt

At times their feet struck hard against rocks in the quickly falling dusk. Loris grasped her hand and tried to recognize something in the twilight. The music was clearly audible now. Before they went by Quadelupe's kitchen, Nives suddenly held him back: Stay with me, she said, and her fingers got lost in his hair.

The plaza was lit up. Yet there weren't any strings of light bulbs hanging from tree to tree, but it was a fire that Jerry and Tom kept going in the middle of the village square; from somewhere they had organized three metal rods, shoved them into the dry ground and tied them together on the upper end; from the contraption dangled the gigantic pot. In the middle of the plaza, Jerry chopped wooden logs and branches that Ivo and Tom and the children of the village dragged to him. Nives and Loris joined them almost unnoticed; it smelled of hot spices and vaporized vinegar; in the pot the turtle was boiling, minced into bite-sized pieces, in a fragrant broth.

Hello, yelled Tom when he discovered Loris. Jerry, while singing, threw pieces of branches into the fire; Maria went from the lit door of the Sanchez' house into the twilight of the plaza and carried an oversized stockpot; she put it, having barely noticed Nives, on the ground, ran toward her and clung around her neck; thereafter, she hugged Loris as well.

Where, then, have you been hiding? We waited for you the entire afternoon; you ought to take a look at that tequila sky in there; she laughed and pointed at the Sanchez' house. Loris wanted to take the pot from her, but she refused: that's my haute cuisine! I bring the blood sauce, stewed in vinegar, nicely boiled up on the gas cooker, with margarine, a treat from Tomas, and onions and roots that only Quadelupe knows. She danced exuberantly with the soup bowl and finally poured the deliciously smelling content into the copper kettle, which Jerry instantly closed again with a wooden lid. The fire almost illuminated the entire village square, and although no loudspeaker messages had informed the people, they now came from all sides; the plaza filled up; the children hopped around the fire, clapping their hands. Chairs, plank beds, and hammocks were occupied in the Sanchez' house; the Indians sat next to the walls, on the window sills, in the corners and nooks all the way out to the garden; Maria and Nives cut the bread that Tomas had fetched from his mother's little bakery on a mule; Steve leaned next to the record player with a joint in his mouth.

Loris listened to old Reyes, who was telling a story under the roof of the widow Sanchez; it was the story of the talking bird, who allegedly was the cause for young Reyes' power to learn the alphabet all on his own. Nives kissed old Reyes on his bald head and danced ahead of him through the room of plank beds; Ivo poured him a bit of tequila; Reyes finished it, licked even the rim of the glass, and began to tell of the time when he supposedly washed gold dust in the Sonora. Loris listened only with one ear; he looked for Jerry; he wanted to know why he—never mind, maybe Jerry really didn't know where Rey had gone.

Ivo brushed past Loris and said: Be careful—or not—but you must stay in control under all circumstances.

Tom had started to dance with El Loco; they hopped wildly back and forth for a while, and when Loris crossed the room to go into the garden, Tom shrieked out in joy and sang: This world is so confusing—

In the mean time, under the thin stream of the water pipe, Jerry scaled the fish that old Reyes had brought along. A festival by the gringos for all! Jerry seemed to be happy with his fish; he raised the hand with the knife as in justification that he contributed his part to the festival in this way. Ivo emerged from the semi-darkness, put a hand amicably on Loris' shoulder, and said: Now you have what you indeed always wanted to have—banana and mango trees in front of your bedroom door.

At the same moment, they heard a noise of an engine, as if a helicopter circled above them or prepared for a landing or as if hands were clapping somewhere endlessly. Ivo pulled Loris under the mango tree and offered him his paper cup with tequila. Loris let the beverage slowly run down his throat and enjoyed the incorporeal taste of the cold cactus bark. After his friend, winking his eyes, seemed to have made off again, Loris tried to get out through the garden toward the plaza, without having to walk through his bedroom again, but he immediately felt Ivo's hand on his shoulder: Stay at the plaza, enjoy yourself, but don't get any notion to go to the bay and to gape at the ocean.

Tom and Maria distributed white plastic plates and the matching knives, forks, and spoons. A present from Steve, they said; he brought the stuff from San Diego on his last trip. Jerry ladled the pieces of meat onto the plates; he was encircled by ravenous, curious children; few adults joined in, a few mothers and grandmothers of the children. A public feeding, said the gray beard. Loris shoved a bite between his teeth and moaned: Spicy! But he had only burned the tip of his tongue. Outside the circle of light that the fire cast, he now noticed men as well who were leaning on the few trees of the plaza or were standing around them; some sat on the floor and watched the gringos who weren't living any better than they and were obviously crazy because they came from the richest part of the world and lived here like they did, maybe a little better but hardly worth mentioning, and they seemed to be unarmed.

He wanted to eat turtle soup with Nives and circled around the plaza; the men laughed with their eyes but barely changed their posture when he passed by them; not one of them tried to speak to him.

He went back into the house; he hadn't seen Nives or Steve for quite a while. El Loco danced with bare feet over the earthy ground, skipped often—so it seemed to Loris—over long musical passages but always stayed in rhythm. Maria and Tom tried to keep up, apparently to encourage the others as well, but they somehow always obstructed El Loco's way; only Jerry managed later, when Maria asked him to dance, to approach the deranged or enlightened El Loco by moving his feet in such wonderful harmony with the rhythm that the children clapped their hands in admiration.

He finally saw Nives and Maria dance in front of the open window in the middle of the street, between the Sanchez' house and the store, in which Tomas had left the light on. Loris watched them for some time; Maria smiled, as if she were in love with the air and her narrow feet, and also beamed at Nives, who sometimes threw her arms up and let them glide in rhythm like wings. When he stepped in front of the door, Nives barely lifted her head but waved at him with a contorted hand and kept on dancing, and only when he was in the house again, leaning on the wall next to the record player and, time after time, lifting the needle from the empty groove, only then did Nives reappear and let herself drop next to him on the clay floor. She took his hand and guided it to her face, pressed his fingers on her cheek, against her eyes, on her mouth, and suddenly said: Rey is back.

Strange, Loris thought, that I don't care.

What does that have to do with us? he asked.

Nothing—basically nothing, it is not important; she started to laugh while coughing slightly, but it almost sounded like weeping.

Where is he?

Probably where the helicopter came down a short time ago, not far from Steve's tent, and Rey's truck is no doubt there by now as well; I can give you an exact account sometime later. She laughed again in her hurt voice.

Come, she begged him, let's dance; I want to dance with you.

She looked at him with narrow eyes, as if she were to take measure of his hands, his shoulders, his three or four-day-old beard, his lips, his forehead, his hair falling down his neck; she hugged him more and more while dancing and said: We can sleep in Tony's cabin today.

And Rey?

What does that have to do with us?

In the mean time, the whole village had come together on the plaza, and with an embarrassed giggle one or the other took a bowl of soup with maybe a bite of turtle in it.

In the entrance to the Sanchez' house, they came across Rey, who squeezed Nives against his sweaty shirt. All three shoved themselves into Ivo's bedroom; it seemed to take Rey two attempts at his memory to remind himself of Loris again: The man in Jerry's hut, he yelled almost cheerfully, matching the half-embrace that had briefly included Loris as well. Loris didn't push him back. He was merely frightened by the similarity that occurred to him just now in this room—the similarity with himself.

Nives brought Rey a full bowl of turtle soup; he spooned it up while standing. She, however, placed a stack of plates in the middle of the room so that everyone had to make an attempt to avoid it, including Rey; she sat down without haste and leaned, barely noticeable, with her shoulder against Loris. He felt her quiet, urging power and knew that she was capable of challenging anything, that she indeed was waiting for a provocation. And into this joyous lack of a conversation roared suddenly fragmented words from the plaza's loudspeakers, barked Spanish words that Loris did not understand. But here, in this room of the Sanchez' house, nobody seemed to care much about that.

Rey circled around the tower of plates. How did you fish this soup meat out of the ocean? he asked. With a noose, answered Nives, unbelievable, isn't it? She said it without any ridicule. Jerry's vibrating voice came unexpectedly from Ivo's iron bed: Anyone who wants power is insane.

Man, sighed Tom, is there still a drop of tequila somewhere that might be passed from mouth to mouth?

Just a moment, said Rey, called for Nives and asked her to get a bottle from the truck: You know, of course, where. But she didn't move. From the plaza one heard the shrill cries from children, and Rey took a few steps toward Nives, who still sat next to Loris. Suddenly, they heard that dance music was coming from the outside loudspeakers as well, interrupted in short intervals by an announcer's rattling voice.

Come on, said Rey, and Nives shook her head. Come on, Rey said it one more time, and Nives let herself be helped up and followed him out onto the village square.

Loris pressed his shoulders to the wall; she can be what she might not even want to be, he thought; outside, he saw her head surface in the square every now and then; Rey danced with her to these consumptive, heart-troubling Latino tunes; Tom shoveled the last embers into a pan, carried them into the house, and then sat down next to old Reyes in front of the hut that was a chapel; El Loco stomped a magical dance on the other side of the plaza yet was hardly noticed by more than a few children.

Translated by Harald Becker

© DIMENSION² 2.3 (1995): 437–445.
© Carl Hanser Verlag München Wien 1995.

josef haslinger

migratory birds

at a place to eat operated out of a camping trailer, a man reclining in a shabby chair enjoyed the sunset. he had been busy all day long plotting the course of a celestial body that he had discovered the previous night. computer records were sufficiently accurate to draw conclusions about the form of the object based on the behavior of sunlight. it was an asteroid, large enough that in a single day a human being would not be able to traverse the earthwards-facing oval in its flyby. the calculations showed that it must have had a crater and was surrounded by a cloud of debris. the astronomer traced this back to a collision that the object underwent in the last millennia, only a short time ago. its high rotation speed also spoke in favor of this assumption. all the asteroid needed was approximately five hours for a rotation around its own axis.

sitting next to the astronomer were a carafe of wine and a plate full of mussel shells.

the simple eatery had just recently opened. it belonged to janica, a woman around fifty wearing black. there was no menu, there was also nothing to order. there was only what janica put on the table, wine, water, and a multi-course meal whose individual dishes were known in advance to her alone. the astronomer had his glass in hand and observed us as we approached. he had vertical wrinkles on his forehead.

igor, an actor whom i was visiting, had brought me to this place. we had wanted to drive to rovinj. because of a backup on the main road he'd opted for a detour through the coastal villages. igor had

really only stopped out of curiosity. he wanted to know if just anyone could set up his trailer here and offer himself as a restaurateur.
a hand-written wooden sign had indicated that this little speck of a
camping area was a restaurant.

as janica caught sight of my friend igor, she dropped everything
and ran up to him.

janica! igor cried. janica, what are you doing here?

this is my restaurant, janica said. she embraced him and rested
her head on his chest. igor took her head in both hands.

how long have you been here? i thought you were living in
switzerland.

i didn't know you were back either, janica said.

igor hugged this almost rural-looking woman dressed in black
tightly. for one moment she seemed about to cry but collected herself rather quickly.

she asked: where are you living now?

in vienna.

he let janica go and introduced me.

janica said in german: oh, an austrian. then she turned back to
igor again.

when did you go?

igor's answer was a little snippy: i'm the one who left four years
ago—not fourteen, like you.

she was irritated for a moment. she said: you have to tell me everything. i'll come over to your table. right now though i've got
some cutlets on the stove. she got two camping chairs out of a shed,
unfolded them and set them at one of the three tables. it was the
table where the man with the vertical wrinkles on his forehead was
sitting. then she disappeared into the steaming trailer.

the astronomer stood up to shake our hands. he was around
forty and wore a short-sleeved shirt.

my name is zlatko, he said in english.

janica brought a carafe of wine and glasses.

are you having wine too? she asked me.

wine and water, i said.

the water'll be a while.

she took the plate with mussel shells and wiped the table off with
her bare hands.

i have to let mirjana know, she said. as she left, we heard her say one more time: i have to let mirjana know. through the trailer window we could see her dialing on a cell phone. she was so loud that everyone could hear. guess who's here, she screamed excitedly into the telephone. no, i won't tell you, you'll have to see for yourself. no, i won't tell you, come over, then you'll see.

as she spoke, she kept looking over at igor.

i had gotten to know igor in vienna. he was an actor, on various evenings he had told me the long and short of his story. since describing himself in an interview as yugoslavian instead of croatian, he was never again to be seen in any croatian film. there was a long dispute about him carried out in the croatian press. when you walked into his apartment in vienna, the first thing you saw were these newspaper clippings. they were lying on the chest of drawers in the entryway. it was igor's luck to have acted in one german thriller before the war. he had succeeded in reestablishing old contacts. now he primarily made films in austria and germany.

igor had two marriages behind him. he had traveled to pula to see the twelve-year-old daughter from his second marriage and had invited me to accompany him. we stayed in his old two-room apartment. i looked around the city, he met his friends and walked on the beach with his daughter. in the evening we went out together.

so that i wouldn't have to listen to his story yet again, i tried as fast as possible to strike up a conversation with the man whose table we had joined. we spoke english with each other, although zlatko could have also spoken german. he had studied in graz for two years. he enjoyed reminiscing about his time there, he said. whatever had happened to him careerwise he owed to graz. that was when the comet shoemaker-levy 9 slipped into jupiter's gravitational field, shattering into 21 large pieces in jupiter's dense atmosphere. they'd been able to observe balls of fire larger than the earth. to show us how the comet that got thoroughly devoured by the large planet had no chance, he circled the small european wineglass around the carafe, before dropping it inside, where, however, it got stuck.

shoemaker-levy 9, zlatko said, was my guiding star of graz. it showed me the way. that's when i began to specialize in asteroids and meteoroids. they became my pets. a certain segment of the asteroid belt is easier to observe from istria than from any other point on earth.

zlatko invited us to visit him in his observatory. it was close to poreč but somewhat difficult to find. he'd draw us a map.

igor asked, how many of these asteroids are there really?

countless, zlatko answered. if we take only those that are at least one kilometer in diameter, there might well be a good million of them just between the orbits of mars and jupiter. not to mention the smallest ones.

we sat there for a while in silence.

that'll be the end of the world, igor said.

possibly, zlatko answered. there's certain to be a few time bombs among them.

and then he told about the asteroid that he'd discovered the previous night. from encounter to encounter it'll come closer to the earth. during the twenty-second encounter, its orbit could intersect the earth's. it's large enough, zlatko said, to penetrate the earth's atmosphere. if it slams into the sea, it could mean a proper tsunami. in which case it'd be good to live in the mountains.

zlatko had written his thesis on tsunamis resulting from meteor collisions. afterwards he had frequently lectured on the topic.

but all of you can keep on sitting here in peace for a while, he said. our friend requires 258 years for its rotation. so it'll take 5676 years for the twenty-second encounter.

he let the effect of his impromptu mathematics sink in a bit before adding:

we could all come up with a name for it tonight.

let's christen it the redeemer, i said.

that won't go over, igor said. there'd be too many hopes pinned on it. let's christen it marilyn instead.

zlatko laughed. 30 years ago, he said, one marilyn was christened after another. today they want to get away from women's names, because in the meantime the entire firmament has been overpopulated with women.

and then zlatko began to tell of a failed european space mission that, as he said, would've relayed information of incalculable value about precisely that segment of the heavens he specialized in. as he launched his ariane 5-plus rocket fork and let it crash directly in the sand, two guests got up in order to, it seemed, take a stroll on the beach, and, while zlatko demonstrated to us how a wineglass by the name of rosetta should've landed on a carafe named virtanen—but had missed the last possible launch time because of an accident with the rocket—i noticed that, instead of strolling, the guests were relieving themselves behind the smattering of cliffs stretched along the beach.

hey igor, janica called over to us, mirjana's on her way!

really? mirjana? i haven't seen her since you two left. she was ten years old then.

eleven, janica corrected.

someone or other told me that mirjana's living in canada.

and that's true, janica said. but she's here for the summer.

she came over from the camping trailer with a carafe of wine, stood behind igor, and put one hand on his shoulder. igor took her hand and pressed it against his cheek.

we were just christening a star after you, he said.

a star?

more like a clump of ice and rock, zlatko said.

i don't want some clump named after me. if anything, then a shining star. she pulled her hand away from igor, raised it theatrically, and portrayed the shining star.

sorry, zlatko said, a star is out of my league. i'm only in charge of the clumps.

she brought the carafe of wine to the next table and went back into the trailer. igor said: her husband was a well-known actor.

what became of him? zlatko asked.

he disappeared. maybe you've heard of him. ivo radić.

she's the wife of ivo radić? really? zlatko suddenly got very excited.

yes, igor said. once she was also an actress. janica and mirjana left in the summer of 1991. ivo insisted that they leave. through the playhouse in zürich he was able to arrange their first stop in switzerland. but whatever happened, he himself wanted to stay behind. back then we were still acting in films together. he had the lead; i played the seventh dwarf. it frustrated him that janica didn't get any parts in switzerland. however, she hadn't done too much acting here either, after having mirjana. he sent her money. janica was required to continually present bank statements in switzerland. she soon got into trouble since ivo radić had quit acting. at first i had no idea. it was only when i ran into him in pula one day and asked him how janica and mirjana were doing and what he was filming at the moment that he said he couldn't give a short answer in passing. so then we sat down in the café across from the castropola bookstore. he told me he wasn't acting anymore, and that he had more important things to do. janica had found work in davos, à la thomas mann, so to speak. ivo came off as relaxed and confident. he said he'd be leaving for bosnia soon. i asked him did you register for the army, and he responded, you could say so. but he didn't want to clue me in on exactly what he was going to do. he acted like he himself didn't even know. there was martial law, you were always meeting people carrying out special assignments, you just had to trust that they were doing something useful and important. we met for about an hour, then he had to rush off. that was my last encounter with ivo radić.

ivo radić, zlatko whispered. i revered him. he was uncompromising, the man who wasn't for sale. who never shied away from confrontation and ultimately won out. after a film i'd imitate his walk. those hulking shoulders, zlatko said getting up and walking back and forth a few paces like king kong. you remember, he said. when he swaggered through a movie, you couldn't hold him back. that was ivo radić.

igor said, maybe he tried to be the same way in real life too.

but all at once igor seemed to lose interest in continuing to talk about ivo radić. as zlatko started in all over again, igor said, sure, he was a great actor, a bit melodramatic perhaps, but that was a while ago.

but zlatko didn't quit and asked: did he fall into the hands of the serbs?

i don't know, igor said. ask janica. he disappeared, that's all that i know.

janica had started to bring out new plates and bowls from the camping trailer. she kept looking over at us, in the unmistakable joy of seeing igor again.

i asked zlatko: how many celestial bodies have you actually discovered?

the exact count is now at 314. this number is the first part of the name. i've always done it like that. first the ordinal number in the sequence of my discoveries, then a first name.

314 zlatko, i said.

zlatko laughed. i have to confess that i immediately named my first asteroid after myself. 1 zlatko. that's right, it exists. since then there's been a 67 zlatko also and a 211 zlatko. neither is related to me.

zlatko picked up his monologue once again. he said that so far he'd successfully refused to catalogue his foundlings according to the method that had been established over the last few decades. first the year of discovery, then a row of letters or digits. which letters and digits they were to be could be figured out from an american website. the name which would be required as a result of this system ran—and at this point zlatko pulled a scrap of paper from the breast pocket of his shirt and read aloud: 2004 YN6. he had noted down the name to be on the safe side, in case he couldn't come up with a better one by tomorrow.

ivo radić, i said. wouldn't that be a good name for the asteroid? then he wouldn't be so gone.

zlatko had objections: first and last name together, that won't work, i'm afraid. i've already christened ivo, for ivo andrić. and radić could be misunderstood. it's not my job to bless the national saints of our government.

it's got to be a woman's name, igor said. if we can't go with marilyn, how about sophia?

what's so special about sophia?

then christen it after a woman you know, a girlfriend.

at the moment, zlatko said, i don't have a girlfriend, and i've gone through all the old girlfriends too. i even used the name egle twice, 17 egle and then later 83 egle, because we backslid into our affair again. and then i borrowed a couple of women that i never had in real life.

something can still pan out, igor said. tell me who they are and i'll drop some hints around town.

these women are unfortunately married.

what about it, igor retorted. if they find out what you've done for them and don't leave their husbands right away, they're not worthy of you.

just then a white-haired man at the table next to us laughed out loud, the others chimed in. we leaned around towards them, but saw at once that they had laughed for other reasons.

our hostess came with a pan of lamb cutlets. she went from table to table, apportioning the meat onto the plates. in the distance you could hear the whine of a moped.

that's her, janica said. that's mirjana.

she left the pan sitting on the table and got an additional plate and a camping stool out of the trailer. the moped got louder. it drove along the forest road and appeared on the beach. there was a young woman with black hair tied into a ponytail. she didn't wear a crash helmet. in her upright posture, with her back arched, she seemed to be tall and slender. the straps of the shoulder bag running in a slant across her upper body made her breasts protrude noticeably. although she was riding through sand, she had no trouble taking her hand from the handlebars and waving at her mother. she leaned the moped against the camping trailer.

mirjana, her mother called, snapping the camping stool open. here.

she pulled the shoulder strap over her head as she slunk over to us, taking her time.

igor went to meet her. they stood in facing each other for a while.

uncle igor, mirjana said. bad uncle igor.

mirjana, igor said. you were just a little girl back then.

they embraced.

why bad? igor asked.

that's what my father always said. because every time you came over, it was with another woman.

igor introduced us. about zlatko he said: he's a world famous astronomer and we were just in the process of figuring out a name for a planet that he discovered.

it's only an asteroid, zlatko said.

i'll do it, mirjana said. i know a guy in canada, he'll do a divination for the name.

zlatkos vertical wrinkles contracted a bit. mirjana sat down on the stool, took some tobacco from her shoulder bag, and began to roll herself a cigarette.

why does it have to be divined, zlatko asked.

mirjana gave him a surprised look. why not? you can't just give a planet any old name. instead you have to figure out which name is its name.

but it doesn't have any name at all, zlatko said.

how are we supposed to know that, mirjana countered. we only know that we don't know its name, but we're not sure if it's already got one.

no, it doesn't, zlatko said. it hasn't been registered yet. i went through the databases for the entire region. it would be a huge disgrace if i reported an object that someone else had already documented.

meanwhile mirjana had finished rolling her cigarette. she lit it, blew a puff out, and took a long and appreciative drag. as she slowly released the smoke, she plucked a shred of tobacco from her lips.

don't let your meat get cold, janica called to us. she served the side dishes, hurrying back and forth between the trailer and the tables. the white-haired man at the table beside us closed his eyes in rapture while chewing. janica, he called, you're worth your weight in gold. for one moment, janica interrupted her incessant fussing. her sharp mouth began to smile in satisfaction.

mirjana crossed her right foot over her left knee. she wore sandals with a strap over the big toe. her legs were shaved. she wanted to lean back, but the stool had no backrest; she seemed on edge. igor poured wine for her. she said: we can't act like we invented everything there is.

and we aren't acting like it, zlatko said. he was talking with his mouth full.

you are too, mirjana stated. naming something means taking power over it.

she still hadn't started to eat. zlatko swallowed. what a funny theory, he said, and began conducting the flow of his own sentence with his knife. an asteroid that we name has a recognizable identity for us, but that doesn't mean we have any power over it. when it wants to drill through us in 5000 years, then we'll have to see if we can get power over it beforehand. the name by itself is totally useless. he ended his presentation by slamming the knife on the table.

a scrawny brown dog came running along the beach. he sniffed around the rocks that the guests had visited earlier. mirjana sliced her cutlet in two. she held out the part with the bone to the dog. he came over and snatched it, only to run away again instantly and disappear behind a rock. it didn't take long before he was back in front of mirjana with his mouth open. she cut off another piece and gave it to him. again he ran off.

igor asked: what do you do when you're not feeding dogs.

i play the glass marimba.

what's that?

you just have to imagine a normal marimba, but the pieces that resonate are made out of glass instead of wood or metal. wine-glasses, bottles, glass cylinders. anything that sounds good. i made the instrument myself.

and where do you perform with it?

in bars. we have an english name. birds of the balkans.

she laughed and added: with a lead instrument from africa and a mexican guitarist. but people like that.

mirjana had a swiss accent. in the meantime i had finished eating. mirjana took the bones from my plate and gave them to the dog. then she fed him the rest of her cutlet.

so how long has there been a restaurant here, i asked. three months, she said. her mother'd been working in a kitchen in davos, in a good restaurant, but it unfortunately had to close last year. for 13 years, she said, her mother worked in that swiss restaurant. but in the end she was treated as though it had been only 13 days. igor poured more wine and made a toast. then he said: we live in a world of primates. everyone thinks he can play master over the rest. every-one presumes to have some kind of hereditary rights. everyone be-lieves that his birth furnished him with a privilege as opposed to the rest of us. there may be privilege, but who has a right to it? those are primates.

we haven't even been around for very long, zlatko said. maybe sometime a human being will descend from us.

he turned to mirjana and started waving around the knife again. you're right about one thing. names aren't completely without meaning. they're an intervention right now into the data systems of the distant future. that's why christening celestial bodies is always such an exciting thing. in the end the name of the asteroid might even last, while it'll have vanished into a larger planet. it's much worse for my colleagues who name distant galaxies. they don't know if what they're seeing and naming has existed at all in the last millennia. that's why they simulate more and more existences until, sometime in the distant future, there's a rupture in the flow of data on earth.

zlatko opened his mouth to yawn amply. he turned his head to the side. since he couldn't stop yawning, he held up the knife to his mouth.

mirjana turned to igor: are you acting in a new film?

in two months we'll be filming an episode of a police drama in frankfurt.

and what are you playing?

a supporting role, i only play supporting roles. usually in mysteries and i'm the good old balkan mafioso.

a small boy came along the path with a wheelbarrow carrying two six-packs of mineral water. he turned towards us and, after a few meters, got stuck in the sand. janica ran to meet him and took the mineral water from him. she patted his cheek and slipped him some money. the kid dragged the wheelbarrow from the sand. then he turned his back to the wheelbarrow, stood between the handles, and took off again. janica tore open one of the packages and distributed the bottles to the tables. the jars she brought from the camping trailer had once contained dijon mustard. she cleared away the empty plates. i'll be right there, she said to igor, who was pouring the water. it was pleasantly cold.

mirjana rolled herself a new cigarette. i couldn't resist the sight of it and asked her if i might roll myself one too.

help yourself, she said, and slid the package over to me.

do you come to istria very often? i asked her.

no. my mother is trying to make a life for herself here again. but i plan to stay in canada and perform here during the summer for a month or two. in the last few years we were mostly in switzerland and france, now we're traveling over here. a migratory bird. that's exactly what i am.

she paused for a moment, took a drag from her cigarette, and her mouth frowned. my mother wants me to stay here. but i can't, even if i did spend my childhood here. war is the only thing talked about. everybody lost someone, or they know of someone who disappeared. that's all i hear. i don't think about it in canada. but here it's ever-present. it doesn't matter whom you meet. they all tell you whom they lost. my mother talks about it every day. every day.

mirjana stood up and took her bag. i've got to go now. my performance awaits.

she gave us the address. igor knew the bar. we promised to come later.

ciao, she said to me. i answered, ciao, balkan bird. she smiled at me in response.

zlatko said he wouldn't be coming later. he had to get some sleep.

what about the star, mirjana asked.

not a star. it's only an asteroid. zlatko's wrinkles contracted. i'll look and see if there's already a 314 mirjana.

in that case, mirjana said, we can forget the divining.

she shook his hand.

mirjana waved to her mother, who had begun to plant torches in the sand. you could hear the moped whining for a bit before it was swallowed by the dense mediterranean forest. barely had mirjana left, and janica was back by igor, her hand lying on his shoulder again. with her other hand she drank from his wineglass.

igor asked: when was the last time you heard anything from ivo.

i got his final letter in the summer of 1993 through the red cross. in it he had written that he was involved with supplies for sarajevo. since then I've gotten no leads at all. as though he had simply vanished from the face of the earth.

igor said: they probably snatched him up and now he's lying somewhere in a mass grave.

janica looked out to the sea. between the rocks you could see the still-red horizon, from which, on the other side of the bay, dark smokestacks rose. janica had started crying.

igor stood up and took her in his arms. he's still alive, she sobbed, i know that he's still alive.

igor said, 1993, that's twelve years ago. eventually you've got to come to terms with the facts.

then she tore herself from his arms, and in a voice broken by tears she screamed so it could be heard far away: he's alive! he's alive! he's alive!

silence fell. the guests quit talking. only the waves crashing on the rocks were audible. janica sat down on mirjana's stool, poured herself a glass of wine and emptied it in one gulp.

before i go, zlatko said, speaking into the quiet embarrassment, i have to give you directions. from his shirt pocket he took the scrap, on which he had noted the name for his asteroid—required according to the system—and in the light of the torch he sketched out, turn by turn, the way from pula to the observatory. down below he wrote his telephone number. you'll find it, he said. call me beforehand. then i can prepare a few nice pictures for you.

zlatko wanted to pay, but igor said he'd take care of it. while saying goodbye, we had to promise zlatko that we would come for sure. then he was gone. by now it was so dark that you couldn't see the street anymore.

the guests came to pay one after the other. janica charged them all the same price. she just set the money on the table. later, when she went to get cigarettes from the trailer, she left the money lying there. igor sifted through it. he weighted the bills with coins so that the evening wind couldn't carry them away as it picked up. through the window in the trailer we could see janica light a gas lamp and put it out right afterwards. when she returned, she not only held cigarettes but also a new carafe of wine. she slid the more comfortable chair, on which zlatko had been sitting, over to igor. she just sat there for a while, drinking and smoking, without anyone saying a word. igor linked her arm with his.

what makes you think he's still alive?

she held back on the answer for a while, then she whispered: i just know it. she slid right up to igor, leaned onto him, and pressed her cheek onto his shoulder. once again she whispered: i just know it. igor laid his arm around her.

but how? he asked.

she took the wineglass just filled and emptied it. then she lit a new cigarette.

how?

because he comes to me every night.

tears filled up her eyes again. she let them run, staring into her empty glass. behind igor the tip of the crescent moon had appeared. i watched it, narrow and the same smooth shape as the edge of a plate, as it slowly peeled itself from a tree. janica had let her head fall. her cigarette burned to the filter before she took a drag from it. it was as though she had fallen asleep. igor began gently patting her upper arm. he poured her another glass of wine, once again she finished it without setting it down.

she asked, am i old? igor pulled her closer to him.

no, you're not old.

why do i have to live alone then?

i live alone too.

you can't compare us, she said. you've always had ten thousand girlfriends and that won't be any different now. i have no one.

you have mirjana.

do you think she lives here? she's staying with friends in the city. i'm happy if she just comes by every few days. i really can't go to my elderly mother and say, so, here i am again. i've been alive for 55 years, and it hasn't amounted to anything.

you have this little restaurant. you're a great cook. that's a new beginning.

the authorities never even approved the power line. that's not a restaurant, they said, it's a camping trailer. and they're right too. all i've got is this ridiculous trailer. but they can't drive me off, this piece of land belongs to my cousin.

you could build a restaurant.

with what? what i made in switzerland mirjana got for school. and the bit i'm making here—she indicated the little stack of money still lying on the table—that's just enough to live on.

suddenly she laughed out loud and added: and for new undies.

for a new panties? igor asked. you mean for new panties?

yes, janica said. i bought myself beautiful panties.

i got up because i felt the urgent need to go behind the rocks. but by then it had become so dark that it was enough to go a little ways from the torches. while relieving myself and looking back over my shoulder, i saw janica stand up and lift her black dress. igor grabbed between her legs. janica's lower body jerked back and she let the dress fall. they both began to laugh. igor stood up and wrapped his arms around her. then they kissed. i had finished my business by now and didn't know what to do next. it was too dark for a walk. there was no lighting at all in sight, only the three torches, the crescent moon and a few stars. i could slowly make out the contours of the rocks. far out in the bay, the lights of a village were visible. or maybe it was a large ship resting there at anchor. so i just stood there for a while watching igor and janica kiss. they moved in greater agitation, lost balance, stumbled over something, fell down. igor laughed out loud, janica said: oh god, am i drunk. she was quickly on her feet again and sat down on the chair. igor too pulled himself up and sat down on a chair again. she took a cigarette from the pack, he offered to light it. then he put his arm on her shoulder again. when i came back, i found them in exactly the same pose as when i had left.

i said to igor, if you loan me the car, i'll pick you up here tomorrow morning.

that's an excellent idea, he said. i wasn't sure if janica was too excited by it. in any event, she didn't say anything to the contrary, and then i asked her for a flashlight so that i'd be able to find the car. igor told me the way to mirjana's show. the bar was located in an old austrian navy fortress, you couldn't miss it. tell her, he added, the bad uncle igor sends his regrets.

no, janica contradicted him. tell her, he was so drunk that you had to bring him home.

at first i didn't find the bar. three times i drove by the building, erected out of massive stones and corresponding exactly to igor's description, but saw only a restaurant advertising grilled specialties in big neon letters. since there was by far no other comparable building on this street, i wound up stopping in front of the restaurant in order to inquire with a waiter. barely had i locked up the car when i saw the sign fixed on the wall, which a fleeting glance could have taken for a traffic sign. although the word bar was printed on it, it was inside of the same white arrow on a blue background that otherwise indicates a one-way street. the arrow pointed to the right side of the building, where a narrow alley began. in it bursts of noise were audible, but no music. there were narrow windows resembling openings for firing weapons set into the wall but too high up to see through. several mopeds were sitting at the side of an arch, one was leaning against the wall; i assumed it was mirjana's. behind the arch, a small courtyard emerged, where the guests sat, divided among approximately ten groups of tables. in the corner to the left of the entrance, on a stage made of stone, which earlier might have served as the base of a cannon, stage lights illuminated musical instruments and an amplifier. young people smoking and drinking beer sat on both of the steps leading up to the stone base. the musicians, who were obviously taking a break just then, were nowhere to be seen.

i went to the stage. there were two piles of birds of the balkans cds stacked at its edge, and i inspected the glass marimba for a while. on top it looked like a xylophone with a keyboard made of two rows of small plates. the glass containers hung below, arranged according to size like the pipes of an organ. the higher tones were produced by little shallow glass cups, the midrange tones by cylindrical containers, and the deeper tones by large bottles. on a little round side table that otherwise could well have served as a stand for a flower pot there lay a row of mallets of varying size, some of them were capped with little balls of felt. from one of the mallets sticking out over the edge of the table hung one of mirjana's red hair bands. i couldn't pick her out from all the people sitting around tables or standing together in groups, entangled in laughter and lively conversation, but so far i really hadn't been anywhere but the courtyard. the bar proper lay behind an open door, which i hadn't seen at first since it was concealed by the bough of an old knotty tree.

it was even busier inside the bar than out in the courtyard. young people stood packed together at the counter, calling out their orders to the two bartenders. i got in line at the back, but that was a mistake because everyone who came up behind me appeared in front of me shortly thereafter. you somehow had to squeeze through and get one of the bartenders to notice you. i didn't know what i wanted to order, so i took a quick look around the place, but mirjana was nowhere to be found here either. the bartender addressed me because everyone standing right at the counter was already taken care of. i ordered an espresso. at the very moment i passed the money to the counter, over everyone's shoulders, the marimba began to play outside. there was a run of high notes and the notes were sounded twice each time, one after the other. soon deeper notes came along, the guitar joined in and finally the bass too. to my ears the music, in its quick sweeping rhythm, was more caribbean than balkan.

i balanced my espresso over all the heads, out to the entrance, stopping under the tree. mirjana now wore a white dress, colorfully embroidered around the plunging neck line. her long black hair hung down unfastened; by contrast, her red hair band tied the guitarist's almost equally long hair into a tail, which flew through the air when he vigorously shook his head now and again. the mexican was shorter than mirjana. he tried to compensate for the difference a little with stacked heels, while mirjana was still wearing her thin leather sandals.

the glass marimba was the center of the music, everything was arranged around it, but the mexican was responsible for the stage show. sometimes he drew very close to mirjana with his guitar held up to his chest, they laughed together and their bodies fell into the same rhythmical movements, while the mallets in mirjana's hands flew across the small plates in a swiftness that made them discernible purely as streaks cut into the air. the bassist, a seriously morose looking young man with a moustache, kept to the background. it was only after the audience burst into applause and let out screams of excitement that his mouth smiled gently. rather than pausing to take in the applause, the birds of the balkans went right into the next song.

with the espresso cup in hand i stood under the tree and thought about janica and igor, maybe they were already lying in the trailer, groping each others' bodies in the glow of the weak gas lamp. i imagined igor complimenting her and janica gratefully receiving his tendernesses, how his tongue touches her body and how he uses all his experience to stimulate her nipples and clitoris, how finally he penetrates her and janica suddenly begins to cry.

mirjana's breasts danced under the neck line of her dress, the mexican was standing just left of her, body on body they circled their hips to a melody that now sounded clearly balkan, while the rhythm was still caribbean. i couldn't rid myself of the thought of janica and igor. even when i concentrated on the music, on mirjana and the ease with which she swung the mallets, the image of her mother was in front of me. i saw igor's harsh thrusts, i saw janica's tears, and i heard her screams at the same time as her daughter's music, the daughter who couldn't stand it anymore that her mother would never quit a dead father. when i sipped my espresso, my upper lip felt something that had fallen into the cup, a sliver of wood maybe or a beetle. in the darkness beneath the tree i couldn't tell. i set the cup on the ground and slowly made my way to the exit between the groups of tables. here i stopped for a while and hoped in secret that mirjana would look over at me, but she didn't and couldn't have recognized me at all because of the stage lights, which lit her from where i was standing. they played a song that sounded like slavic folk music; its rhythms kept picking up. each of mirjana's hands held two mallets, they flew like two victory signs over the glass marimba and got faster and faster, while the mexican twisted his body about, letting his bound hair dance through the air. the people around the stage began clapping in rhythm, the others joined in. the images of janica and igor returned, and all at once a feeling of disgust rose in me. i couldn't look at mirjana any more without thinking of her mother, fucking and crying, of igor, who, not to be deterred by her wailing, keeps thrusting harder and harder, who drills into her further the more she cries and screams, further into janica, who wails out with every thrust but who doesn't fight it, in whose crying and whimpering there lies an immeasurable joy; it spurs igor's lust until he falls into rage and hammers into her, as though he could fuck the memory of this damn war out of her once and for all.

i left the courtyard and sat down on mirjana's moped. in the mean time the music had reached a tempo that knocked the wind out of you, the clapping guests couldn't keep up with the speed that mirjana played the glass marimba. they fell out of rhythm, they gave up. meanwhile the crescent moon was high up on the firmament. there were a few stars to see. i waited for a shooting star, a comet or something like it. somewhere out there in the dark, zlatko's pets were at pasture, 1 zlatko and 17 egle and whatever the other names might be. the piece of music galloped towards its end in roaring applause. the birds of the balkans broke off the tempo sharply and played on in a reggae rhythm. i grabbed the handlebars and twisted the throttle. all i wanted was to steal the moped. all i wanted was to take off over the mountains with it.

Translated by eugene sampson

© S. Fischer Verlag Gmbh, Frankfurt am Main, 2006.

Robert Menasse

Long Time No See

A Story from the End of the Postwar Order

When I see an abstract picture, all I see is an abstract picture. The Rorschach test triggers nothing in me but a recognition of a Rorschach test. If I see a floating woman, then I see a woman who appears, with the help of a series of magician's technical arrangements, to be floating. The illusionist is paid just so that we don't see the arrangements. So, here too, I can believe my eyes. And when it comes to the eternal plausibility of the little world in which we live, I can never really rightly see anything that can't be. What is possible I can't say, but when I see it, I know it's real.

Of course, none of that is right, but I had to learn to see that.

Not just because I once saw something with my own eyes that I would never have believed possible. But that's where it started. I was taking my dog for a walk around the block like I did every evening. I had passed the Queen of Spade's bar countless times without ever thinking of going in. Why, on this night, I suddenly went in to drink a beer, I don't know. Perhaps my lust for life was stronger at the moment than the fear, which usually calculates every disappointment ahead of time and therefore avoids it—especially when it is as easy as walking by a dubious pub in a Viennese suburb, even when laughter is pouring out into the street.

I must have looked like a blind man, as I stood with my dog in the pub, staring with wide open eyes through my steamed-up eyeglasses. What I saw like through a fog that was slowly dissipating and what I couldn't believe for a moment that seemed to last forever was a horde of drunken, howling men, standing around a table—and on top of the table the Lechner girl was dancing.

Maria Lechner. I knew her from our high-school days as the very definition of well-behaved and proper. We were in the same grade together. She never let anyone copy off her out of fear that it might adversely affect her own progress in class. At the final examination she still wore her hair in two braids; of course, she passed with honors. Right after the exam, half the class went into town to celebrate. We were surprised when Lechner wanted to come along—then she was the only one who wouldn't sneak onto the streetcar without paying, and we all had to wait forever while she found somewhere to buy a ticket. She drank nothing but soda water with raspberry syrup. Webora seemed wicked to us all with her perpetual sweet martinis. Then she suddenly disappeared with Humer, who only ever ordered ouzo.

Later I saw Lechner once in a while by chance, but into her thirtieth year she remained absolutely a ten-year-old who did her homework like a good little girl. At twenty-four she graduated from law school; at twentyfive, after an internship year at court, she passed the bar exam; and, four years later, she was appointed to a permanent judgeship. Everything went smoothly for her, without conflict, without interruption, right on schedule, and then she became a judge, and I had lost sight of her.

And now, maybe five, no, almost six years later, I saw her again, drunkenly shrieking and laughing, dancing on top of a table, continually almost falling off, scornfully fending off the hands that stretched toward her under the pretext of helping her, under the pretext of fending them off.

I noticed that the music that filled the dingy little space of the bar came from a radio because the news came on when the song was over. German Democratic Republic. The Berlin Wall, said the reporter, was being torn down. The postwar order was dissolving. The phrase *postwar order* could be heard distinctly a second time coming out of the radio over screaming and laughter. Maria stood on the table with her hands on her hips. Suddenly, she saw me and started to laugh, either because she recognized me or because the men who helped her from the table . . . no, because she recognized me, because she came right up to me. She had a steady, shining gaze, like glass eyes that are stuck in some soft mask that looks as though it might dissolve at any moment. She stumbled, she just about threw her arms around my neck, screaming. She said, Hello Holzer, long time no see. My dog began to howl, I broke out in a sweat. My eyeglasses, which had just begun to clear, started to fog up again. We have to celebrate this, she said, but not here.

I can still remember the tight pink sweater of the waitress who suddenly stood in front of me and, shortly after that, the thought of a woman's body made of glass, filled with raspberry soda; the waitress's large purse, which opened like a dark gorge, glistening at the bottom; an arm in a blue-and-white-striped shirt that came out of somewhere and was pushed back, I don't know how or by whom. So much movement all around me, and so I froze.

In the street, Maria hung on my arm. Tell me! I had to laugh suddenly. I had nothing to tell.

Up until now I had led a life about which nothing is remarkable except that it had been particularly consistent in never being worthy of mentioning. At one time, when I began to feel a certain pride in the fact that I was leading a sensational life, I just as quickly realized that my banal excuse for pride was nothing more than dumb and petty schoolboy pranks. And when, a second time, I thought that I was on the verge of beginning a life of ferocious intensity, I realized that I had almost taken inconsequential college skirmishes to be much too important. When I dropped out of college, I took a job in a bank, where I work to this day.

Since then, my life can be completely described in embarrassingly few words: punctuality, cordiality, and the sort of industriousness that smoothly completes all its projects at the same rate that others arise. I have no desire to write an autobiography, but it really irritates me that, if I did, the autobiography would be completed in the act of buying the paper; in all honesty, it would be made up of blank pages. This dissatisfaction is incomprehensible because I have no problems. But it is comprehensible because I have never been happy.

I take after my father. He is a correct man, friendly without exuberance, with a quiet and eternally nervous wife, my mother.

I would rather have taken after my grandfather.

In 1968, when I had just turned sixteen, he told me about his life for the first time. In February of 1934 he took part as a socialist in a workers' uprising, and later he fought in the Spanish Civil War in the International Brigades, then he emigrated to England and returned with the British army as a liberator. Wasn't a victory at all, he said. Why? Just look around. Well, you'll see in time what I mean. And we never got what was coming to us either, all those years of war, not even a good pension. Today there's just enough left to sit on a park bench. Should I feed the pigeons maybe? Nasty beasts.

When grandmother was fatally ill, they both took an overdose of sleeping pills. I was seventeen at the time, and I almost flunked out of school.

My sense of self was definitely developed at that time out of a contempt for anyone whose life flowed smoothly, without problems, harmoniously, for anyone who always had the right answer but never a question. So I despised almost everybody, Lechner too, of course. I was surprised how much I enjoyed seeing her again. Now, at thirty-five, she was displaying, to a grotesquely excessive extent, the simple exultation of an eighteen-year-old who is finally allowed to smoke. But it had an attraction that carried me away; I felt nervous and tense, momentarily excited in some obscure way. And when, after a night of pub crawling that nearly exhausted my strength, we went to bed together, I had the feeling that Maria had made me into a man for the first time. I mean this in the sense of society's characteristic idealized images of masculinity and femininity, images that culminate sexually in an ideal of lust that I had only known from porno films and that seemed unattainable in my own life. I was given such pleasure by Maria, in such a way, while I myself was able to effect the most surprising ecstasies in Maria, that I—I can't say it any other way—I suddenly became another person.

And I saw the world with other eyes too. I asked myself with astonishment how I never questioned it, how what it had offered could have been enough for me. This regulated life that depletes itself relentlessly, this smooth functioning, which, as a rule, doesn't reward one with any pleasure at all. I developed, naturally, a sort of addictive attachment to Maria. We were two people flung onto the right track who suddenly had discovered that the wild abandon and foolishness of carnival, which I had never experienced as pleasurable either, could be created at any time without any consequences. How many pubs were there in the city, and how many pleasures we could afford! And how many places for making love! And we never had to say "I love you." And we never had to keep from saying "I don't." For we weren't lovers but colleagues, rather, who shared a common interest: the production of exceptions.

Exceptions that would become the rule. We planned excesses by our appointment books, consumed pleasures as they came on the market, a market that is just as calculating as the bank I work for. And all of these thrills immediately produced new longings: for a spa vacation, for health food and fruit juices, for a good television show.

When I woke up in the morning, my face was bloated and my eyes were puffy. Two aspirin for my headache swiftly became as much of a habit for me as an egg for breakfast had been before. I could hardly ever manage to read the paper before work anymore, my eyes wandered over the lines without grasping what I read. When I walked to work through the city park, I was afraid of being asphyxiated in the storm of pigeons swirling like gigantic gray tufts around the old women and their bags of bird feed.

Last Friday night, when I went to pick up Maria at her house, she wanted to watch the TV news before we went out. It's wild, she said, every day now something unexpected happens. The Soviet Union, the GDR, Czechoslovakia. Look at that, she said. She seemed tired and stressed. When the domestic political report came on, she started to tell me the incredible case she had to handle in court that day. An absurd request, she said, that she had to deal with.

It had to do with an order of guardianship. I asked her what that was. In plain language, a disability hearing, she said. A person who suffers from a mental illness or is emotionally handicapped and is not able to manage all or a portion of his affairs without danger or injury to himself may, at his own request or the court's, be provided with a caseworker. OK, so picture this: an eighty-nine-year-old man who constantly walks around District One blind, jostling people, stumbling, almost knocking people down. In short, a public disturbance. The man is known to the police because there are constant notices at the precinct, complaints, even charges filed, or because it comes to scenes in the street that have to be broken up by passing police. The problem is, mainly, that the man doesn't make his blindness evident by wearing the yellow armband blind people usually wear here, and he doesn't use any sort of aid that would help a blind person get around the streets, like a cane, for example, or a seeing-eye dog. A seeing-eye dog is very practical, as you know; you have one yourself, she said, grinning. Anyway, it turns out that the man isn't blind at all. He isn't registered as blind, and an examination at the central city precinct revealed that, aside from the farsightedness of old age, there is no impairment of vision. He was given a warning, but he persisted in his simulation of disability, that's how it's written in my report, simulation of disability, which led to regular disturbances of public order. Then the police requested that the court carry out an investigation. Since there had been no attempted fraud, such as trying to falsely obtain disability payments—he hadn't even begged from the people on the street; instead, he knocked them down—there couldn't be a criminal trial, and finally I got the report on my desk in the courthouse and I'm supposed to decide whether a caseworker should be assigned. This is the sort of hair-pulling nonsense I have to spend my time on, Maria said.

I asked her why the man acted like he was blind.

That's just what I wanted to know, she said. So I made an appointment for the hearing and it was today. And you know, I think, the man is just a grumbler. Do you know what he said? I know, he said, that disability is the most sought-after privilege in Austria and, therefore, the life's goal of every Austrian. But he didn't want to present himself as disabled, nor did he want any privileges. Nor any alms. That's why he hadn't even accepted the so-called honorary gift, the four thousand shillings that the Republic of Austria presents to survivors of the persecution of the Jews. It is simply the case, he said, that he just couldn't look at everything that one sees when one walks through the streets with open eyes. It's a natural and healthy reflex that he closes his eyes to it. I asked him what it is that is so terrible about what there is to see. And in answer he told me his life story, in all its miserable detail. I tried to interrupt, but he just kept on talking. I told him to answer my question. That's exactly what I'm trying to do, he answered.

I asked Maria what he had said.

What do I know, she said. He talked and talked; he wanted to tell me his whole life story; you can imagine, I mean, everyone knows it was difficult for that generation. But I just can't stand these old men anymore, always wanting to talk about the war, or the civil war.

Which civil war, I asked, First Republic or Spain?

What? Oh yeah, Spain. Yes, he wanted to tell me all about Spain too, I think, I really don't know, he just fought a lot, and so I asked him once more: what is so terrible then that you see, are they pictures from the past that you can't get free of?

The television was still on. Now it was the commercials between the weather report and the culture news. I was extremely annoyed and wanted, most of all, to get up and turn off the thing, but I was afraid to interrupt Maria.

No, the old man said, it's pictures of the present. I don't understand that, I said, he should be happy that there is peace and no more political disorder, and no more terrible suffering. And just imagine what he said next. He said: Don't you see it at all, your honor? No, I said, I don't see what's so terrible. And he in answer: You see, your honor, I would like to fit in better in my old age, that's why I close my eyes so I won't see it either.

He said that? I asked.

Yes, said Maria, the man's sick in the head.

And what did you do?

Nothing. I was supposed to decide whether there was cause for a caseworker. There isn't. I can't give him a caseworker as a seeing-eye dog. The man is probably running around the city like a blind shell right now. A little nut, what can you do?

I leaned back in my seat with closed eyes, in my head Maria's voice was echoing while a detergent commercial rumbled on.

Can't we turn this damned thing off? I asked.

No, wait, she said, I want to watch the culture.

I couldn't say another word to her. Of course, she noticed right away that something had been torn, although she didn't understand why. We went out to eat but didn't speak a word, except to order. I drank faster and more than usual. Maria looked at me puzzled. When she finally asked me what was wrong with me, I didn't comprehend at first. I didn't have my senses about me. I had expected to see a speech bubble when she said something and to have to read what was said instead of hearing it. But I couldn't see the sentence. What's wrong with you? she asked again.

I gave no answer. When a rose vendor came into the pub, Maria leaned across the table to me, touched my arm, and said: Buy me a rose and leave me alone!

Translated by Genese Grill

Original story first published in *Manuskripte* (Graz, Austria), © Suhrkamp Verlag.
Translation published in *Fiction* 19.1 (2004): 172–178.

Gerhard Roth

Winterreise

Nagl felt that the most normal thing in the world was to surrender oneself. Everyone keeps fighting until resistance dies out and self-surrender creates the secret hatred, the desire to see how others surrender themselves. That is the only satisfaction and the only meaning. If all people give themselves up, it is obviously necessary. A law.

It happened by itself, but he often felt a small ache of humiliation, which he quickly blocked.

He had walked up to the bus stop and had sat down next to the woman in the dark-red Volkswagen.

In the vending machine outside the store, all the shelves were torn up and stuffed with banana peels, paper cups, and other refuse. They had been in that state for months. No one took the garbage away to throw it out.

The car stopped with the screech of brakes that always got on his nerves, and the policeman's wife leaned back and fished for a plastic sack containing a woman's boot.

"I've lost a heel," she said.

He didn't want to stay in the car and he followed her into the courtyard. Outside the shoe-repair store there were decayed racks with honey-colored wooden foot models, which had been used for custom work. A few were cracked or smashed, only a piece was left of some, and the dust made them look like junk. The wooden models had female names written on them.

Nagl peered through the window into the workshop, a small room, where the shoemaker was sitting. Next to the shoemaker stood a kerosene lamp with a gaudily decorated shade. Nagl's grandfather had made lampshades like that at the turn of the century. He had manufactured medicine vials, paperweights, glasses, and vases, almost none of which probably still existed.

When the policeman's wife came back, Nagl said he had changed his mind.

"Shouldn't I come along?" asked the woman.

"No, I've changed my mind."

"I'll drive you home," said the woman as she sat down, placing the empty plastic sack at her side. When he shook his head, she drove off.

It was a cold winter day.

It was the last day of the year.

"I always think that life still lies ahead of me, as though I had organized my previous life only for a short while and I were about to start my real life not too far in the future," thought Nagl.

"It all simply happens to me," he kept thinking. "I live from day to day, without asking many questions. Mostly I take everything for granted so that I don't think about it. I don't resist, nor do I give in, nor do I tell myself I have no choice."

Outside the barber shop at the end of the village street, he chanced upon the veterinarian's funeral.

The brass band had already marched by, now it was followed by men in folk costumes and loden coats, firemen in uniform, and a fire engine, which was towing the wreath-adorned, steam-powered delivery van on a rope through the loam-yellow snow because the engine couldn't get started in the cold. Since it had rained that morning, the farmers carried folded umbrellas. In their faces, Nagl saw the darkness from which they came and to which they had to return, the drudgery and the loneliness. The children, he noticed, ran along anxious and obedient under the low-flying clouds, the children looked as if they knew everything by now. Death, darkness, loneliness were not alien to them. They were not allowed to speak to their parents and grandparents, they had to stare straight

ahead as though hypnotized. Only the priest and the altar boys emanated, he felt, something wonderful. But in the faces of the children, he could read only victimization, frugality, and poverty.

He unlocked the school door and sat down in front of the blackboard in the empty classroom. From one side he could see the frozen fishponds, where children were ice-skating. He enjoyed sitting
in the empty classroom. He did it often. He liked the washed green
blackboard, the sharpened pieces of chalk, the sponge, and the stiff
dried washcloth. Sometimes he put a stack of uncorrected note-
books on a bench and worked until it got dark.

He had recalled an outing to the open-air museum of Stübing,
where he had viewed and entered various granges, smithies, smoke-
houses, mills, dairy farms, charcoal-burner cottages. Darkness had
reigned almost everywhere: in the woodcutter huts, in the parlors,
in the stables, in the workrooms. Sometimes, from inside, at the
small windows, he had seen the green leaves of flowers that were
planted in pots and gave the impression of shielding the house with
a radiant green umbrella. But what had truly reigned was darkness,
while the scant light, filtered through plants, had merely given a
false impression. The smithy had been so dark that, instead of peering into the house through the glass window, he had seen his mirrored face behind the flowers. Not far from the beehouse, Nagl had
discovered a small wooden chapel. A big vase of sunflowers had
stood on a table. The wall had a votive picture showing a man with
a conspicuously long nose and raised hands in front of a bed, and
next to it, the wife with the child in her arm. Above them, in a blu-
ish cloud of smoke representing heaven, Mary, who was known
here as Our Dear Lady of Heilbrunn, with a crown and the boy
Jesus, her eyes a mixture of pride, sorrow, and love, staring into
space, which gave her something of the sacrosanctity that strict and
just fairy-tale kings have in the minds of children. "In thanksgiving
for the manifest danger, when my six-year-old daughter lay danger-
ously ill, the Virgin Mary's intercession brought about her recov-
ery." Those were the words he had read under the picture. It had
hung there like a luminous document, a proof. He recalled it while
thinking of the funeral at the same time. "Perhaps," he suddenly
thought, "it was really the smartest thing to entrust oneself to life

the way one entrusts oneself to death, even if the nearness to life means a nearness to the terrors of life."

A map showed the Austro-Hungarian monarchy, with Vienna as the capital. The rivers were drawn as thin as capillaries, the mountains like melting ice floes; the map had always hung on the wall. Nagl had noticed it the very first time he entered the classroom, now it was as normal for him as the photograph of the president of the republic and the cross over the teacher's desk. He locked up the classroom and the school and cut through the orchard toward the pond, where he could still see the children ice-skating. One child lay on his belly, banging a hockey stick on the ice.

"Why are you banging the ice?" asked Nagl. The child laughed and zoomed off.

Right after that, low, sluggish, and whizzing, a blue helicopter flew over the school.

The children crowded together and screamed in excitement.

Then the helicopter was only a tiny dot in the distance. Nagl stared at it until it vanished.

The teacher had always wanted to see Mount Vesuvius. He had read books on vulcanism, on eruptions of Mount Etna, Stromboli, Fujiyama, but he had been most interested in Vesuvius and Pompeii. Pompeii seemed to him like a graveyard of dreams whose images had stiffened and frozen. How often had he thought of vanishing in Pompeii or plunging into Vesuvius, but suddenly, while still gazing into the distance where the helicopter had melted into thin air, he thought that the time had come.

The room was straightened up. The silver peasant watch with the eggshell-colored face and the tiny decorated golden hands, which he had inherited from his grandfather, lay on the table, on the newspaper, where he had left it that morning after winding it. He took the watch in his hand, it was cold, he held it to his ear and let it tick. The back of the watch was worn down and decorated with an engraved pattern of flowers and leaves. He thought of the farmhouses in Stübing, of time, which was passing, of Fujiyama and Vesuvius. He had forgotten the policeman's wife, but suddenly he thought of Anna, who had been unfaithful to him. He saw her in front of him: small, dark, with big eyes and the face of a child. He

felt like seeing her and talking her into coming with him. All at
once, it made no difference what had happened or would happen.
The thought was a relief for him. He found a book with color photographs of volcanic activities and leafed through it: sulfurous ef-
florescences in front of the ice wall of the Torfajökull Glacier in
southern Iceland, the white-hot lava flow from Mount Kilauea in
Hawaii, geysers in Yellowstone National Park, lava with a blue,
glassy surface in Idaho, violet ash deposits on the Lipari Islands,
and a view into the crater of Vesuvius, with pale billows of smoke
rising from inside. He put the book away and called Anna. Although he had been friends with her for a long time, he was
strangely wrought up. The moment she answered, he thought of
hanging up, but once he began speaking, he was suddenly overwhelmed by such powerful joy that he had to pull himself together
to keep from laughing the whole time. When he said he didn't know
how long he planned to stay away, she thought he was joking. Everything went as a matter of course. He knew she had a taste for
what she considered adventurous. Moreover, she was naturally
frivolous. Her father was an optician, he would somehow manage
to get along without her. Suddenly he wasn't sure whether she was
taking him seriously. Did she believe he was merely joking? Was she
making fun of him? But she was taking him quite seriously, and
now he realized she did so with great intensity. He gazed out the
window. In the street, the movie-house owner was walking along in
his rubber boots with his lively Pomeranian. All this would soon be
a thing of the past for him.

Carrying his valise, Nagl left the house. No sooner had he taken a
few steps on the path, which was hard with trodden snow, than the
policeman came toward him. His eyes were a watery blue as if
soaked by the shimmering aqueous humor. He smelled of alcohol
and made a hateful face.

"I'm serious," he said.

Nagl thought of the policeman's wife, and it struck him as ridiculous to maintain a guilty silence.

A moment later, the policeman had pulled out his gun and aimed
it at his own hand. He held the gun in one hand, stared into Nagl's
face, squeezed the trigger, and then gazed in disbelief at the other
hand, from which blood was running.

"Let's go upstairs!" he promptly snapped at Nagl. Nagl took a handkerchief and wrapped it around the policeman's hand before taking him to his room, still carrying the valise. He held the hand over the washbasin and took off the handkerchief. The blood ran into the washbasin, and Nagl turned off the water.

"You have to go to the doctor," he said.

The linen blinds were lowered and they filled the bathroom with yellow light.

So that was the last day of the year: a hurried meeting with the policeman's wife, the funeral procession, the empty classroom, a memory, the helicopter, an abrupt decision, Anna, a valise of ironed clothes, and a jealousy-crazed policeman shooting himself in the hand. He was Vesuvius vanishing far away. Anna would sit in the train and travel alone. It was grotesque. Anna would look at the murals in Pompeii, climb Vesuvius, see the ocean, while he scuffled about with the policeman.

"You can see I'm serious," said the policeman.

"Yes," answered the teacher. He took his valise and left.

Evening was gathering.

The clouds flew low and fast, and when Nagl looked up, he felt he was peering into a tremendous ocean overhead, streaming above the earth.

Now the earth was an isolated marble for him, sapphire-blue and streaked with white, in the blackness of the universe, a tiny particle floating in the void—as he had seen it in color photographs. This picture of the earth was not something he had in daily life. Usually the earth was the school building, the fish ponds, a mood of the sky that he wrote down in a notebook, children's faces, the earth was the smell of kerosene, floating dandelion, the children's drawings on the walls, the policeman's wife—no, not even those things, it was made up only of things that were taken for granted. The most usual and normal, the most humdrum things, which were repeated a thousand times so that he didn't even register them any more—that was the earth. From far away it was something that seemed like his conception of life: something wondrous, mysterious. But the closer he came to this life, the more it dissolved into details, into tiny things, through repetition. Life was a vegetating thing, just as the earth was nothing special in the universe, a triviality. He rode in the train and noticed that he was thinking about the earth as though it were an alien star, so remote in the infinity of space that one could not tell it was inhabited by human beings, as though he himself were living not on it but outside it. He felt as if he had fallen from the earth. It was an oceanic feeling of loneliness. Perhaps his inner emotion was something he ought to be ashamed of, something he was indulging in. For his grandfather, survival had been the meaning of life, while for him the meaning was a question of survival. From far away, in the deep-black ocean, he saw the blue globe of earth, which carried along his everyday life. It was as if he had nothing more to do with it. The policeman may have been sitting in his bathroom with a bleeding hand. There was no difference between the policeman and him. Only random things separated them.

The train stopped at a depot with wrought-iron columns on the platform and on the station house, which was covered with wild grapes in the summer. Under the clock with numbers full of flourishes, the stationmaster stood in his red cap, whistling the train to a halt. There was silence, only the swinging door into the waiting room made a noise when a traveler, who had come out in curiosity, vanished back into the waiting room. What Nagl saw was everyday life, in which there were only the most obvious things and small demands. "But that was my mistake," he thought, "I never got beyond the most obvious things in everyday life." Everyday life was always holding back his thoughts and political opinions only because it was necessary to do so for the principal or the school inspector, it was having to teach the children a life of values even though he knew that a life of values had to be something radical, had to be a life of truth. He felt pleasure in resistance. The thought of rebelling made him suddenly feel strong. He knew this feeling would pass, and he wanted to think about something else in order to keep it for a long time. Slowly the train began moving. Nagl stood up and saw the seemingly untenanted farmhouses with drawn curtains, and a vast field of snow, in which a man with binoculars was observing a flock of crows that had flown up at the approach of the train. Nagl didn't want to see the landscape any more because it reminded him of what he had always ignored. He looked at the windowpane, but saw his own reflection, transparent and wraithlike, so that he felt he was watching a self which had been his until then. The landscape drove through him, leafless trees, high-tension poles, scattered haystacks, a river. Outside, the world had perished, the myth of work no longer existed, work, which was full of constraints, which had always basically humiliated him, which had nothing to do with his wishes, his thoughts, his imagination, or his dreams. Amazed, he realized that his only hope had been old age, the only salvation the thought of retirement, when he would no longer have to ransom himself, month after month, from drowning in debts for the barest necessities of life: a roof over his head, food, and his own thoughts. He sat back and suddenly felt it was a great comfort to have fallen from the earth. He was no longer a victim of victims. He saw the policeman before him in the bathroom, the blood running from his hand. It was as if the policeman would have shot himself in the hand no matter what. Then he thought of the low-flying streams of clouds, the children who had run beneath them at the funeral; then he saw the globe of the world again from the outside, covered with white whirls of clouds, a bright blue planet of such great beauty as though embodying, in the deathly hush of space, both meaning and survival.

"I ASKED MYSELF why I just up and took off with you, and I ask myself now why it all seems like such a matter of course," said Anna.

Her gaze alighted on the dining-car waiter, who looked up like a frightened bird in his white jacket when a glass clattered, as though the clattering of a glass announced orders. She sat opposite Nagl and looked young and full of curiosity. Nagl had at first wanted to tell her about the globe of the world, but then he held his tongue.

"I had always wanted to tell you, but I was afraid of losing you. My fear made me do it again. All at once you asked me about it and you wouldn't let up," she said after a pause.

"I sensed you were lying to me. I didn't want to be lied to any more. But at the same time I wanted to be mistaken." He bared himself in order to free himself. He no longer had the wish to appear superior to her as he usually did with a woman, although it had always surprised him that he could seem superior. "I think it was more of a desire to find out that none of it was true, that I was mistaken," he went on. "But it was also an obstinate urge to find out everything from you, although meanwhile I've lost it."

"You acted so sure of yourself, as though you knew something," said Anna, amazed.

The glasses and the wine bottle clattered against one another. "The only thing I could go by was the way you answered. The way you at first tried to wave off my questions, the way you approached the truth while pretending to be frivolous, as though nothing had really happened. Then your sentences got more and more cautious and simple, until you just kept saying no and staring at the ceiling. And you put on an offended look to intimidate me. You didn't move either, because any movements would have given you away. You had gone so far that anything would have given you away: any reproach, any hurt feelings about my distrust, any gruffness to show me how ridiculous my reproaches were. All at once I knew my suspicions were right. It hurt so much that I wished you could convince me I was imagining it. But, on the other hand, there was something in me that couldn't stand being lied to. At the same time, I began desiring you. Strangely enough, my being hurt got me so excited that I absolutely had to sleep with you. I never wanted to tell you that."

The dining car with the white tablecloths, the folded napkins, the white upholstered seats, the curtains at the window, and the resolute motion of the train gave him a pleasant sense of calm.

Anna had put the pocketbook on the table and snapped it open. She took out a tortoise-shell compact, patted the tip of her nose, and shot a quick glance at Nagl from the corner of her eye. Nagl leaned back, took hold of the glass, and had a drink, while letting enough time pass to change the subject. He asked her about men she had gotten to know in the meantime; she lied to him, he sensed it but didn't want to stir it up, he didn't want to know anything at all.

Anna gazed out the window and said nothing. He had somehow hurt her feelings, but it didn't bother him. She sat in the dining car and couldn't leave. He let her feel hurt. He had been hurt, too. It was precisely the shallowness of her acquaintanceships that had hurt. He would have preferred her to fall in love with someone else and leave him, rather than secretly cheating on him.

On this remote blue-and-white globe, which turned on its own axis and flew through the cosmos at great speed, he had once taken that very seriously. This thought made his suffering seem small. But it hadn't been small. It had been so big that it had taken him a long time to find his way out. Anna was still gazing out the window. Back then, when he had found out that she had one-night stands on the side, he had sensed for the first time that he was replaceable. It was something novel to find out that other men could instantly take over for him. And then, a few weeks later, when he had fallen sick, a teacher from a neighboring town had substituted for him, and the principal and the children had liked him very much. Upon returning, Nagl had to admit to himself that he would soon have been forgotten. What did the other man have that he lacked . . . ?

In the dining car, there was a young Austrian, in wire-rimmed glasses and a windbreaker, quietly reading a book, and there was an Italian, with bug eyes, staring at him, so that Nagl stared back until the man turned away. When Nagl took Anna's hand, the man laughed out loud and peered shamelessly into Nagl's eyes. He was wearing a black suit, a white shirt, a dark tie, and his hair was severely brushed back. Even when Nagl gave him an angry glower, he would not be stared down, he just kept looking at him. Next, he stood up, halted before Nagl, and said: "I only looked at her." He stood there, the way the policeman with the bleeding hand had stood there, then he reeled and walked down the long corridor of the dining car between the tables, without turning around. Outside, there seemed to be only blackness, and Nagl recalled what he had read about the end of the world. The oceans would freeze down to the very bottom and eventually vaporize. The last trace of life would vanish, and falling meteoric dust would be affected by the oxygen and cover the entire surface of the earth with a brick-red coat. When the oxygen was used up, the meteoric dust would retain its green color and lend it to the earth's winding cloth. He had read this many years ago, and he wondered why it came to him at this very moment.

The passage to the sleeping car was an opening and slamming of doors, a groping through long chasms in the droning of the train. Anna had taken off his pants, squatted next to him, and fondled his penis, but Nagl had been so drunk that he had fallen asleep. He had woken up in the middle of the night because he felt that someone was in his compartment. The shade was down so that very little light came in. To his horror, Nagl really did see a man at the foot of his bed. The man stood there upright, searching Nagl's jacket. Nagl at first didn't know what to do. The train was rumbling, and the man was taking his time. Suddenly he stopped and looked toward Nagl. He looked at him for a couple of seconds, then he left the compartment. Since Nagl had seen that there was light in the corridor, he leaped up and flung the door open. The corridor was empty. But Nagl had flung the door open so violently that the sleeping-car conductor in his glass cubbyhole awoke with a start and confusedly asked Nagl what was wrong. Nagl answered: "Nothing," and stepped back into his compartment. He locked the door behind him and waited for the dawn.

When he opened his eyes at six o'clock, he saw the radiant red silhouettes of pine trees whisking past on the horizon.

THE HORIZON WAS yellow and merged into a slate-gray bank of clouds. The moon was still in the sky. Then the train dipped into fog, which shrouded everything in a blue veil: vineyards and leafless fruit trees, houses. He looked out the window and felt good. The fact that a man had come into his compartment at night seemed unreal to him now. Perhaps he had only been dreaming? Or perhaps the man had entered the wrong compartment? . . . But why had he searched Nagl's jacket? Nagl had checked during the night, but nothing was missing, neither the money nor his passport. The fog was gone again, and the earth shone red. He remembered he had been drunk that night. Anna had cried in the dining car. They had babbled about the alcohol, in wistful misunderstandings. In a box near his head, he found a bottle of water and glasses, and he thirstily gulped down half the bottle. How beautiful the landscape now seemed to him as he viewed it while still lying in bed. He lay there very quietly and watched.

They managed to catch the Naples train by jogging over to it. Breathlessly they stuffed the baggage into the train compartment, and Nagl felt happy upon hearing the foreign language, which he didn't understand. Anna had come up the ladder to him and had lain down naked next to him. He had told her about the unknown man who had entered their compartment during the night. All at once, he had suspected that the man had something to do with his death. The train had rumbled. It had been dark. In a hidden memory blurred by sleep, the veterinarian's funeral had emerged, and the image of the policeman, whose hand had bled into the washbasin, his picture of the earth in space and of the end of the world. The man had stood in the darkness and looked at him. He had studied him patiently and precisely, then he had left the compartment unhurriedly and vanished a second later. The more Nagl thought about it, the more probable his explanation seemed: death had been accompanying him for a long time, and only now did he notice that it removed the confusion afflicting him. Death had shown itself to him, not to frighten him, but to comfort him and help him obtain peace of mind. The dash to the moving Naples train, the throng in the corridor, the foreign language, and Anna's happy face had seemed to him for the first time like something that was free of guilt.

The sun shone brightly on olive groves, canals, in which Nagl could see tangled green plants below the surface of the water, wind wheels revolving on high wooden structures, green cactuses, and trees with yellow oranges and pink buds glowing amid the leaves. The thought of ephemeralness made him see the growing, greening, and blooming more clearly and he was amazed that it was winter. Anna sat next to him on a valise and stared through the compartment door at a crocheting nun. Anna remained silent, squeezing his hand every so often as if to make sure he was there. Then, suddenly, dazzling bright, the ocean heaved into view, covered by a delicate shimmer of light in the distance. The ocean revealed itself to him, splendid, vast, and big. Small ships seemed to be standing on it, it put up with them, even-tempered and good-natured. Nagl couldn't remove his eyes. Death had entered his compartment in the darkness, in the confinement, while the ocean lay there in light, inviting and beautiful, vast and indestructible. A seaplane flew above the ocean, settled on it in white foam, next to buoys that looked like tiny drops of blood.

Then the train rose, up a stony mountain, past a pink station, with palm trees in front and freight cars full of oranges, which Nagl could see through wire grating. The ocean now lay beneath them, the sun glittered and glimmered upon it, and Nagl felt as if he could make out the curve of the earth behind the vast ocean, as if he could see that the earth was a sphere. Now he also knew what he had wanted to talk about with the policeman, the whole time from the moment he had shot himself in the hand until Nagl had left the house: it was the emotion he had felt at the first view of the sea. And now, as the train moved inland again, it seemed to him as if a longer view would have removed the wonder from the manifestation. He had seen the ocean for the first time. Normally he had only gone to his parents in town or to the small vineyard cottage, which was surrounded by high grass, fruit trees, daisies, and sweet William, and in which he had loved Anna. The encounter with death altered nothing in his feeling of happiness. It was as if death were a neighbor whose arm he felt as a pressure on his arm but whom he knew nothing about.

OUTSIDE THE TERMINAL at Naples, they were surrounded by a waiting host of cab drivers, porters, unemployed men, and elderly people. When Anna asked for the Hotel de la Gare, a wrinkled man in glasses, a coat, and a hat stood in their way and explained that the hotel had gone bankrupt. The next instant, a man in a camel's-hair coat and a velvet cap appeared, shoved a calling card into Nagl's hand, and took the valises. He charged toward the wide street, which was jammed with traffic. Cars honked and the street lay in harsh light. Nagl ran along behind the man, who wound through the cars and was often invisible except for the black velvet cap. Nagl held on to the calling card without finding time to look at it. The man turned into a side street. When Nagl raised his head, he saw potted plants on iron balconies, laundry hanging from windows, ocher houses with crumbled plaster and posters stuck up haphazardly. A blistery cardboard sign announced LABORATORIO DENTISTICO, huge false teeth were drawn underneath. The man crossed the street and vanished in a nondescript blue house. Nagl, not wavering for even a second, ran across the street and pulled the door open. He heard the man's footsteps on the staircase and followed them. First, he stood at a door, where he could glimpse a piece of a back court through the mail slot, then he ran up the staircase and found himself in front of a dismal hotel lobby. On the glass door, the words HOTEL PRINCIPE could be read only in fragments of golden letters. Nagl rang and instantly the hotel clerk appeared with the man and showed him three rooms from which to pick.

Nagl took the brightest room, with a view of the street. It was unspeakably filthy, just like the others, but Nagl had not had the nerve to ask for his valises back. Between the filthy white curtains hung a string with a brass button that shone in the sunlight. The walls were uniformly papered, the bedspread had cigarette burns, the tattered rug was dusty. The wall had a photograph of Vesuvius behind the Bay of Naples, a mighty shadow that spewed flaming clouds, as though the earth were about to turn into a ball of fire.

WHILE ANNA WAS SHOWERING, Nagl had opened a curtain and seen her in the mirror with nipples stiffened by cold on the white, girlish breasts, the soft, dark pubic triangle, and the painted toenails. All at once he was so excited that he pushed her down on the bidet. Her body was cold, but her mouth was warm. For the first time since meeting her again, he kissed her, thinking of the men she had slept with. From the corner of his eye, he glimpsed her naked, parted thighs, he opened his pants and pulled out his cock. She was wet and hot and tight, he felt her hand, her smooth, tiny bird-tongue, which licked across his face and in his mouth, and he heard her high, loud moaning, which had always driven him crazy, but it occurred to him that she had moaned with other men, too, and he was both excited and offended. Then he heard the door opening and someone putting the valises on the floor. They paused and listened and held back their violent breathing. The other person seemed to be listening, too, for they could hear only the noise of the cars in the street. Furiously Nagl yanked his pants up and tore the curtain aside. A bellboy in greasy black-and-green livery stood in the room, laughing with a mouth that had lost a couple of teeth. Nagl's voice was hoarse from the embracing and whispering. Naturally the bellboy knew what was happening. After all, Nagl had come out of the shower room fully clothed while Anna remained concealed inside. The bellboy smiled again before vanishing from the room. Nagl went back behind the plastic curtain, his face angry because of the interruption, but Anna pushed against him, whispering and sighing, so that he picked her up and put her on the bed. He began to tell her about the policeman's wife, the way she had knelt before him naked on the bed and he had made love to her, until Anna moaned, with spots in her face, while she pressed him tightly to her body.

Piazza Garibaldi lay in the sunshine. Nagl had made up his mind to go to the harbor, first changing money on Piazza Garibaldi, and then, without looking for it, he had seen Vesuvius in the distance.

Meanwhile, Anna had entered a pet shop and crouched by a cage in which a small dog sniffed between the bars. Nagl waited for her, his hand rummaged in his coat pocket, finding the calling card. It said: HOTEL PRINCIPE. Via Firenze 16 and the telephone number. Nagl pocketed it again and looked over at Vesuvius, whose peak was draped with clouds.

The closer they got to the harbor, the narrower the streets became. Oranges and lemons on carts and in fruit crates gave way to crates of firm red peppers, cucumbers, and zucchini. Vegetable dealers in caps and aprons hauled crates of leeks, radishes, cabbage, fennel, pears, and apples past them, the air smelled of fish and meat, fruit, onions, and cheese. Up ahead, a fat woman sat at a tiny table, offering a carton of Marlboros for sale; behind her, a scrawny crone was twisting the fat woman's hair into curlers. Anna touched the fruits and vegetables. It was a touching and displaying of innards, mountains of cauliflower, tomatoes, and lettuce, as well as green-and-white peritonea, hearts, and brains of living creatures, and the longer Nagl walked down the streets, the more he seemed to be passing through bellies of slaughtered mammoths, whose entrails hung in clusters down to the floor, strange organs, like artichokes and carrots, that still contained oxygen and blood, melons that were gigantic blinded eyes. Widows with elegiac and sorrowful gazes sat before the innards of strange creatures, throwing pathetic glances at the passers-by or stuffing fruit into paper bags on the teetering surfaces of round scales. Nagl saw the shrines for the Virgin Mary in wall niches, they were framed by neon tubes or electric bulbs as though in a wreath of light, Mary with the child Jesus, in front there were dried carnations in ugly glass vases on filthy crochet work. The effigies resembled the pictures that Nagl had gotten in his childhood as rewards from the priest after confession. He recalled Stübing, the small chapel, the dark farmhouses. Religion struck him as an artistic handiwork from the hands of death, and it seemed only to be announcing death. Amid this butchery of the earth's entrails, the shrines were strung together as if to point out sorrow, suffering, ephemeralness. He thought of Anna, the way she had hugged him naked on the bed, her white skin, the life she could give, a transparent fetal membrane in which an embryonic person moved. Embryonic people walked about, were old, sat on chairs next to cartons frull of wonderfully large eggs, fossilized fetal membranes, next to cages of densely crowded brown hens, hutches of speckled and white hares, with slaughtered and skinned carcasses displayed above them in glass cases. In blue tin vessels, lobsters crawled through water, into which air was pumped through transparent nylon tubes; dead fish were spread out on tables—sardines, eels, summer flounders, mackerels, squids with golden eyes, rays—and others that he had never seen, with bizarre heads, quills, and huge maws, red and mottled ones among gray, dead cuttlefish that looked like intestines. In a bowl, there were large, silvery fish, glittering and flashing in the sun. The shops behind were blue and doorless, and the men wore rubber aprons and looked like murderers. Other shops had dog leashes and bath sponges, which hung in long, thick bundles at the entrances. Beyond a dirty window, Nagl saw a dreary bird shop with iron cages full of canaries, ringdoves, and parakeets. Cooing and twittering came from the shop so that Nagl halted and listened. In the middle of death, of chaos, these birds were singing. They sang with lavish splendor, trilling, chirping, whistling, whispering, while human torrents swept past, ignoring them. Children surrounded Nagl, tugged at him, yanked at his trousers, and scooted off, and Anna peered through the window with huge eyes as though the birds were announcing something she had always been waiting for. Nagl listened: it was something pure, and at the same time it was a memory of a dawn's first gleam, of sick, sleepless nights, of late homecomings after long embraces, of mornings in a chaise longue by the vineyard cottage, watching the birds vanish and sing under the dense leaves of fruit trees. A delivery van came with long blocks of ice, a boy unloaded them with an iron pick, the man in the rubber apron chopped them to pieces, which he poured over the sharks, scampi, sprats, and the other creatures that were lifeless or dying. Meanwhile, the birds sang away obliviously. Nagl felt as if nature were trying to comfort men for her cruelty. Next to a crate of apples, pineapples, tangerines, white mushrooms, and chestnuts, he saw a lemonade stand hung with bursting nets of lemons and oranges so that the vendor could be spied only through a tiny aperture. Nagl tripped over empty lemonade bottles while lemons and oranges were squeezed into a glass for him. He drank and felt the coolness running through his veins right into his fingertips. At a wooden rack, with big green leaves and rows of lungs, tripe, and severed calves' heads with twisted eyes, a young woman stood, pouring water on the meat. Anna halted at a flower stand, bought a bouquet wrapped in cellophane, and looked, holding it, like a little girl. One of the small three-wheeled delivery vans cut off Nagl's view; then he saw Anna again by the fish, she was reading the price signs on long sticks that were thrust into the tables.

He wanted to see the ocean and Vesuvius, which was blocked by the houses, but Anna talked him into renting a room in the next hotel. No sooner had Nagl closed the door behind him than Anna knelt in front of him and opened his pants. He unbuttoned her blouse, took out her breasts, reached between her legs, fingered her vaginal lips and clitoris, and inserted his penis into her. While making love, he lay down on the bed and watched his cock vanish in her and come out again. "Go slower," she whispered. She was breathless, and he turned her around and stuck his cock in her behind. He pressed her to his body, she screamed, wept, but suddenly went silent and began gasping. Then they lay mutely side by side. He again remembered everything that had happened to them, his feeling of shame and despair, his loneliness and the powerful sense of absurdity that had accompanied him. Previously he hadn't reflected much. The meaning had been that nothing had jolted him off course. He had lain awake many evenings, thinking about Anna's embraces and desiring her. Even when making love with the policeman's wife, he had thought about her. Their clothes lay on the floor, and the bouquet in cellophane, and he now felt Anna's tongue, which was tenderly licking the back of his neck.

In front of the hotel, an old man sat on a chair, puffing air from one cheek into the other. He looked up at an aluminum-colored dirigible, which floated over the houses of the city. As a child, Nagl had seen a dirigible with his grandfather. His grandfather had taken him to a barricade, and the dirigible had rested on the other side like a drugged monster. Ropes had fettered it to the ground, and whenever a breeze came, it had rocked jerkily as though trying to tear itself loose. Then, while they were sitting under a chestnut tree in a tavern, his grandfather had told him for the first time that he had once gone to sea, as a stoker. He was a short, squat man with a stiff hip joint, which was why he always carried a cane. His hair was brushed back, and he had worn a trimmed English mustache on his upper lip. He had told about countries and cities that Nagl had never heard of before: Algiers, Christiana, Valetta, Palermo, and for every one of these places he had known stories that struck Nagl as wondrous and confused him. In Graz, they had gone to the panopticon, a dark room with stools along black wooden walls. The wooden walls had peepholes like opera glasses, and Nagl stared in great astonishment at the gaudy images jolting by. His grandfather sat next to him, and whenever a city he knew cropped up, he reminded his grandson of the story he had told him. The colored pictures with three-dimensional depth had stuck in Nagl's mind, he had thought of them while reading, he could remember a few of them even now. He halted and showed Anna the dirigible. It looked to him like a message from a world in which there were other laws, and this dirigible said that everything was interconnected in an intricate way.

A boy trudged past, lugging crates of yellow and red tulips and red and blue anemones. On the sidewalk, next to a brick wall, lay a dead rat with a long, stiff tail and sharp teeth. They had reached the harbor wall and were standing at an iron door, behind it loomed a tremendous building. The white funnel of a ship towered over the roof of the building. But Nagl couldn't glimpse the ocean through any gap.

THE WIND DROVE DUST into their eyes. Via Nuova della Marina, wide, empty, illuminated by hard sunlight, was edged on one side by a high brick wall; on the other side, warehouses and administration buildings rose behind a concrete wall. They walked down the street, and the only things that moved were their shadows. An elec-

tric trolley wire and tracks faded into the distance, but there was no
sign of a trolley car. No automobile drove down the street.

So this was the destination. The dirigible floated silently in the sky.
No sound could be heard from the harbor. The street seemed endlessly long. Far away, he spotted a parked green refrigerated truck
with a fish painted on it. The space behind the steering wheel was
empty. He walked faster and turned around once more to see the
dirigible and realized that wasn't the sky behind the floating dirigible, it was Vesuvius, delicate and dark against the sky. Its tip appeared covered by the sun or a haze. What he saw seemed like a
memory. The endless walking in the street, the buildings, the ship
funnels over the buildings, the brick wall, the electric trolley wire
and the tracks, the parked truck, the dirigible—everything was familiar. He must have been here before at some time or other. As he
hurried on, the view of the earth in the universe flashed into his
mind. He thought of how he had slept with Anna, how his penis
had vanished inside her and slipped out again when she had sat on
him. "It's so dismal here," said Anna suddenly. The dirigible was
very small now, a floating dot of light, and Vesuvius loomed over it
like a dark wave.

At last, a yellow trolley car came rolling up with a singing noise:
right after it, a man pedaled by on a bicycle. "I'm nobody," thought
Nagl. "I was a human being, but now I'm not. And I don't want to
be a human being. That's why I feel as if I had lived through all this
before, because I used to be a human being and came here as a
human being. If I were still a human being, I would have to stand
at an open window with a rifle and shoot at the people going by.
I'm nobody. I can see the earth from outside when I want to. In one
night, in my sleep, I can be in a strange land, among strange people.
I know what the end of the world will be like. The earth will be a
huge, eternal desert. Nothing will recall a human being, no tree, no
brook, no flower, no animal will leave any trace. I can see it.
Human beings are no good. The future is shit. The past is shit. The
biggest criminals are the ones who really believe in the future and
don't put up a fight. I'm nobody. I've invented everything I see. This
street, Vesuvius, Anna, the ships, I've invented everything. Maybe

the policeman didn't shoot himself in the hand, maybe he shot me in the chest." He thought of the children at school and felt sorry for them. He was so overcome that his throat tightened up.

The wind disheveled his hair. The street was livening up now. All at once, Nagl no longer wanted to see the ocean. It even struck him as right that he hadn't seen the ocean. Perhaps it would be more right than anything to stroll up and down this harbor street and sleep with Anna in the hotel room. Or simply crisscross all over Naples until their money ran out.

Anna stopped and asked him what was wrong, and when Nagl merely looked at her, she said he was weird. "Actually I like it in you," she said, "I wouldn't like that in another man, but I like it in you." She glanced at him from the corner of her eye and laughed. A horse-drawn van was coming toward them, loaded with melons. The horse was brown and had a white spot on its nose. It was old, and the driver took a whip and struck it. The horse ambled on imperturbably. Nagl automatically thought of school, the children, the school inspector, of his own life. The brick wall on the right side ended, the street grew broader, and houses started behind a crossing. Two sailors in dirty white kepis and blue shirts were strolling toward them. One was peeling an orange and threw the peel at him, the other laughed. A moment later, Nagl crashed to the ground, he had been tripped. He brought his hand to his nose and saw blood on the fingers. The blood dripped on the asphalt, he heard Anna scream, felt her arms, struggled to his feet, and stood there reeling. They were both stocky, medium-sized boys, and they walked a bit faster when he began hurrying after them. Suddenly they halted and waited for him and the two of them promply leaped upon him. He felt no pain, only the punches that struck him. There weren't many, perhaps four or five, one in his face and the others in his belly and ribs. His head hurt, and everything was bathed in an oddly gray light. The sailors ran away, he saw their collars fluttering behind them like small flags, then Anna came, with tears in her eyes. From the other side of the street, men came running over to him and asked him questions, but Nagl didn't understand. They took him into a side street, where someone brought him a bowl of cold water and a cloth. His nose had stopped bleeding, but it was swollen. His body started aching, but this pain seemed like a protection. It didn't matter to him that his nose was swollen. It was a threat now. He could sense the people stepping away from him as he silently washed his face. But he also sensed their pity. They took him in front of a store with closed shades and offered him a chair. Sitting down, he noticed that a wooden mannequin was standing in front of the next house. He was numb but he felt strong. Anna leaned against him. She talked to him, but Nagl didn't listen. He thought of the policeman with the bleeding hand. Pain could truly be a liberation. Of course, only briefly, for the first moment, but it removed him from people. It made him strong. Now he sensed what the policeman had wanted. It had been a form of salvation, a method of putting oneself in the right. He felt he had nothing to lose. Fear was always merely the fear of something unknown, the first pain. The image of the first pain, which grows to an undreamed-of size, made the heart small and cowardly. He didn't want to fear the first pain any more, he wanted to be ready to take it. That was the whole secret of strength. He thought of the horse. It had gotten used to the blows because it had to get used to them. Because it is normal for a horse not to bite back.

He sat there, thinking and watching the people. A vegetable dealer was walking by with a scale on a chain, which he had attached to the back pocket of his trousers, a small man in glasses, a hat, and a coat was standing at the open window of a newsstand, playing cards with the newsdealer, a man was delousing a young dog that was lying on its back in front of him. Anna pressed a hundred-lire note into a child's hand, but a gust of wind made it flutter away, and the child ran after it.

Aimlessly they walked toward the noise of the city, they found a trattoria with white tablecloths and peaked napkins, and they ordered fish, crab, and wine from a bald waiter. In the hotel, the clerk with the glasses that were missing one earpiece sat behind his desk doing crossword puzzles. Nagl's nose hurt and he was dazed by the wine. They kissed in the hotel room. Nagl pushed her panty hose down and put her over the edge of the bed. He crouched in front of Anna and began eating her. While eating her, he had her clitoris before his eyes. It was big and bright, and Nagl took it in his mouth. He kept licking until she moaned and thrust her spread legs into the air. The filthy blue bedspread was under his mouth, but it didn't disgust him any more, he thought of the globe of the world and that he was no longer a human being. Anna had turned to the side, pulled off his pants, and was whispering that she loved him. Nagl said nothing. He straddled her and wedged his cock between her small breasts. It looked tremendous going into her mouth, he stuck it all the way in, so that she had to open her mouth up wide and gagged and snorted air in through her nose. Her hands squeezed her breasts together and Nagl felt he was coming. They watched him splashing her tongue, until Nagl dropped to the side and fell asleep in exhaustion. For the first time in a long while, he dreamed. It was a confused dream, made up of the things he had seen. He dreamed about the sailors and oranges, about the dirigible and the old horse, which was a white horse in his dream and was able to speak.

In the evening, he had to go out again. His nose hurt worse than before, one eye was swollen, and his thoughts were muddled from the wine he had drunk. He had looked at himself in the mirror and noticed that the pain made him feel he had nothing to lose.

Anna paused in front of a millinery shop and wanted a hat with a black veil, and Nagl went into the shop and bought the hat. Now Anna looked like a widow. She also wanted to go into a church, but the church was locked. The shrines for the Virgin shone everywhere in the streets. A fat man in a tie was strolling with a chair as though it were a cane. In a store for holy effigies, a man was sleeping in a chair and he looked dead. The whole neighborhood honked, yelled, and shouted. A cow's mouth nestled in greenstuff, pig hides dangled from meat hooks, in a store window a young woman was ironing a shirt.

Slowly it became night. Vesuvius lay in darkness. At the street corner, a man was selling cuttlefish soup. A severed arm floated in a red fluid, the fluid was drunk up, and the arm with the thick suction cups was sucked from the glass. He watched Anna in her widow's hat, sucking the cuttlefish arm from the glass, holding the veil over her forehead with one hand. It dawned on her that she had forgotten the flowers at the hotel they had been in that morning.

Nagl had to think of Vesuvius again, he drank the soup, and the cuttlefish arm vanished in his mouth. He stepped into Piazza Garibaldi and felt the wind. The veil on Anna's hat was pressed into her face by the wind. The piazza lay in a penumbra. The houses all around were yolk-yellow and looked like old administration buildings. But the sky over the piazza was enormous, and stars were glittering. For a while they strolled through the piazza to feel the wind. Old furniture was being burned on the street, people stood around warming themselves, and children were playing.

In the hotel room, he told Anna to undress. She was to keep the widow's hat on. Beforehand he had ordered a bottle of wine. "Take your clothes off and look at me," he said. She stood there naked with the black hat on her head and the veil over her face. He told her to turn around, bend over, and spread her legs. The hat lay on the night table. She did it. Then she got into bed with him.

THE NEXT DAY, Nagl bought an umbrella and a bottle of grappa. He went back to the hotel and awoke Anna. His nose still hurt but only when he touched it, and he planned not to touch it. In the street, a bellboy was carrying two cups of coffee and two glasses of water on a tray under a bent umbrella. Now and then, lightning flashed and the soft grumble of thunder could be heard in the distance. He went into the bathroom, drew the curtain behind him, and had a drink of grappa from a toothbrush tumbler. The grappa was so sharp that he choked, but it warmed his stomach.

They walked past the empty restaurants with the white-covered tables and the inverted glasses; in front, under linen roofs and canopies, stood small groups of men, taking shelter, smoking, and waiting. They didn't look at one another, they gazed at the rainy piazza, from which loamy water ran down along the streets. A rubber sheet had been thrown over a shoeshine chair, the stands were cleared off, waiters from the surrounding cafés were serving apéritifs to the people in the street. The subway shaft smelled of chlorine. They jostled their way through the crush of rain-soaked people, shoved into the train, and clung to iron poles as the train zoomed off with a rattle. Nagl stood there in a daze. He experienced the moments so powerfully, but he did not experience them with a clear head. Everything was tangled up for him. The idea of thinking of the past nauseated him. Nor did he care to think of what would be coming. He would not stay on in Naples if he lost his restlessness. Anna had stepped over to a window, wiping a peephole in the steamy pane and looking out. Nagl didn't want to look out. He wanted to make it with Anna in the train, on a mound of folded umbrellas, he wanted to fly across the harbor in a dirigible with the white horse, he wanted his body to be able to obey his thoughts; he wanted anything he could conceive of to be possible. A newspaper lay on one of the seats, but nobody in the overcrowded car came to occupy the seat, so Nagl asked the woman sitting next to it to move. The woman slid to one side, pushed the newspaper into his hand, and indignantly told him to read it. He sat in the train with the Italian newspaper that he couldn't read, and Anna gazed through the peephole in the steamy pane until they got off in front of orange groves at the Villa dei Misteri station.

In a trattoria, he drank a large grappa while standing. He felt relieved when he sensed the alcohol working. The finest moment was when a big finger touched him in the head and made him numb. He sensed his heart opening, he felt he was becoming himself and more invulnerable. He drank for this invulnerability, even if he was more vulnerable the next day. The rain had stopped, and a crowd of sailors poured from the ruins of houses and vanished in them. They had the same uniforms as the two who had beaten him up. Nagl walked with the folded umbrella as though it were a black wing that had broken off. He thought to himself that the watchmen and the tourists with their folded umbrellas stood there and hopped over stones like birds with broken-off wings. The sailors photographed each other at the entrance archways, and, in their uniforms, they entered a restaurant amid the ruins and Nagl wanted to follow them. But he walked on, since Anna had started crying; however, he threw the umbrella over a wall. In front of him stood Vesuvius, dark blue with white strips of fog as if covered with snow. Through gratings he looked into small overgrown garden plots amid remnants of houses and saw fountains of weathered stone, mosaics, and stone tables. Only now did he realize he was alone.

He peered around for Anna and spotted her farther back, walking along with the umbrella. Two nuns in black stood between the mossy columns, poring over a map. When Anna came over to him, saying, "Please understand me," he answered: "I understand nobody."

It began raining again, and she opened the umbrella. "You used to be a good person," she said all at once. "I was a good person in order to feel my own strength," Nagl answered vehemently, "in order to feel a triumph."

The Casa dei Vettii plunged into his eyes, pictures on walls in colors surfacing to the daylight from deep in the ocean. Colors from pollen and from the blood of slaughtered oxen, from air and leaves, colors that were tender as if they had grown as plants, as if they were thoughts made of some living matter. There were people in the pictures, naked children, birds, serpents, lobsters, grapes, dogs and stags, peacocks, columns, and amphorae, they were ocher and russet, black, olive-green, brick-red, lead-colored, and enamel. It was a peaceful kingdom. It showed him an inviolable dignity, its beauty and its indifference to time. Umbrellas rustled, but there was also the twitter of birds, it came from the villa's garden, where rain was falling on the green and the statues, and Nagl remembered the bird shop in the market street. He recalled the man who had searched his jacket in the train, and he recalled the ocean. He stepped up very close to the walls as though he wanted to see that the pictures on the walls were nature, like the jungle, the Andes, or the Arctic. Nagl stood before them utterly dazed, when a guard spoke to him.

He opened an iron box, and inside, in wan colors, there was a man with a tremendous cock. The cock was bigger than the man. The man didn't seem to be suffering, and he didn't seem to be feeling any enjoyment either, he was simply there to be looked at. In a dark niche, colored shadows glowed on the wall. Women with parted legs under men, women straddling men, lying supine before them, holding their penises. And now Nagl remembered the panopticon, the colored pictures he had seen with his grandfather, and he thought of how Anna had straddled him. With the dream colors in his head, he stumbled out of the ruins, over the bumpy stones, he could hear the birds again, and all at once he felt the colors in his mouth as a pleasant feeling, as though his palate were recalling them, and from there they mounted into his head behind the eyes. The birds twittered. All around him loomed the black silhouettes of mountains with the tattered patches of fog. Even the sailors came to him now like childhood memories. All at once, the sun broke through, and the houses and the walls cast delicately colored shadows. In one ruin, the foundation had remained, an oddly distant blue, which he looked at and in which he suddenly recognized life. He climbed down the amphitheater, which was empty, into the gloomy corridors, which were filled with discarded bottles, ice-cream cups, Coco-Cola cans, chewing-gum wrappers, and cigarette butts, and then he stood in the arena; high up, on the steps, Anna sat amid dry, yellow grass like horse manes. In the sky, dark rain clouds drifted by, they were coming from Vesuvius. When he had left the policeman, the clouds had been streaming overhead, too, and on the road in front of the amphitheater, yellow flowers were growing, lizards were crouching in the wall cracks. The sailors had scattered.

They walked toward Vesuvius, which was black, and the rain clouds made it look as if it were erupting.

THE VILLA DEI MISTERI stood among fruit-covered lemon and orange trees. A cat with a scratched-up nose was prowling by the entrance. It nestled against Anna's feet and meowed. Anna had to pet the kitty, and Nagl was alone in the house. He stood in a musty room, where figures appeared on the walls like a fata morgana of death. Mute and big, pale-yellow, dressed in green and violet togas, they hovered on the wall of blood. A winged demon had appeared in this world, lifting a scourge behind his head and about to strike. Nagl looked at the winged demon until he thought that he himself was floating. He returned—through the black vestibule with tenderly shimmering green plants and white herons—into the daylight, the sun was shining and it was raining, bright drops fell rustling into the grass, on the pine trees. A peasant was pissing among the grapevines, another was running toward them, his jacket over his head, and in the zooming train to Naples, Nagl saw a rainbow in the black sky, falling from Vesuvius into the orange gardens, while Anna slept on his shoulder.

HIS FACE LAY on the inside of an upper thigh. He opened the lips of her vulva and blew out his breath. He wanted her to hear the noise of his breath, and he kept blowing, pulling the labia as far apart as possible. The widow's hat lay on the night table, next to it stood the bottle of wine. Nagl reached for the bottle and pulled out the cork. Meanwhile, Anna licked him so that he began to moan. He took a mouthful from the bottle and squirted the wine into her. Anna stopped licking him and leaned back. She enjoyed his sucking the wine out of her and rubbing her clitoris. She was so excited that she sat down on the legs of a chair that had toppled over. She pressed her back between its legs, her thighs were spread apart, and a strand of hair dangled in her face. He reached for her breasts and lay down with his head between the legs of the chair. He saw everything very large, and when he looked straight in front, he saw her breasts and the nipples in the air.

"Look down," he said. She leaned over and peered between her thighs at his face, her face was different now that she was looking down and blood was gathering in it. She sat up again, dropping her head back, and she seemed to be listening inside herself as he rubbed her clitoris. Nagl slid forward out of the chair and saw her ecstatic face and her closed eyes. He always had to see her face when he was excited. Usually her eyes were shut, her nostrils quivered, her lips were open, and sometimes she stuck her tongue out of her mouth. They lay down on the bed and made love until they fell asleep in exhaustion.

THE OCEAN in front of the Castell dell' Ovo was dark, and the silhouette of Capri loomed in the distance. Three fat seagulls perched in boredom on an iron railing. Nagl sat down in a restaurant with uncovered wooden tables and piled-up chairs outside in the open air. The masts of ships towered senselessly into the sky. "Your mind always used to be somewhere else," said Anna. "You didn't care what I was doing, you were independent of me. But you gave me freedom only because you believed I was dependent on you. And I *was.* Anything I did, I did because I wanted to get free of you. I didn't want you to mean so much to me, and yet I loved you too much to leave you. In retrospect, after it happened, it always seemed like nothing. And I always told you it was nothing because nothing of any importance had happened. I was really only scared that you would find out and leave me as a result. I had no guilt feelings, because in retrospect it seemed unimportant to me."

The waiter had peered through the veranda and condescended to take an order. Gaudy rowboats rocked at the breakwater in front of the restaurant. "You always made a point of showing me that I didn't have the least claim on you," said Anna. "Now you don't bother. You say nothing, and I ask nothing of you. I've thought about it all this time and I've concluded you wanted to end it back then. I often had the impression that I'd become a burden on you. I was surprised that what I told you affected you so deeply."

Nagl gazed out. A boat-rental man sat by a small heater in a doorless room. On the stone floor, there were a bunch of rowboats whose paint had peeled off. In a larger boat, which was ribbed and red on the inside, reminding Nagl of the palate in a gigantic fish, a chair lay in rain water.

He was silent. What she said was true. He had never bothered thinking about her. Sometimes he had been glad to be alone. He had also thought of breaking off with her, but then they had had sex and he hadn't gotten free of her. He made it with other women, too, pickups and former girlfriends, but he never told her. She would have cried, a couple of days, a couple of weeks, but she would have gotten over it faster. He was more stolid, more sensitive, more conceited than she. Above all, she was more generous than he. To his dismay, he had realized that he, too, in retrospect, after being with another woman, had only feared being found out, and so he had always ended his adventures quickly. He thought to himself that there were other men who knew how Anna moaned, what idiosyncrasies she had, what she looked like naked. Anna said: "I often wanted to talk to you, but you were just annoyed."

That was right, too. Everything had gone too fast for him. Her intimacy, her practical nature. He had been bothered by her being experienced. To his mind, she hadn't been very experienced. But now he knew that this had been wishful thinking on his part when he'd fallen in love. He had had to take note of it. And again, he had been even more aroused, even though it had also hurt him. That was a strange mechanism. He was scared of the hurt of being cheated on, and yet he had never felt such excitement as right then. The policeman and his wife flashed into his mind. Just as he had treated the policeman's wife, just as he had made love to her, that was how other men had made love to Anna. He could tell about others from himself, about their feelings, their behavior from his own. He looked into her face and thought of her making love with someone else. He gazed out at the veranda again, at the boats. There, where the boats lay, he saw an iron door painted with large, gaudy flowers, as though it were summer. He kept gazing at the same things: the ocean, the boats, and Anna.

WHEN HE HAD spotted the ocean from the train, it had seemed like a huge promise, the flickering light, the curve at the horizon, the vastness, but from here it looked cold and dark, and he recalled the empty harbor street in front of it.

He paid, and they walked up the steps between the boats. Now and then, while walking farther into the city, they glanced at the ocean through side streets and saw large ships, which had come up very close. In front of a green church with peeled-off paint stood a naval officer with gold stripes on his uniform and a luxuriant mustache. Children yelled, clustered around them, and followed them. In the evening, they drank wine in the Galleria Umberto. The light fell through a giant vaulted glass roof supported by iron girders, as in a railroad terminal. Outside, it was starting to rain. The evening sky shimmered yellow, and the clouds were lilac-colored. In Piazza Dante, an old woman in a black coat and white stockings lay sleeping on some church steps. Nagl sat, intoxicated, in a trattoria, under a gigantic fan blade, among white-covered tables, in bright electric light; outside it was night, and the people were walking by, the cars were honking, and the customers were eating slowly and carefully and were beautifully dressed, the waiters were putting dishes down with a clatter, and the radio was playing music.

THE PEAK OF VESUVIUS was capped with snow. Nagl stared wordlessly from the moving taxi. He had woken up at night and lain in the darkness. He had tried to wake Anna, but she had been fast asleep. He felt he could move neither forward nor backward. So he lay in the darkness and breathed. "It makes no difference what I do," he had thought. "If I don't go back, if I leave Anna, someone else will come instead. I have to practice thinking about something else. I'll go to the school inspector and while I talk to him, I'll think about something else. Now that life is no longer ahead of me, now that it's really started, there's nothing else but senseless thoughts. I've done everything almost automatically. I made it a point of honor to have everything I did look as if I wanted it. In reality, it just happened."

The street moved upward, to the left and right there were houses with peach trees blossoming in front, gardens with olives, figs, lemons, and grapes, daisies and mimosas were flowering, and small woods of acacias and pines alternated with each other. But presently, solidified volcanic rock welled up from the earth. Nagl suddenly thought of his grandfather.

His grandfather had believed in work. Work had been the meaning, because he could survive only with the aid of work. It made no difference what kind of work. Living without work was like an insidious deadly disease, it was the awareness of death slowly coming upon him. And so he had worked from his childhood on. In the time of unemployment, he had spent nights over the chessboard, playing against himself, until he found work once more. After retiring, he lived in a dark room that he rented in his sister's home. Outside the open window, which faced a back yard with a chestnut tree, he played chess against himself. After his death, his furniture was gathered together in half an hour. People were disgusted by his furniture because it was the furniture of a dead man. When he was buried, they played "The Song of Work."

Nagl had never understood his own life. He couldn't explain it. So long as he worked and believed in work, it was not difficult. He never wondered what would happen. Below them, the Gulf of Naples spread out, and the city with small houses, and the ocean, which, viewed from afar and from above, was beautiful again and full of hope. In front of him stood Vesuvius, the snow and the clouds now made it sublime for Nagl. The road ate its way through slopes of cooled, reddish-brown lava. They followed the lava streams, they saw isolated chestnut trees and pines and firs from which cones were hanging. Farther up, the lava was covered with snow, at first only in patches, so that the lava looked gray, as though afflicted with a mold fungus; a bit farther on, the road was smooth with snow and ice, and the taxi just managed to creep and skid slowly toward the height. Anna conversed with the driver. Nagl watched her face until she looked at him. "Why are you so silent?" she asked, laughing. The car stopped behind the observatory. A small man in a white coat emerged from the observatory and explained that he would guide them up Vesuvius. He had only two teeth and carried a bag. They wound their way up the snowy path, surrounded by snow and thick gray fog. All the while, the guide lectured on volcanic eruptions. Behind a curve, the fog shone sulfur-yellow. In some places, black lava peeped out from under the snow. Nagl climbed without pausing, even though the guide halted several times, gasping for breath. But when he saw that Nagl forged on without him, he hurried to make faster progress. If Nagl moved too far away, the guide stopped and yelled after him, and as soon as Nagl turned around, the guide showed him a bottle of wine that he carried in his bag, or else he shouted senselessly that he would have to spend the whole day on Vesuvius. They climbed higher, and the lava dribbled under their feet with a clear noise and trickled down the steep mountainside into the fog.

NAGL LOOKED UP AT THE SKY, but the sky above him was the same opaque fog in which the snowy slopes disappeared. A narrow path was well beaten by footprints, and he followed them. Suddenly he stood at the crater. The trail had vanished, but he had ignored it, and he stood so near the edge of the crater that he could easily tumble in. He was dizzy, he felt a throbbing in his temples, but he stayed put. A gigantic hole yawned before him, full of snow, cooled lava, and fog. No human being was in sight. He stayed put and gazed deep down, into the earth. There was nothing below. Rather than gazing into the earth, he seemed to be gazing at an alien star. Not even the fog rose or sank. Had he taken one step, he would have hurtled down. He could just barely make out the other side of the crater's edge. It was as though he could survey a large part of the world, and empty as the world may have been, it still had its beauty and rightness.

The guide and Anna stepped over to the crater's edge and the guide shouted into the crater so that the echo came back. Nagl felt an emotion that he didn't immediately grasp. He had pictured something different, but what he saw looked far more obvious and natural. He saw only that tremendous hole, the fog, and the snow, and sensed that the emotion pacified him. He thought of his class, the children's faces, he thought of their amazed way of listening. But he also knew that everything would be at a distance as though invented. The children would listen, unable to picture anything. It would be the mysteriousness that would astonish them, and since he knew this, he would tell everything mysteriously. He would soon give up convincing himself during the telling, it would be enough for him to see the children sitting there with gaping mouths.

He bent over and touched the lava. He knew what emotion, what appeasement was in him, the very fact that nothing was happening, that nothing was changing, calmed him down. A cold wind made him feel his sweat like water from elsewhere. Anna shouted their names, and they came back as an echo. They clambered down a narrow path to the crater. Vapors rose from the rocks, smelling of sulfur, the rocks were hot when Nagl touched them, and finally, the mountain guide, holding a lit cigarette to a narrow chink, produced vapors that thoroughly enveloped and soaked them, their hair became wet and curly, and the stubble on Nagl's unshaven face dripped water. Thus they stood in the volcano, coughing and enshrouded in an ash-colored fog, when all at once the sun came up, irradiating the fog with a golden light. Nagl saw the outlines of Anna and the mountain guide. This weather lasted only briefly, then, abruptly, the radiant fog, which had protected them, tore apart, and sheer below them, deep down, law the bottom of the extinct volcano.

THE WIND WHISTLED COLDLY as they went back. Anna walked in front of him; below and above them hung rosy fog, all around them were only snow and lava. The light was dazzling and silvery gray, and wherever the lava had blended with the snow, violet spots were shimmering. They walked silently and quickly. Nagl saw his feet before him, the soaked shoes, the snow, the fog, the lava. No one came their way. The sky and the earth were so close that they touched. It seemed to Nagl as if someone would have to picture the world like that upon first viewing it in space. He had felt as if he had fallen out of the world, and now it was as if he were really experiencing what that was like. He felt a yearning for people. When they came to the observatory, the valley lay black underneath them. The driver was freezing behind the wheel, he had pulled up his collar. Cautiously he drove down the icy road.

AFTER THE LAST CURVES, they veered off toward the freight harbor in the sunlight, and there lay the big steamers from London, Marseilles, Hamburg, and Dubrovnik. Looking out the rear window, he recognized Via Nuova della Marina. When they left the wide harbor street, he could see no people and no vehicles except for a streetcar that grew smaller and smaller. He thought of his grandfather and automatically looked for the dirigible in the sky. A park with palms, deciduous trees, and a fountain glided past them. People were strolling in the park, and Nagl felt the same yearning for them as he had felt on Vesuvius. He remembered the Sunday mornings when his grandfather had taken him and his older brother to the city park in Graz to hear a concert in front of the fountain. The band had sat in the pavilion, and patterns of light had fallen on the audience through the chestnut leaves. Actually, the fountain concerts had always been boring. Nagl had liked going only because of all the people. On the way home, his grandfather had bought them cold, watery raspberry ice-cream cones. That was special, because it was special for the grandfather to buy them something. He never offered an explanation, but because he whispered tender words to them and stroked their hair, Nagl had concluded that his grandfather had been thinking of his own childhood. He had been born in Istanbul. His father, a glass blower from Austria, had worked there in an Italian factory. The grandfather had alternated between two stories on those Sunday mornings: about how his brother had died and a ship had taken him across the Bosphorus, to a Christian graveyard; and about how he had tried fishing for crabs in Istanbul. The big ships with the black clouds of smoke from their funnels had always played a part. Now they were driving along railroad tracks and scattered dirty houses by the ocean. Nagl's shoes were soaked and his feet were cold. Anna looked uninterestedly through the window, but her hand lay on his penis, squeezing it. Whenever she spoke to the driver, she would lean over so that he couldn't see anything, and only once did she send Nagl a look that jokingly sought concurrence. He was wearing a Burberry, and she had slipped one hand under the coat, unzipping his trousers and grabbing his cock. He was able to twitch his cock, and every time he twitched, she squeezed it.

Now they were driving inland, leaving the ocean behind. In front of a small garden with fruit trees, a man with a tree spray on his back was washing his boots with a hose. The trees had no leaves, but beyond them, green olive groves covered a mountain ridge. Anna took her hand from his penis and put her face out the window. Vesuvius lay far behind them. Not only was it a silhouette against the sky, it was also an oddly remote memory for Nagl. He thought of the gigantic crater and of how he had stared into its depth as though looking at an alien star. And then the sun had made the fog around them fluorescent as though they had suddenly found themselves on the sun, enshrouded in glowing gases.

THE DRIVER HAD STAYED BEHIND, and the cashier in the checkered hat over the dark-skinned face led them across the bottom of the solfatara crater, where their footsteps rang hollow. It was a flat, vast stretch of earth, leaden-gray and lifeless, without plants. Nagl felt the warmth under his feet and yet he sensed no alienation in the vermilion cone, which was overgrown with woods and where the earth bubbled, steamed, and simmered, and where he inhaled the stench of sulfur. The pines at the crater's edge seemed like ink blots on the sky, yellow broom flowered on the slopes in between mimosas, palms, rubiae, and eucalypti. On Vesuvius he had been closer to heaven than earth, but here, over the boiling heat, he felt very close to the earth. He thought of the market streets, the lush fruits that had reminded him of organs, and a wax cloth panel at school, showing the inside of a mine, bracken, and prehistoric animals. The guide had twisted a torch out of a *La Stampa*, lit it, and waved it across the ground, which was dirty-yellow from the sulfur. Giant

clouds of hissing smoke had risen from the earth and flown overhead as dark shadows. On the other side of the volcano, the abandoned Osservatorio Friedlaender bobbed up in the smoke. The
walls shimmered with flowers of sulfur, the house was made of
stone and had only one room with a barred window. "Here, on the
thin floor of the volcano, a man once sat, observing what happened
in the crater," thought Nagl. He had meticulously recorded the
ground cracks on a map, taken the temperature, studied the seismo-
graph. But the ground under the observatory had grown thinner
and thinner so that the station had to be abandoned. Was it sheer
chance that he thought of his grandfather again, in his dark room,
over the chessboard? During all the chaos of the Austrian corpora-
tive state and National Socialism, Nagl had always pictured him in
his dark room, over the chessboard. He had been a Social Demo-
crat, but had felt no triumph at the collapse of the monarchy; in
1934, during the Austrian civil war, he had not fired a rifle at the
army from the apartment house, as his brother had done. He had
remained out of work, living off his wife, who was a cleaning
woman in a pencil factory. He had watched National Socialism
with disgust at the authorities and with amazement, since he had
found work again. He kept silent when he was supposed to answer,
and shrugged his shoulders when he was asked questions about his
silence. After the war, he had campaigned for the Social Democrats,
driving sick people to the polls and sitting by the radio till late at
night, entering the election returns into lists. Thirty years later, he
had been forgotten by the party; not even red carnations, which
he used to wear in his buttonhole on the First of May, lay on his
grave. His very name was misspelled by the obituary in the *Socialist
Workers' Newspaper,* as though someone else had died.

A stone, flung by the guide, hit the ground with a hollow boom.
It was an odd sensation walking on the thin crust over the seething
earth. At the exit, the guide picked fragrant myrtle branches and
heather for Anna. The observatory, wrapped in sulfurous steam,
perched on the leaden-gray plain of the crater, and the farther they
receded, the more it looked like the icy surface of a volcanic lake.

On the staircase, there was a woman who had hung a small
mirror on the banister knob and put her handbag underneath. She
had long, dark hair and was making up her face, while a young man

with a mustache stood next to her briefly and then silently went away. Nagl had told the clerk they were leaving the next morning, and when the clerk had asked him where they were going, he had said Rome. Outside, it was pouring. In Piazza Dante Alighieri, there was the trattoria with the large fan blade on the ceiling. Nagl was hungry, and in the hotel room he had felt like drinking. It was still early evening. They were the only customers in the place. Nagl drank rapidly, but it started bothering him that Anna wasn't drinking. He felt fine and merely wanted her to feel the same well-being that he felt; but Anna gave him a disapproving look, which he knew was meant for the drinking. He remained silent and kept on drinking. He felt more and more strongly that Anna was cheating him of his well-being and his good conscience. During the meal, he picked an argument, asking Anna about past lovers and explaining what mistakes he would avoid making with women in the future. He sat on and on until he almost passed out in his fatigue. The trattoria had filled up with customers, but it still wasn't late. They went back to the hotel. If Anna ran away from him, then let her run away. In front of the hotel, a squashed red cardboard valise lay in the street, and Nagl said she ought to take the valise and go. The last thing he saw was Anna setting up the open umbrella to dry on the bureau. In the night, he awoke and spotted the umbrella, which looked like a gigantic open flower. He felt threatened by it, got up, and put it away. Through the open balcony door, he could hear the rain. Only now did he realize he was still dressed. He took off his clothes and felt he no longer meant anything to Anna.

WHEN HE AWOKE in the morning, he took two Alka-Seltzer tablets in a glass of water and wondered how to start a conversation with Anna. He could play the innocent, just slowly remembering everything, he could ask her to forgive him, or do none of that and answer her reproaches and offended looks with terse, angry explanations and change the subject to whatever was important. He dressed and went outdoors. Across from the hotel there was a photo studio, which he had seen from his window, and he entered it. A man in a black smock came toward him, the woman sat behind a cluttered desk. They obviously had no orders. A pair of glasses with smashed lenses lay on the counter, a rope with clothespins hung straight across the room. The telephone cable was artfully entangled. The walls had photos of married couples posing stiltedly in front of palms and on bridges. It was a dismal store. Nagl asked them to take a photograph of him, the woman held the lamp, and the photographer crept busily under the black cloth. After an hour, which Nagl spent sitting in the office, the photographer brought six copies, on which Nagl gazed at the viewer, unshaven and absentminded. During the waiting time, he had kept his eye on the hotel entrance, which was visible through the photographer's display window. Anna had not come out of the hotel. He had asked himself what attracted him to Anna. She had aroused him, that had been the most important thing. Her face had something innocent about it, and that innocence had kindled his fantasy. Moreover, she had let him notice how much she loved him. It had been a child-like urge, but later on, Nagl skeptically wondered whether she hadn't been calculating. She had put up with his indifference and his deliberate aloofness. But then again, she had shown him how much she suffered. It had been very convincing, it may even have been true. But throughout that time, she had secretly had other men, with whom she had tried to still the pain. He didn't have that reason on his side: he had slept with other women because they had aroused him or because he had been in love.

He sometimes had uncontrolled fits of rapture, which resulted in complicated obligations for him, the stolid man. He then squirmed and wriggled, trying to find excuses, and he himself couldn't tell what he did out of obligation and what he did out of inclination—He paid and asked for an envelope, into which he inserted the photographs, then he wrote his name and address on it and dropped it in a mailbox.

In the hotel room, the linen had already been removed from the beds. The towels lay crumpled on the floors. He could hear Anna in the bath. She came out and was intent on showing him that her feelings were hurt. When he approached her, guilt-ridden but cheerful, she would reject him and play the deeply injured woman. He said nothing and stepped out on the balcony. The bustle in the street bored him. He turned around and saw Anna sitting on the mattress and staring into space.

"We have to go," said Nagl.

"Is something wrong?" asked Anna. "If you want me to travel back alone, then say so." Nagl looked at the street again. "You have no reason not to answer me," said Anna. Then she suddenly threw her arms around his neck and kissed him. He put her across the mattress, stripped her, stuck his cock into her, and moved very slowly. Her nipples were pink and solid, and he licked them with the tip of his tongue. "Stand up," he whispered. She leaned against the table, bent over, and pushed out her white buttocks. They were so fleshy that she had to spread her legs wide. She stood on tiptoe, her breasts dangled, and since she bent her head way down to see between her legs, her hair fell out from the back of her neck and rocked back and forth with her head. They plunged upon the mattress, her buttocks still pressed against him, but her legs were closed. It struck him that the balcony door was open, but the thought got him even more aroused. He glanced at the door to the room, and it struck him that he hadn't locked it. He told her, and she waited until he had shut it and come back. Now he lay between her legs, which she curled around his back. She slipped a finger into her cunt and scratched his cock, she wound the other hand around his buttocks and tickled him. The bed squealed, they licked each other's ears and shoulders, and when Anna came, she bit him in the throat.

Spit was running out of the corners of her mouth, his cock was still inside her. Anna whispered that she loved him, and he whispered back. When he was alone, he yearned for just such moments: to sleep with a woman, lie beside her, feel her warmth. He had often embraced a woman because he was alone, even though he hadn't particularly liked her. He felt his cock sliding out of her. "We have to go," said Nagl. "Wait a few minutes," said Anna sleepily. She opened her eyes, yawned, and smiled.

THE TWILIGHT DESCENDED upon the white statues, the green gardens, the fountains, and the gilded churches. On the square in front of the terrace-shaped white monument to Victor Emmanuel II, monks were strolling with umbrellas and naked feet in sandals. Nearby stood a couple of old men, gathering signatures for some cause or other. All afternoon, they had drifted through Rome, riding about aimlesly in pale-lime double-decker buses, past beflagged houses, on which sheets of paper proclaimed CASE OCCUPATE and posters demanded BASTA CON LA RAPINA DELLE IMMOBILIARI DEL VATICANO! CASE PER I LAVORATORI! For a while they stood superfluously among the old men, then they went to the gathering point for the buses, which priests in broad hats and black clothes were entering.

THE TRAIN RIDE had been tiring. No sooner had they stepped into a compartment than a short Arab, sucking lemon drops, asked them what their nationality was. He had offered them cigarettes and said he was waiting for a friend. The friend was a tall, slender Algerian with sunglasses and curly hair, he had been drunk. They had ridden through the green of the landscape, and the Algerian had tried to start a conversation with Anna. When he had begun inching closer, she had sat down next to Nagl; then the Algerian had addressed Nagl in French. He had slipped his hand between his legs and laughed. Nagl had gazed out the window. In a vineyard, where creepers hung like nets between tree trunks, a peasant had been trudging with a lame dog. Later, Nagl had seen a child relieving himself behind wrecked buses. All the time, he had wondered what to do about the Algerian. But nothing else had happened. The Algerian had dozed off, and his head shook with the rattling movements of the train. In Latina, a corpulent man got in and read a wide-open *Corriere della Sera*, so that neither his face nor the Algerian's could be seen.

They had found a pensione, on the fifth floor of an old mansion at the corner of Piazza Esquilino and Via Cavour, with flowery tapestries in the corridors and a chest in front of a connecting door. The window looked out on the faded brick-red of the rooftops. Nagl's stubble was a few days old, his hair was unkempt and the Burberry crumpled. They had heedlessly left their baggage in the room and had gone outdoors.

IN A SMALL CHURCH, richly decorated with gold and marble, sat two nuns. They were wearing glasses and reading. Their habits were the color of eggshells, their veils white. People stepped through the swivel door, reached into the baptismal bowl, crossed themselves, sat down on one of the chairs, and vanished again. Nagl sat there drowsily, surprised that he felt all right. He had left the Church ten years ago. Whenever he had been in a crisis, he had thought of God. He had also prayed whenever something was important to him, but as soon as it was past, he had forgotten it. Sometimes his only hope was that God existed. When pain and loneliness had compelled him to speak to God, he had not doubted God's existence. But when he vegetated monotously, when the hours wore on and he did not sense himself, then he did not consider it likely that there was a God. Sometimes, however, he did feel that God must exist. Everything was thus given a flickering meaning, it was no longer shallow, it was coherent. Often, inside his vineyard cottage, in the darkness of his room, he had aimed his air rifle at people, at dogs, cats, chickens, crows. Now and again, he had thought of really firing. It would have seemed like a relief to him. At school, in such moments of dumb, senseless fury, he had asked the children about their homes in order to soothe himself. Only seldom had he felt for no reason at all that there was a God. He had sat there calmly, the peasants planing corn, mowing, hanging the grass up to dry, harvesting currants, the leaves of a tree shimmering in the sunlight, the children in school, with pinched lips, studying a letter of the alphabet, and everything had emanated a force that gave him certainty.

In a corner sat a bearded man, he laughed, sprang up, and went outside. Curious, Nagl followed him, he opened the door, and the man was squatting on one of the steps, begging.

In a store opposite the church, he saw various jackknives and switchblades. Without reflecting, he bought a switchblade with an ivory handle, which he fingered in his jacket pocket while walking.

BEAUTIFUL WOMEN in light-colored leather boots and soft fur coats passed by in clouds of perfume. They sat down in a bar, Anna ate and Nagl sat opposite her.

"Don't you want to eat?"

"No."

"At least a bite?"

"I'm not hungry."

A couple of times, Nagl took out the switchblade, put it on the table, and snapped it open, but Anna didn't like it.

"You once told me you look back at women on the street and imagine sleeping with them," said Anna suddenly. He didn't realize he had told her that, and he said nothing. Anna ordered a taxi. It came only after two hours, and by then Nagl was drunk. In the pensione, Anna said she was tired. Her panty hose and her bra hung over the back of the chair. Nagl hugged her warm body and kissed her, but Anna wanted him to let her sleep.

In the morning, Anna pushed back the blanket and took his penis in her mouth. He pretended to be asleep, he was still tired, but it was fun lying in bed, squinting his eyes, and watching Anna excitedly sucking on his penis. Anna got out of bed, pinned up her hair, and put on her makeup at the mirror. The hair, which she normally never pinned up, fell slowly into her face. She crouched over the bidet and began washing herself. Nagl saw her lovely hand with the red-lacquered fingernails rubbing the lips of her vulva and stroking the inside of her thighs. Her face was an image of unobserved joy. Nagl got out of bed and stood in front of her and had her soap his penis. Closing her eyes, she did it with an absent expression and excited tenderness. He washed his stiff penis with cold water and sat down on a chair in front of the bidet. He had to urinate but felt only a burning cramp when he tried. He closed his eyes and thought about something else, but it didn't work. Then he inserted a finger in her crack, waited, and noticed that she was waiting, too. All at once, he pissed in painful waves, he felt his urine striking her labia, felt himself pissing into her crack, and suddenly he felt that she was pissing, too. She sat on the bidet, their knees touching, and her body leaning back. He waited until she was done, picked her up and put her on the bed, and lay down next to her so that her legs stretched across his thighs and his cock vanished inside her. She began rubbing her clitoris, and Nagl told her about sleeping with a woman in a car, sticking his cock into the woman, pulling it out again, and eating her. At that instant, Anna moaned so loud that he had to put his hand over her mouth. She sat up and licked his nipples. He sat in front of her with a stiff cock and saw her lovely face and the small tongue darting over his nipples; then she asked him to lie on his belly. She licked his hips, and the hair on his arms stood up, then she licked his back up to the nape, from there across the shoulders and under the arm. The sweat ran in single drops over his face. He felt sick from drinking and he lay there naked and motionless, with closed eyes.

UPSTAIRS IN THE pale-lime double-decker bus, he felt sick, he had to get out and wait for the next one in the fresh air. In the next bus, he also felt sick, he had a hard time breathing, there was a pain under his breastbone, and his throat seemed pressed together by some invisible force. It was the same tightening he had felt in the train when he had awoken and seen the man. He sat down with Anna in front of a column in gigantic, circular St. Peter's Square. A bit farther on, there was a man with a light-colored hat and black band, black horn-rimmed glasses, and a collapsible umbrella; he was scrutinizing Nagl with interest. Nagl was pale, he took a deep breath, stood up, and saw how tremendous the inky sky was above them. There were black rain clouds, and the farther one gazed, the blacker they grew. Instead of flying on one plane, they merged into each other like dense, heavy smoke. On the merlons of the buildings, the statues of saints loomed white, like optical phenomena, against the dark sky. They stood next to one another, and in order to see them, Nagl had to lift his head. He thought of the veterinarian's funeral and the children, who had stared as though hypnotized. The children knew a lot, he thought. They saw how animals were killed because people needed food, they worked in the house, in the farmyard, in the fields, they saw how a storm wiped out all efforts, they saw people dying, and they slept in the same house with the dead. When it was warm, blood ran from the corpse's nose, flies scurried over the waxen faces of the old grandmothers and grandfathers. Outside, the work went on. The fathers came home drunk, the children could hear them lying in the same bed with the mothers. And he had to act as though he didn't know that, as though it didn't concern him, he had to represent a normality that did not exist. He had to act as though this nonexistent normality were all that existed.

Anna stroked his hair, and he reached for her hand. Even if he had the impression that nothing had anything to do with him, he nevertheless sensed how rich life was. He remembered the way he had sat on a chair at the fruit harbor in Naples, with a swollen nose and full of anger. He reached for his nose and could still feel the pain.

THE CATHEDRAL HAD such a tremendous impact on him that it took his mind off his body. The walls and decorations were of black, green, yellow, and gray marble full of golden mosaics and stucco-work. Instead of a heaven, a golden ceiling radiated above; and all the way in front, at the center of four powerful columns, stood an altar. Nagl stepped into a side chapel, and there, in a glass coffin, lay the flat, gold-covered body of a Pope, he was wearing red velvet and appeared to be breathing. It was the most ordinary thought that flashed through his mind. Anna marveled at the dead Pope, but Nagl felt his own ephemeralness so strongly that he couldn't go on. He thought of the world, revolving in space, sapphire-blue and radiant, the crater of Vesuvius, into which he had gazed as though it were an alien star, Anna straddling the bidet and soaping herself, and the policeman shooting himself in the hand. Now he again felt everything he had felt while sitting in the train with Anna and thinking about the end of the world, when memory had tortured him and the present had afflicted him. And then, in the night, the strange man had come into his compartment and had searched his jacket without taking anything. Anna had walked on and had knelt down in a confessional. He wondered what she planned to confess. Life seemed so full of suffering to him that it was arduous just living at all without surrendering oneself. A bit farther, he saw Pope Josaphat lying in a glass coffin, his head was decayed down to the bones, and his face covered by a net, through which Nagl saw the shape of the skull. But in front, at the altar, a honey-colored window with a white dove was shining, as if to mellow his dismay.

HE WALKED THROUGH the shimmering marble cathedral, golden leaves and flowers adorned the bronze columns of the great altar, and the dome over the red baldachin seemed to be a gigantic window into the violet universe. Nagl gazed past golden stars, on and on, into dizzying heights.

He climbed to the roof of St. Peter's Cathedral and was so close to the rain clouds up there that he believed he could touch them. The sun shone, lighting up the giant saints as he looked between them down to the city. The spiral staircase to the dome was narrow, and the rust-colored walls had names scratched all over them. Through an opening, they stepped out on a balcony which ran all around the inside of the dome. The people beneath them looked so tiny that Nagl grew dizzy. He took one step back, touched the gold and blue mosaic stones, which had been so wonderfully luminous when seen below, and then he went back to the stairs. His legs hurt when he climbed around the spherical dome, then he and Anna walked out into the open, the rain clouds lay beneath them, and through the rain clouds they saw the white figures of the saints.

Nagl was exhausted and felt sick. He thought of what it would be like when he came back. He could only push this thought away without finding a solution. He wanted to drift along, but it didn't work. He recalled how stupid he had felt as a child in school. He had learned arithmetic like a machine, he had written like a machine, without knowing why. He had only felt an inescapable constraint, a hopelessness, which struck him mute. "It makes no sense," he had often thought when giving up, as if what came next would have made more sense. He had raised the children to keep quiet and make no waves, because he believed that would be best for them. Of course, the children had to be cheerful. Actually, they had learned how to conform and dissemble, they had learned how to conceal and how to put themselves in the limelight. Those who hadn't learned these things had stayed back.—Two choirboys in white-and-red robes and with a holy-water basin lifted their robes like chaste women as they climbed the steps to St. Peter's Cathedral. Nagl gazed after them. He lacked something, but he had never spoken about it. Other people didn't complain, either. Anna had gone on ahead, buying ice cream from a street vendor and laughing as she came toward him.

From far away, they saw the stone angels on the Bridge of Angels, it was noon and the light was mirrored on the brown, sluggish Tiber. In front of the Bridge of Angels, there was a half-rotted boat with a wooden house and a terrace. Above the many whirls in the flowing river, the angels loomed white and beautiful, with large wings and pleated robes, like creatures of an icy, light-flooded planet. In the hard sunshine, which pierced through the rain clouds, the angels seemed to radiate a distant northern light, giving the water underneath a silvery shimmer. Nagl went down to the river, and from there the angels had their backs to him.

Anna sat on a step and stretched out her aching legs. Nagl's legs ached, too, he was full of earthly gravity, and he recalled the story that his grandfather had told him about his, the grandfather's, brother. He had died of spasms. For two days, he had lain in state in a cleared-out room with a scrubbed board floor, the sun had shone upon him through the window, and his face had looked alien. His mother had shown him a picture of an angel, saying his brother had become an angel. Two days later, they had put the brother in a coffin and taken it across the Bosphorus, to Büyükdere. Huge ships always sailed on the Bosphorus, gigantic steamers, and waves from behind them hit against the house. His father, after coming home, had sat in front of the house until it was dark, and the brothers and sisters had whispered. The next evening there had been a knocking on the big window shutters. He had closed them, thinking someone had called him from the house and the roaring of the ocean would drown it out, and then something had flown away from the window. He had looked but seen nothing. It must have been a seagull, he had thought later. But at the time, he had thought it was his brother.

THEY HAD SAT DOWN on a bench under leafless trees by the river. He was tired and thought of the dead. In order to find work, the great-grandfather had wandered to Wies, from Köflach to Vordersdorf, from Voitsberg to Moosbrunn, from there to Reifnig. In Köflach, he had married a woman from Schneegattern in Upper Austria. The wedding was a new hope, a brief surfacing from unconsciousness. At the end of the summer, he had moved to Piran and then on to Istanbul to work as a glass blower in an Italian factory. Life had been work. The grandfather had been born on the Bosphorus, the Asia Minor side, and had, without realizing it, always looked toward Europe.

When he gazed out on the Bosphorus, he thought he was seeing the whole world. Everything was contained in the Bosphorus, visible and concealed. Gigantic ships sailed past with strange people, and fish and seashells washed up in front of the house. Even human knowledge seemed to come from the Bosphorus. Sometimes, his mother had sent him to a glass polisher, who gave the children lessons, he had gazed through the window at the Bosphorus, and since he hadn't understood anything, he had thought there was some peculiar connection between the numbers and letters on the blackboard and the Bosphorus. Then the great-grandfather had wanted to go back into the world. The world was foreign countries first, and then the Austrian monarchy. He had no time. He looked for hope like a faithless beloved, whom he couldn't live without but who never stopped cheating on him and leaving him. In Trieste, it was cold. The new hope, life, the world were impressions of coldness for the grandfather. Icicles hung from the ships. He saw snow for the first time. The place they lived in was moist and dark, only the ships in the harbor were messengers of hope. The great-grandfather moved to Reifnig, and since he couldn't support his family there, he moved to Vordersdorf, to Köflach, back to Moosbrunn, then on to Osredek and Salgotarjan. How strange it was for Nagl to sit here on the Tiber and think about the life stories of dead people. In the distance, he now saw the angels as dark shadows against the sun. Oddly, the stone angels were more real than what he was thinking about. It was gone as though it had never existed. The sufferings were gone with the dead, and the people had lived by coming to terms with their lives.

THE PRESSURE HAD vanished from his chest, and as they passed a clothing shop for priests, he remembered that they had left Anna's widow's hat in Naples. In the store, cassocks hung on racks, there were priestly hats and miters. The proprietor came out wordlessly and pointed a finger at the heavens. Nagl couldn't help looking up, and there, an endless flock of thousands and thousands of songbirds was soaring over the houses. The man who had come out of the shop was gaunt, tall and stooped, and over his arm he held a cassock he was working on. He adjusted his glasses and spent several minutes staring up at the birds, which flew across the city like a swarm of locusts. When Nagl looked down, the gaunt man raised his finger again. The birds were flying so high that their wingbeats and voices could not be heard. They disappeared behind the houses, where the rain clouds were deeper, and the man with the cassock nodded and withdrew into the shop again. On Piazza Navona, children were yelling between the tea-colored, olive-green, and iodine-brown houses and the white fountains. A pretty girl in a yellow dress and a flowery hat sat outside a café amid gaping people and waiters who juggled coffee and liquor on trays. It was like spring. They sat there until darkness came. Nagl felt a familiar arousal when Anna began whispering obscenely into his ear. She had told him about a lover who had asked her to say obscene words. While sleeping with her, he had told her what words to say, and she had repeated them until they no longer embarrassed her. She had often told Nagl about him, and at first it had pained him, but then, when he slept with her, he had asked her to tell him about the man. Nagl smiled in silence. In the hotel room, he had Anna sit down with her back to him and bob up and down on his cock. He could see her legs next to his thighs all the way down to her shoes. The dress slid over her behind, and he rolled it up and tucked it into the cloth belt. He opened her blouse and tugged on the nipples. From the side, the breasts looked white and strangely deformed. She was scratching his thighs, holding tight to his knees, and bending forward to see his cock vanish in her hole. Nagl grabbed her beautiful hair, pressed her away slowly, stood up over her, and pushed his cock into her mouth. When he leaned back, he could see her rubbing her clitoris, in front he could see his cock going in and out of her mouth. Right after that, she came, her face was painfully distorted, her eyes were shut, and she splayed her legs in the air. In bed, they licked each other's tongue. He had stuck a finger into her behind, and she threw her head back and forth. A short time later, someone knocked on the wall. Nagl had to put his hand on her mouth, they listened, but there was silence. He placed Anna's head on his shoulder and looked at the ceiling, and she held on to him tenderly.

When they slept, Anna always crowded against him; if he woke her up then, she would turn over on her side, only to nestle against him once more. Suddenly, he didn't know how or why, he was weeping. His face twisted, and tears ran over his cheeks. He wept very softly, a sound came from his chest only now and then. He had such a strong sense of leave-taking now, he thought he would never see the children at school again. Even Anna would leave him. It was like on the train, when he felt that he had fallen out of the world. The earth in space was no comfort. All that comforted him was despair overcome in the past. He would live again and forget, sometimes he would think back, but the memory would not pain him.

Nagl awoke in the morning because there was a loud yelling in the street. As he went over to the window, he remembered weeping in the night, and he washed his face. In the middle of the street, a young woman was squatting. She had one corner of her coat in her mouth and was yelling. She had raised her dress with her hands and tugged her panties up to her belly so that it looked as if she were naked and were relieving herself. The passers-by ignored her, only the cars drove slower. Policemen ran across the street and took the woman to a jeep. When Nagl dropped the curtain, Anna was standing next to him. The sun fell into the room through the curtains, and suddenly she asked him whether he had cried during the night. "I had the impression you were crying," she said. "I was tired, I was almost asleep, and then I heard a noise as if someone was crying. But I didn't have the strength to wake up."

"Maybe I was dreaming," answered Nagl.

He felt tired, he was indifferent and left everything up to Anna. They strolled through the parks of the Villa Borghese, first across the Piazza del Popolo, with the reclining sphinxes and white statues, then past stone lions and green trees to a square that lay in the bright morning light, edged by pines and palms. Children were running across the gravel and riding the merry-go-round, and their grandfathers stood in hats and spectacles near the baby carriages, which were parked in the sun or under rosy, blossoming trees. After a while, they walked down a lane with trees spotted elephant-gray and with white busts and green benches in between. Children sat on a stone lion, reaching into the open mouth, the nostrils, and the ears. Shitting horses, whose riders gazed in boredom, caught up with them on the street.

At noon, they were sitting on the glassed-in terrace of the Café Doney among bereft blue chairs. On the peach-colored tablecloth stood the apéritifs with ice cubes. Nagl thought about it being winter. The glassed-in terraces on Via Veneto were empty. For once, Nagl felt he had time. He made up his mind to continue traveling. He didn't know where he wanted to travel to. He thought about going to Sicily, to Catania or Messina. Then he had the idea of going to Florence or to Venice. Basically, it didn't matter where he went.

On the flower stands, anemones, gladioli, tulips, and roses were blooming. Anna stood in front of a glove shop and studied the red, dark-blue, black, and white gloves of suede and leather with worked-in patterns. In the vestibule of a church, a nun in black was sewing a striped hospital nightgown on a bench. The sunlight shone from small side chapels upon gold-and-blue murals. Nagl lit a candle for the dead whom he had thought about. He had known many of them himself. A black-haired great-aunt, who had yodeled at folklore evenings. Once, she had yodeled on the radio, and her brothers and sisters had spoken admiringly about her. Nagl had seen a picture of her in a folk costume, posing with a regional song-and-dance group; she had artificial edelweiss plaited into her hair and sat next to a zither player, who was gazing very solemnly into the camera. And a brother who had blown bottles until he was seventy-five, who had spoken slowly and left him a bicycle. He had had powerful arms and had been an earnest man who sang chorales at funerals. When he spoke about his father's death, tears came to his eyes. He had gone almost totally blind because of a gray cataract, but he had to do unskilled labor in the glass factory until the very end. He had died of tuberculosis, and the doctor had written "consumption" as the cause of death on the death certificate. At that time, the grandfather had gone looking for work himself. From Graz to Vösendorf, from Vösendorf to Meissen, from Meissen to Torgau, then on to Frankfurt an der Oder, Fürstenwalde, and Berlin. In the hostels, they deloused him and checked his work book. He moved on, from Berlin to Dresden, from Dresden to Aussig, from Aussig to Prague and Brno, then back home again, to Grafenschlag-Ottenschlag and Mariazell. In 1910, he made up his mind to go to America.

They couldn't get out of the church right away because the main entrance was locked. They tried different doors until they stood outside, on a white stone step, in the daylight, amid ocher and tobacco-colored houses. A Dalmatian lay sleepily in front of the church. A woman stood next to it and spoke to it, but the dog didn't stir. Anna wanted to pet the dog and talk to the woman, but Nagl didn't care to stop. They went back to the hotel room and slept the rest of the day.

I⊤ WAS 6:00 P.M. when Nagl awoke. He peered out the window: below lay Via Cavour, the street was closed off, and from the railroad terminal a demonstration was moving toward the inner city. Anna wanted to go out, and they took the elevator down with a panic-stricken waiter who was delivering coffee to an office. Nagl looked at himself in the mirror, he saw his unshaven face, the tousled hair, the greasy coat. Human masses swept through the street, policemen with billy clubs, steel helmets, and shields stood around imperturbably. Suddenly, a cobblestone zoomed through the air, tumbled under the wheels of a police van, and stayed there. As though at a signal, the police charged toward the demonstrators while cobblestones came flying from various sides and tear gas spread over the street. The demonstrators had pulled back on the sidewalks, behind trees, and into side streets, and Nagl thought that the gathering was about to break up, when a car burst into flames and shots cracked out. That same instant, he saw a young woman being carried past them. She was blond, eighteen or nineteen years old. Her eyes were open and black blood was in her mouth. When the men who'd been carrying her let her drop, a pool of blood spread from her mouth. One of the young men spoke to him. Nagl didn't understand, but finally he grasped that the man wanted to hide. They took the elevator up to the pensione. From there they looked down at the street: the girl lay in a big pool of blood, and a police official and an orderly were kneeling beside her. The car was burning, scattered people were dashing across the street, throwing cobblestones and getting beaten with rubber truncheons. From above, they seemed small and unafraid. Slowly they retreated, followed by the police. The young woman still lay in front of the building. The pool of blood was black, her arms were at a peculiar angle. A policeman was covering her with packing paper, which he weighted down with cobblestones. Nagl had once seen a man die in the street. He had been hit by a car, flown a bit through the air, and then sprawled on the ground with a broken neck. He had been about sixty, a bald man with glasses. The glasses had lain smashed on the pavement, his head had dangled away from him, small and bloodly, like the head of a slaughtered chicken, and black blood had spread around him.

The man in the room was tall and dark, his face was pale, and he sweated. He spoke in a broken German. Nagl gazed down with him at the dead girl. Smoke poured out of the car, the street was strewn with cobblestones, and the man watched to see what they were doing with the girl. "She suddenly lay in the street," he said. Then it dawned on him that he was in a strange room, and he shook hands with Nagl and Anna. He told them he was studying zoology and botany, but it sounded as if it meant nothing to him.

Nagl was still looking between the curtains at the dead girl, who was covered up with paper. He recalled the woman who had screamed in the street that morning, and the birds that had flown over the rooftops.

America had been his grandfather's dream, the escape from self-destruction, from the senselessness of just barely keeping his head above water from day to day. America, he had supposed, was peace. He had made a mental picture of a new life in America, which he always thought of: the sun in a gigantic sky, with him walking along underneath, very small. It was this picture that he traveled toward. In America, there would be good work. He had no intention of getting rich, but he had worked so much that he hadn't perceived anything else. He had worked, eaten, slept; sometimes, on Sunday mornings, he had danced. Perhaps it was a trip to America that made Nagl think so much about his grandfather. Suddenly, he had gotten underway. He had sold everything he owned to take the train to Bremerhaven. There he had seen the ships again and the strange people, as on the Bosphorus. He had had no money in his pocket. A rucksack contained tobacco, a shirt, underpants, a comb, a pocketknife, and a photograph showing him with a tramp:

the grandfather sat there, smooth-shaven, with a fleshy face and a cap, a flower in his buttonhole; the other man wore a big, floppy hat and a chain of silver coins around his belly. At night he had stowed away in a coal bunker of the *Martha Blumenfeld,* which was putting out for America. He lay in the stuffy blackness, waiting. He had to make sure and come out of the bunker at the right time so as not to be buried under the coals in a seaway. He lay there, tiny, between the slopes of coals. But the *Martha Blumenfeld* sailed to Cardiff, and the sun went down in the prairie without his grandfather ever seeing it.

At night, Nagl dreamed he was swimming out to sea as a child. The sea was vast and endless. He felt he was getting cold, but he swam toward a big ship. The closer he came, the eerier he felt. The ship lay deep in the sea. Under the surface of the water, the ship was green with seaweed; and above the water, it rose so tremendously to the sky that he was terrified. Anna woke up and turned on the light, and Nagl watched her with squinting eyes as she crouched on the bidet and pissed. She sat in the dirty-yellow light with her white body, the dark pubic hair, her girlish breasts, and the lovely long hair, on the porcelain bidet, and he could hear the gush of the piss. Later on, he had confused dreams, and in the morning, relieved at the daylight, he embraced Anna, who had nestled against him and whose warm, soft body he had been feeling for some time. They didn't speak, they only hugged and caressed each other.

VIA CAVOUR HAD BEEN CLEARED of cobblestones, leaflets, and banners. Where the dead girl had lain, he spotted sawdust. The burned-out auto wreck had been dragged over to the side, but there was still a huge black stain on the asphalt. He heard bells ringing, it was Sunday. Sailors, policemen, and soldiers were ambling in front of St. Peter's. The church was peaceful, as if nothing had happened. They peered into a side chapel, bald priests were sitting there in white and black lace garments, singing in a withdrawn state. —An old man trudged toward them with a tapping cane and a hat in one hand. He pressed the hand with the hat and cane against his own body and held out his other hand, open, to Nagl. He didn't look at them, he had merely stopped without moving, without speaking. Nagl gave him money, the old man looked into his eyes and walked away, groping. Nagl thought of the roaring train, the sleeping car, and the man in the compartment. It was as if the man were following him all through the trip. It was only outside, in the open air, that he could think of anything else. The statues of saints on the merlons no longer interested in him. The nuns and priests bothered him. They merely seemed to be blocking out everything. A strong wind was blowing, and it was cold. A man appeared at a window in the side tract, far, far away from the people: the Pope. A dark-red flag billowed under the window, was twisted about by the wind, and got entangled in the shutters. The Pope spoke in the wailing tone of a very old, sad man. In his white robe and white cap, he had spread his arms out wide and was blessing the people under him; then he vanished into his room, slowly and heavily, and a priest pulled at the flag for a long time until he managed to draw it into the window.

In a cold, brightly lit restaurant, which looked like an ice-cream parlor, a young woman was slicing noodles from sheets of dough. They eyed the woman and waited to be served. The woman was cudgeling sheets of dough as large as a tablecloth, scooping flour on them, and cudgeling on. The staff ate silently and earnestly at the next table. Nagl saw the meat, fish, and vegetable dishes on a long table. They were served wine, and Nagl drank so hastily that he spilled some while pouring. But the stain on the tablecloth looked beautiful to him, it was pale-red, like a red splotch of ink in an exercise book. The more Nagl drank, the gloomier he got. He thought about leaving and began talking about saying goodbye. Anna suddently wept. Tears ran down her cheeks, she was silent and did not make a face. Instead of drinking wine, she had ordered ice cream and now refused to eat any more. Nagl took the ice cream, ate it, and Anna held one hand in front of her face. He suddenly became furious and made nasty remarks, but she kept crying until he stopped talking. The waiter came and put a plate of spaghetti on the table. The waiter pretended not to notice, but they were sitting directly against a wall with a mirror, in which they could be seen by everyone else. A child at the next table laughed so loud that the guests at the other tables joined in the laughter. The child went toward the toilet and there it could be heard laughing, too. When it came back, it knocked over a bottle, and covered the lemonade stain with a mound of napkins. They drank silently, and Anna laughed at the child, then she was serious again. The child, too, was always serious right after laughing so loudly. The guests were now looking openly at them, Nagl wanted to talk to Anna, but she threatened to keep crying if he didn't stop talking away at her. She said she couldn't help crying if he started talking about it again. Nagl kept quiet and was glad that no one was staring at them any more. The child pointed a finger at Anna, and Anna laughed. Nagl remained serious. Her laughter offended him all at once. Nothing special had occurred, basically nothing had happened, but Nagl felt he'd been put in the wrong. Anna suddenly stroked his face, pinched his cheek, and hummed gaily to herself. He felt that his politeness made her insecure, and he kept on. In the hotel, she embraced him the instant they shut the door behind them, but Nagl was tired and felt this fatigue like a reinforcement. She snuggled against him, but he fell asleep.

IT WAS ONLY in the huge concourse of the glass terminal early the next morning that Nagl had decided to go on to Florence. As they rode there in the train, he still didn't know where they would get out. In Florence? In Bologna? Would they change to the Milan train? Or go to Venice? He gazed out the window: yellow fields lay under the heavy rain clouds; all around, the various greens were shining: grass-green, the green of cypresses, the turquoise-green of shrubs, the green of pines, the green of olive groves, and the rain water lay in the fields, reflecting the green of the sky. Behind a cypress wood, trees were shimmering in white blossoms. Wherever the hills rose a bit, they were covered with patches of fog and looked dismal. He was riding there and thinking about his grandfather. His grandfather had wandered around Cardiff for a couple of days without money, never sleeping for fear of the police. The shipping offices turned him away, he had no papers, no passport, no documents. Finally, he submitted his work book, with the stamps of glass factories in Dresden, Prague, Brno, and Berlin. But those were peculiar names for ships, said the officials in the offices. The book had Fürstenwalde, Gloggnitz, it had the names of hostels like Mürzzuschlag and Bruck. They checked the records. No ship in their books had a name like that. The officials mulled it over. Finally they asked him for money. No, he had no money. They closed the registry book and told him to come back when he had money. He came back the next day. They gave him a job as trimmer on a German ship. He had to shovel the coals over to the stoker. The ship was named *Anni*. It was sailing to North Africa, to Algiers, Tunis, and Temnis. It was hot and dark in the ship, but a cold wind blasted on deck, and the earth was blue all around and infinitely vast. He went on deck and felt as if he were floating on a blue liquid sphere. When he came ashore, his pay was gone in just a few hours. He sailed to Sicily with coal and lumber aboard, back with sulfur or oranges from Gibraltar or Valetta. They sailed to Lisbon and Cartagena, Barcelona, and Valencia. He was a stoker now, and the ship had been sold to a Norwegian company and was named *Skagerrak*. He wanted to see the Bosphorus, but what he saw was towns that came before his eyes like a colored veil, or the vast blue sea when he came on deck. Sometimes he pictured in what direction America lay. Then he forgot it. He shoveled coal into the boilers. He didn't know what was happening to him. Was that what he wanted? Was it happening to him? He had no time to brood about it. No one asked him. He didn't ask himself. When he came back to Austria, he joined the Social Democratic Party. He said everything had been senseless for a single person. The fact that he was nothing was something he alone knew. Everyone only knew about himself that he was nothing.

Nagl's eyes fell on another passenger, whose face was continuously overrun with twitches. He was a tall, well-dressed man with a small beard and dark eyes, and he was reading a book. He moved his mouth silently, cleared his throat, coughed a little, shrugged his shoulders, and cracked his knuckles by pressing his fingers individually behind his ears. Then he tugged his beard, gasped for air like a fish, put the book aside and read a newspaper, put the newspaper aside and read the book. Now and then, he napped. The man got off in Florence, but Nagl stayed in his seat. The trees were bare, and the houses of the city vanished like shadows in the yellow fog. Outside, it was winter. They were alone in the compartment now, and Nagl put his head in Anna's lap and gazed out of the rolling train.

AFTER THE STATION AT MESTRE, the train moved out toward the ocean. Gulls perched on wooden pilings or screeched above the water in front of Venice.

They carried the valises down the steps of the terminal and climbed into one of the overcrowded taxi boats. Palazzi rose out of the water, in colors that seemed to come from the ocean, yellow and orange, purple and salmon, with stone balconies and closed, heavy shutters. Ships came toward them or past them or rocked between blue-and-yellow and tobacco-brown and white pilings with golden balls over the tops.

They rented a hotel room on the Ponte di Riato; men in yellow sou'westers stood erect in cargo boats; on the street by the canal, single people were walking with gaudy umbrellas. Nagl went outdoors and strolled along the water with Anna. Everything struck him as alien and not meant for him.

THE CREAM-COLORED Albergo Marconi & Milano with the golden letters was closed. The lower half of the window to the sidewalk was curtained, and Nagl peered through the panes. Inside, the furniture was covered with linen sheets. The farther they walked along the street by the canal, the more the houses seemed to have died out. Even the streets were empty. He thought of breaking into one of the dead hotels with Anna and making love with her on the white sheets. A black boat moved across the canal in the rain. A golden globe of the world with two spread wings and golden lions shone on the keel. A wreath of red flowers lay on the cabin, which was hung with curtains, so that they couldn't see anybody. Only a man in an oilskin stood in the fore, piloting the boat. They walked through narrow streets between houses with their bricks visible behind the crumbled plaster like a wound. On stone balconies, green plants were wrapped in transparent nylon covers.

The closer they got to Fondamenta Nuove, the harder it rained. The side canals smelled of salt and rotten seaweed, and an old woman walked ahead of them, arduously bucking the wind. A squall blew her umbrella into a canal, and it sank slowly, its handle upward, into the water, while the woman leaned over the stone balustrade, furious and despairing. Anna fled into a church, and Nagl followed her. The white marble in the church interior was decorated with flowery and plantlike intarsia, as though shadows of flowers growing outside were shimmering through. Maybe dying was really a streaking review of images from life and a rising over the earth, thought Nagl. Maybe what he had experienced since the moment he had turned his back on the policeman had been the moment of dying, a dying in which he saw what could have been, a clash of forces that were still inside him, and the extinction of consciousness. He stood in this church and thought of the votive picture he had seen in Stübing, the blue cloud in which Mary had floated. Religion was easier to understand than life. He found it odd that faith, and not life, was the problem for human beings. Religion struck him as a shield against madness, everything was colorful and radiant and had its intended purpose. He could imagine that he had died and that dying took so long. His naked, struggling life jeered at faith. It needed his rational mind to survive, and this rational mind gibed at everything in him that sought comfort. But in a state of long dying, when he grasped life as a dying, religion struck him as something quite simple, to be taken for granted.

He looked around for Anna, who held a wet kitten in her arm and petted it. Next to the church, there was a tumbledown house with paneless windows, cats had been running around in front and jumping in through the windows when they had come. One cat had remained squatting in the rain, Anna must have picked it up and taken it along into the church. The kitten peered over her sleeve and meowed.

Since he had ridden away in the train, something had occurred that he experienced but hadn't grown quite aware of: he constantly saw himself. Sometimes he saw himself from above, he saw himself running, walking, standing, he saw himself hugging Anna, or he felt he could observe himself from up close. It didn't bother him. He saw spit oozing from his mouth and he saw himself standing on the edge of Vesuvius and gazing into the crater . . . And he had noticed something else: the feeling of having already experienced something, the conviction, the knowledge of it, had first surfaced at the harbor street in Naples. But it had always stopped again, and he had always pushed it aside again as though to shield himself.

He had gone to church with the schoolchildren for various religious occasions: the harvest festival, first communion (for which the girls had come in little white dresses and the boys in dark jackets with candles in their hands), midnight service on Christmas Eve (when the children knelt in church and were suddenly alien people because of the presence of their parents), and Easter, when everything was green and the children brought pussy willows and blossoming twigs to church. He now saw all those things very rapidly as though they had happened one right after the other. And just as he had felt a yearning for people on Vesuvius, he now felt a yearning for school. The children had been shy and timid, there had been no transition, no gradual winning of confidence; suddenly, the children had shown up in front of his house to wait for a piece of chocolate, and all he had to do was claim he had no time and the children vanished for days.

They stepped outdoors again. The green, shimmering through in the church interior, had had something mysterious and stimulating about it, but here, in the street, a cold wind blew and the rain was pouring down. Anna carried the kitten under her coat, only its head stuck out. The kitten was quiet and allowed her to carry it off, it enjoyed the warmth and tenderness. Anna pressed it against her face and made sure it was under the umbrella and didn't become wet.

THE OCEAN MELTED into the fog. Nagl saw the piles, on which iron lanterns warned of sand banks, and, farther out, he saw the brick walls and the cypresses of San Michele towering over them. When they stopped at the wharf by the cemetery, Nagl noticed that the water next to the vaporetto was turned milky by the engine.

The black boat they had seen on the Canal Grande was rocking in front of the entrance. The sides of the boat were decorated with tucked-in golden braids and tassels carved out of wood. Anna's kitten held still. The ocean sloshed over the stone steps, and the boat rocked. The steersman came, climbed into the boat, and drove off in a foaming curve, but another boat put in that same instant, a sailor bent over, a coffin was slid onto his back, then loaded in a small metal wagon and covered with flowers and wreaths. Two

children stepped out of a yellow vaporetto with red-and-white life
preservers.

They walked through the dark gate of the cemetery. On the stone
slabs, there were red petals, laurel sprigs, red and red-spotted carnations tied to wood by wire; they had all been torn off in haste,
and the carnations were like the paper ones that the grandfather
had worn in his lapel on May 1. As a child, Nagl had never understood why his grandfather had worn red paper carnations. His
grandmother had had whole bouquets lying on the kitchen table,
they vanished the next day in a sideboard drawer, where the picture
postcards and the few letters were kept. He could see the small
kitchen in the factory apartment, the yellowed sideboard, the black
radio on a wall shelf, the kitchen bench into which the dirty laundry
was stuffed. His grandmother laughed as she stroked his hair. She
was a good-natured, corpulent woman, who always pressed an aluminum two-schilling piece into his hand at every visit. If he remembered correctly, she had been the first person he ever knew who
died. He had felt a mixture of importance and incredulity when he
heard about it. The terrible thing had been the horror of his mother
and his grandfather. He had seen how powerless they were and he
ascribed it to religion. And the notion of a life after death had suddenly crumbled in the face of his mother's and grandfather's despair. Nagl picked up the carnations and followed the funeral. A
woman spoke to him. Nagl could make out that she was asking him
how he knew the deceased. The funeral official carried the wreaths
ahead, and Nagl merely nodded. There were six or seven friends
and relatives in gray suits and patterned raincoats, eyeing him in
amazement. They were also astonished that Anna was carrying a
kitten.

They didn't follow the coffin any farther; instead, they halted by
a small room in which there were photographs of deceased people,
pictures hewn out of gravestones. Nagl bent over and saw the faded
pictures of people who had once lived. They stared at him out of
fixed moments, in which they had stood before a photographer's
lens, thinking they could feel the supposed endlessness of their lives.
All people now seemed naïve to Nagl. Through a gate he looked
into a densely overgrown part of the cemetery, rank with pines,
palms, and laurel bushes. Ivy leaves wound up the tree trunks,

blackbirds sprang down to the gravel walks and twittered in the trees. In a stone hall, there were gravestones, cast-iron lamps, and marble angels. There they stood again with their robes full of folds, their huge, beautiful wings, their absent faces. The room was white, and the kitten had leaped out of Anna's coat and was rambling among the figures. They looked for the funeral and came upon it in a meadow strewn with crosses and sliced by lanes.

On the way to the exit, glancing through a cast-iron gate, they suddenly caught sight of the ocean and the brick wall of Fondamenta Nuove. They walked faster now, going astray once again in marble streets, where there were heaped-up graves with flowers and photographs of deceased people. Something in his chest was strangling Nagl and making it hard for him to breathe. He spoke to an old man with glasses, a beret, and a briefcase. The man had a hoarse voice, he turned around, stooping, in the rain, the briefcase slipped out under his arm, and he vanished.

Anna held the kitten and ran her fingers through its fur. The motor-boats were chugging on the sea. People were jamming into the small waiting-cabin, which rocked in the water. Two old women in blue stockings and marcelled hair perched on a bench, smoking. Over-crowded vaporettos drove by; Nagl finally managed to squeeze into one that stopped and to pull Anna in.

THEY HAD BROUGHT the kitten back to the front of the church. A velvety-gray, white-spotted cat sprawled flat on the ground, vomiting. On the next floor, over the window, canaries had been twittering, and when Nagl had thought of Naples, of the market with the fruits, the meat and animals, the vegetables, the people and flowers, he had suddenly felt that everything had its validity. On the street, one of the dogs was trying to mount a cat. The cat put up with it, but children drove the dog away, and the cat went on vomiting. Anna knelt down to it. After a while, she said he was callous. Nagl kept silent. It was as if his sensations were different.

The children were all that gave variety to his everyday life, but their fear, helplessness, and submissiveness, the same from generation to generation, had utterly perplexed him. He often spoke about it to other teachers and was astonished that they viewed the children's invariable and consistent behavior as natural and at best cracked jokes, making light of it. They were not bad teachers. He liked some of them a lot, but even they seemed to take their experiences for granted. He lacked something. He always had the feeling that something was lacking. It left him dissatisfied and, since he couldn't talk to anyone about it, lonely. He no longer spoke about it either. He said nothing. But for quite a while now he had looked upon his work as something temporary, as though he would be doing something else before long. That helped him; but on the other hand, his life wore on like that, day after day, and nothing happened.

"You're a cold person," said Anna and ran off. The water in the canal was green, two men passed by in a boat, which they rowed standing up. The fact that the water made everything alien kept him calm. He walked back to the hotel. Shop windows reflected the Canal Grande, the passing boats, the gulls, which perched on the red-and-white-striped pilings, and the pale-blue wharf cabins for the vaporettos, cabins with many small glass windows, the wooden steps leading to the jetties, and the empty gondolas, covered with tarpaulins, while lost oranges and small pieces of white wood floated between them. The glass door of a restaurant was clouded, and the brass knob, which had the form of a bird, was afflicted with verdigris. Through a chink, Nagl saw a piano in a big room and bottles in a corner. The sidewalk in front of the restaurant was torn up, and a man carrying a plant on his shoulder squeezed past him awkwardly. "It's winter at home," thought Nagl. "There's snow on the ground, here it's cold and empty." Behind an archway, he noticed a dark corridor with posters of horses with flying manes. There was a smell of fish. He stepped into the corridor and waited until his throat no longer choked. His withdrawn character was often mistaken for coldness. When he had loved a woman, he never let on that he disliked some quality about her. Even though he felt he was suffering from it, he could still act positive and friendly. But precisely because he kept silent, smiled, was polite, while thinking about something else deep inside and persuading himself that he nevertheless wished what everyone else wanted, he did not seem warm to other people. He did not disguise himself with any intentions. At times he suspected that most people were just as dissatisfied as he was, only they appeared more imperturbable. Perhaps they didn't expect much else, while he was always full of expectation. And he had been too unsure of himself. He had often been forced to realize that he had secretly been right. He had held his tongue about something, but allowed it to happen, and then it had come exactly as he had thought. With differences of opinion at school, for instance, he had often not ventured to express ideas; a good deal later, others had had the ideas and been praised for them. He had then felt superfluous. What should he have said? —A boat with empty fruit crates sailed by. Nagl saw the time on one of the round bronze clocks that were installed on street corners. Near the hotel, he wandered into a narrow mews, in which houses were connected to each other by iron boxes with glass windows. The panes were dark and filthy, and the mews looked gloomy. He turned around, nobody was following him. A tiger cat was squatting under a tom on a pile of black wooden blocks. The tom stroked her with a paw and slowly moved down with his stiff, pink penis. The cat's hole was open, but the tom was biding his time, he slowly drew back, then he was in her lightning-fast. The cat screamed, the tom moved, but a moment later the cat had vanished with a snarl, while the tom remained behind, dumbfounded. When Nagl walked on, he saw a large, lovely angora cat lurking between the blocks, appearing to have noticed everything. He went past a trattoria, in front of which the dishes and prices were chalked on a blackboard covered with a transparent nylon tarpaulin. Two velvet mannequins stood in a boutique. When he had been beaten up by the sailors in Naples, he had been put on a chair, and there, too, he had seen a mannequin. Everything was full of parallels now. Whenever he was offended or felt hurt, he was receptive to any bit of advice. Despair and pain were not merely despair and pain. Deep down, he also had a feeling of pleasure, a secret strength, and the longer his despair wore on, the more strongly he felt this pleasure and strength. In despair, he was capable of things he would not otherwise have risked. He was more courageous and more honest. He was past shame. In despair, there was a self-humiliation which rippled through his body like a pleasant shiver. How often was he amazed that someone else had felt guilt and despair because of his self-accusations. But anyone else's despair had always taken away his secret strength and pleasure. He had been rapidly fed up with them and grown furious. —He walked down the stone steps on the other side of the Ponte di Rialto and paused before the hotel. He knew that Anna would be lying in the room. And still he walked up the steps with a bizarre emotion. He bought a bottle of wine and joked with the waiter. He said he wanted to surprise the signora and ordered two glasses.

HE OPENED THE BALCONY DOORS to glance at the canal, then stretched out in bed with his back to Anna and drank.

For a while, they lay side by side, and he knew she had put her arm on her forehead and was staring at the ceiling. She probably sensed what he sensed. Whenever he had argued with Anna or felt hurt, he had a need for tenderness. He wanted to be released from his pleasant sadness. He would first put up a resistance, make a furious gesture, but what he wanted was precisely for her to continue being tender to him until he started accusing himself and felt how much she loved him; and he, too, would want her to feel how much he loved her. Suddenly, Anna slipped naked under his blanket. A mirror was attached to the chest door. They lay sideways to the mirror, and Nagl could see her body nestling against him, pressing against his cock, he could see her buttocks, which were tightly squeezed together. Their eyes met in the mirror. In Naples, he had bought a cigar with a lovely painted tube, he took the cigar out of the valise, had Anna kneel before the mirror, and put the cigar tube into her behind, and Anna peered between her legs into the mirror and moaned.

Once, when visiting a county fair, he had gone into the burlesque tent. Drunks on wooden benches had howled and cheered the girls on as they stripped on stage. Sitting down on the edge of the bed and taking Anna on his lap, he told her about a blond woman who had unbuttoned the lederhosen on a man with a "shaving-brush" hat and pulled out a rubber dildo. It had been white and long, and the woman had stuck it in her mouth. The man had laughed into the audience while the woman had sucked and licked the dildo. Then she had knelt and pretended to stick the dildo into herself, while moving her hips. It had been wretched and lewd. The woman had been almost naked, she had spread her thighs, her breasts had hung out over the décolleté, and the man in the lederhosen had lain down between her legs. While the audience laughed, he had spread her legs in the air and acted as if he were fucking her, then they had sat down on a folding chair, and Nagl had seen the man really stick the rubber dildo into her. The audience had become still, and a few minutes later, the woman pulled the dildo out and squirted its milk into her mouth. The milk had dripped down her chin, and the woman had laughed, and now the audience, too, had burst out laughing. They were peasants in Styrian costumes, with careworn, red-cheeked wives, drunken workers, and adolescents of fourteen or fifteen, sitting there with red faces. It had been toward noon, and the performance had lasted half an hour. Flat-chested girls had stumbled over tattered veils to the music of a band, fat women with undersized wigs had shaken their breasts, bent over, and pulled their buttocks apart, while spectators had squirted beer on the stage. Nagl could not say it had repelled him. In some peculiar way, what he had seen was true and, above all, not alien to him. It had been a mixture of dream and life, rather moving in its wretchedness. That night, he had slept with the policeman's wife while thinking about the burlesque, and he had been amazed at how greatly the thought of it had aroused him.

Nagl's eyes alighted upon the canal, and he had the desire to note everything. He saw himself in the mirror between Anna's legs, which had curled around his back, and he felt a voluptuous sensation making him numb.

Anna lay in the bathtub, and Nagl drank wine. His grandfather had seldom gone to his wife's grave. The worst thing had been her abandoning him, he had said. As a stoker, and later on as a worker, he had always felt he was nothing, he had said, but now he felt like someone who had been definitively and irrevocably abandoned. Nagl thought of his feeling of being abandoned while sitting in the train, and he saw himself on the edge of the crater of Vesuvius, the wind tugging his coat, with snow and fog all around him.

Anna was asleep. Nagl was riding to San Marco on the fore-deck of a vaporetto. As soon as the vaporetto had left a jetty, the overhead light was switched off and he sat in dark coldness. A gondola crossed the path of the ship. Nagl saw only the black shadow. The solitude made him feel a pleasure in solitude. He no longer feared it. He knew the pain of being abandoned, and he knew how much was based on lies. His job was based on lies, his relations to other people . . . Lies, nothing but lies. Without secrets, it had not been possible for him to live. He spoke not as he really was, but as he wanted to be. Perhaps every sentence he uttered meant something different from what he intended. Perhaps he had taken on opinions which he could advocate without their being really his own. Perhaps his true philosophy was lying. Throughout his life, he had told more lies than truths. His brain made up a life for other people, a life that had nothing to do with his real life. He spared others with lies, he saved himself conflicts, he made wishes come true, everything only with lies. Nagl gazed at the dark water. They were approaching a jetty, the conductor in the navy-blue coat with gold buttons shivered as he pulled aside an iron grating, and Nagl stepped off. "That's what's so bizarre, telling the truth isn't automatic," thought Nagl. "I automatically lie." Whenever he spoke, he simultaneously wondered if it was absolutely safe to tell the truth.

The roller shutters behind the arcades were down, there were puddles on the patterned stone floors. In front of the Café Quadri, yellow plaited chairs with MARTINI written on their backs were dumped in a pile. Through the panes of the café, he saw the olive-green chairs on the covered tables, between the marble columns and the mirrors. The arcades melted into the darkness. A lamp over the large square rocked, casting a swaying light on the wet stones. While Nagl gazed at the clock with the sky and the zodiac signs and the lions against the blue-and-gold starry sky, while his eyes ran along the geometrical pattern on the ground, finally reaching the campanile, which towered darkly into the night; while he looked up at the ornate, orientally curving fairy-tale turrets and mosaics of the Chiesa di San Marco, his mind was elsewhere. Only the starry sky on the clock tower behind the golden lion distracted him. The yearning for the stars, for the universe, the yearning to see it and survey it, to lose himself in it, that yearning was inside him as a conception of the beyond. He then thought about there being one hundred quintillion stars in the univese. Sometimes he had had the children look at the moon through a telescope and had told them that number. The huge variety on the earth itself was already inconceivable—there were a million different animals and four hundred thousand species of plants. Water, air, and land were permeated with organized matter, which absorbed a countless number of substances, changing and growing, multiplying and developing subspecies, killing and being killed, to make room for or be food for new grass seeds, eelworms, whales, nightingales, or crocodiles. In a steadily variable form, and despite seemingly catastrophic changes in the earth, life had managed to survive over four billion years. While riding in the train with Anna, he had thought about the end of the world, but now he thought about this life, and it was equally beyond him. For these ungraspable, incomprehensible facts were things he had read, and knowing about the end of the world did not make him live any differently, nor did the awareness of manifold life on earth comfort him. The gondolas in front of Piazza di San Marco rose in the water, and the gulls rocked on the sea like little paper boats.

THE IRON TAFFRAIL, clanging and clattering, fell back into the vaporetto, which swept past closed or abandoned hotels that looked even more dilapidated in the dark. Inside the illuminated cabin, there was only one man, he sat quietly with a violin case.

Once again, Nagl thought of his grandfather. He had been out of work for five years. Even though he had thought of work as a constraint, he had longed for work. He had played out chess games by Alekhine, Morphy, Botvinnik, Capablanca, and Euwe until he knew them by heart. He had given his one self a rook and sacrificed a pawn to the other self. He had racked his brains, wondering why he had lost against himself, where he had gone wrong. Even with the coming of National Socialism, he had kept on playing against himself, although he was thankful for the work. Until then, for five years, he had felt every day, every hour, that he was nothing. Now he was needed. He was still nothing, but he could forget it. He had believed in life, and this belief had been enough for him.

AT NIGHT, Nagl embraced Anna. He let her sleep and kissed her tenderly. It was dark, the balcony door was half-closed, all he could hear now and then was the drone of a vaporetto. Anna's mouth tasted of sleep. Nagl propped himself on his arms and began making love to her. She moaned softly, remained quite still, and let it happen with blissful murmuring. But she didn't awake, and Nagl felt his fatigue again, his movements grew slower, and he fell asleep.

The rumble of the vaporettos, the din of motorboats and human voices, were the first sounds he heard the next morning. The buildings shimmered through a milky light, while the rooftops lay in a shadowy fog. He crept deeper into his blanket and studied Anna. One of her eyes was half open and moving. He touched her, but she was really asleep. He had always sought the feeling of love. He had always experienced it as something that changed him, that overwhelmed him with raptures of bliss and yet made him despair. He was so sure of himself when loving that he felt capable of anything, yet at the same time he was the most ridiculous of men and suffered. He believed he had to live in terms of an image that he assumed the woman liked. Anna had made him both dependent and self-sufficient at once. Her cheating on him had made him more honest. Actually, while being with Anna, he had always looked for a woman to help him forget Anna. He never let things run that far, but he had wondered what woman he could go on living with after Anna. He had slept with other women, returning to Anna with a bad conscience and full of malaise, and she had behaved no differently from him. The time would come again when they would seek replacements for one another.

At the start of a love affair, he had always been carefree. His only real goal was to embrace a certain woman and become her lover. Whatever had happened before him hadn't interested him. If he heard about it, he would put it out of his mind. But if the affair went on, the woman's past would become something torturous, making the present uncertain, and yet letting him feel new physical desires. Sometimes the affair had been so dull and indifferent that he continuously felt he was missing something. He had fallen in love with another woman because he couldn't stand the thought of missing opportunities. He had been surprised that just when he had started loving a woman, he had had a light touch with flings. But if he had been unhappy, he had also been stolid and awkward.

He looked at Anna and was astonished by his thoughts. She probably had similar thoughts when she spoke to him or when he wasn't with her. She never told him right away that she liked a man. It was only afterward, a long time later, that she made a cautious remark. She had learned to shield herself against him and hide from him. Nor did he behave any differently. And yet this knowledge was no longer a hindrance for him to love Anna. He loved her in a new way. He felt drawn even more strongly to her, he distrusted her, but he recognized sides to her that he had previously overlooked. She was more courageous than he and more honest. He still presented his past as though he had always been faithful to her. He imagined he could thereby force her to be faithful to him in the future while, when admitting he had behaved no differently from her, he feared she would no longer feel guilty and launch more recklessly into an adventure. By claiming he hadn't had any other women but her, he enjoyed her trust. She had to watch out for his distrust, to which he now had a right. But he also sensed that he was dependent on her. He didn't want to lose her. If he had to, he would do anything to keep her. He liked her cheeriness and warmth and her passion. He liked her feeling hurt by him and her being jealous. And basically, he liked the fact that she was unpredictable and that he had learned through her that there was no such thing as innocence. Love for him was now a cheating and being cheated on, and if he loved, he had to commit himself, even though he never acknowledged it to himself.

THEY DRIFTED AMONG the market stands and bought oranges. The fog was thick, they didn't know where they were. Nagl recalled the market in Naples and the fog on Vesuvius. A fish vendor reached into a cup and pulled out a living gray eel with a white belly, which twisted around his hand; the vendor chopped its head off with a huge knife. But the eel had wriggled so violently that he missed, cutting away only part of the head, and he had to strike again. Anna wanted to leave, but Nagl kept watching the vendor as he took a piece of iron, nailed the end of the eel to a plank, sliced its belly open, with the tail fins twisting upward, and cut out the backbone, while the eel twisted spinelessly on the bloody plank. An old Venetian woman with white hair and wrinkled hands asked the vendor to wrap the eel in paper, where it lay sticky. The woman had a long nose, and a case from which she removed a pair of spectacles to evaluate the merchandise, taking them off, putting them on again, and finally stowing them in the case, which was so worn that Nagl could see the aluminum under the cloth. Another dealer lopped off the head of a huge, ugly, salmon-colored fish and split the body lengthwise in two, then paused and gave Nagl, who had halted in front of him, an inquisitive look.

THEY SAT FREEZING in the vaporetto, Anna was so cold that she whistled between her teeth when she breathed. In Murano, they entered a glass factory, and once again, Nagl had a vague sense of leave-taking. When picturing his grandfather's life after his death, he had imagined him in the open sea: He was standing on the deck of the *Skagerrak* with his back to him. The wind was disheveling his hair, and he stood there calmly, watching the sea. Upon imagining this, Nagl told himself that he was happy. He had left the earth behind, and infinity lay ahead of him. It had received him, and he stood before it, amazed and incredulous, and full of gratitude, and within him there was peace.

Nagl realized he had not taken leave of him. He had been incredulous about his death. Sometimes, when hugging his grandfather, he had felt the stubble rubbing his own face and thought that his grandfather was old and would probably die soon. Or he had clutched his hand, feeling the warmth of his body, gazing into the inflamed eyes, and thinking that some day he would remember this moment when the grandfather was dead. He had spoken a lot and done a lot with him, knowing that soon the present would be only a reminiscence of him. Sometimes this thought had been so strong that Nagl had deliberately had to talk about something else. Then again, he had listened to him for a long time when he had told him about digestion problems, insomnia, shortness of breath, nervousness, difficulties in speaking, and fatigue. He hadn't wanted to die. He seemed never to have had any doubts about life, thought Nagl. Basically, he was thankful for everything that had happened to him and for everything that he was spared. He had taken it all as a matter of course, a price to pay for life. The price had been suffering. He never said he had suffered a lot; instead, he told about suffering only in a specific context. Suffering had always been tied to life. Never in his life had he looked for the experience of suffering. He had come to realize his suffering only when it couldn't be ignored any longer. The older he had grown, the uneasier he had gotten at the thought that time was passing. He didn't know how it had happened that he was suddenly so old. He remembered everything precisely, as though it had been ten or at most twenty years ago. Then Nagl discovered that his grandfather was expecting something. He didn't know, he merely felt that something else had to come.

Nagl, too, believed that he was secretly always expecting something which he was living toward. And entering a factory, he thought of how he sometimes benumbed himself by persuading parents and children that there was an ultimate expectation for every human being to live for. As the thought of his grandfather aboard the *Skagerrak* on the vast blue sea disappeared in the fog with the vaporetto, he saw workers in a factory, their faces illuminated by the glowing glass. Fires burned in the ovens, the men sat there calmly, twisting the glass, cutting it; now and then iron clattered and a ventilating system roared. They hurried to produce their colored pieces of twisted glass, as though the world were desperately waiting for glass penguins. His grandfather had manufactured bottles, first thirty-five-liter bottles with the iron blowpipe, his cheeks were squeezed out of his face and the lungs and arteries in his body were about to burst. Then, during World War II, his grandfather had stood at machines, observing the dials and thermometers and checking the chemical mixture. With the "Strength through Joy" campaign, the National Socialists had sent him and his sister to provincial villages on Sundays, he had played the guitar and his sister had sung the Archduke John yodel. He had performed with the comedian Panzenbeck, acting as straight man for him. The next day, he had done the same chores again; the next Sunday, he had played the same songs and acted as the same straight man. Basically, however, he had only told about incidents, and Nagl had once thought that his real life had been the incidents.

In a trattoria which had dark wooden paneling covered by wallpaper full of bubbles an old woman was scooping wine out of her glass with white bread. The woman nodded amiably at Nagl and imitated the twittering of a bird, then she took the plate of fish bones and squeezed-out lemon and conversed with some card players. She forgot the plate in her hand and watched.

Anna said that, before dropping off to sleep, she had begun to fear that Nagl would kill her with the switchblade he had bought in Rome. She said she had pictured dying and not feeling anything more even though she knew what was going on around her. Nagl, unwilling to answer, peered through the dirty, yellow, semitransparent curtains at the factories and the sea. He sat down next to her and put his arm around her shoulders.

At FONDAMENTA NUOVE, a weeping woman with a plum-and-raspberry-striped umbrella got into the vaporetto. In the water, Nagl saw the small circles emanating from bursting raindrops. The shutters and doors of the buildings were closed, no one was walking in the street. While calmly registering everything, Nagl was suddenly convinced that death would not snuff him out. He had never felt this certainty before. As a child, he had grasped life no more than the thought of life ending. Everything that tortured him on earth, everything he suffered from, would dissolve. He didn't know how, but he was now convinced it would happen. At Piazza di San Marco, sparrows hopped about amid pigeons, and empty gondolas swayed and rocked, and while they got into another vaporetto, everything struck Nagl as enchanted. The notion of his immortality animated his thoughts. They sat on the foredeck, and it was cold. A huge red-and-black steamer emerged in the fog, it lay at anchor in front of San Marco. The gigantic rudder blade loomed out of the water. The vaporetto droned along a park with statues and pines and cypresses, then it turned and sailed out into the open sea.

NAGL NOW STOOD by himself in the cold, on the foredeck, since Anna had sat down in the cabin; a drop hung from his nose. He felt as if he were plowing through something new. When they left the jetties, rain pattered down upon them. They stepped under a glass canopy, with piled-up garden chairs and round tables shimmering green beneath it. Next, there was a shop with whitewashed panes. The entrance door had paper glued over it, and the paper hung down in shreds. He didn't want to return to life, to a country that took care of him but demanded, in exchange, work that had nothing to do with him. Human beings longed for work, not because they loved work, but because they would otherwise be expelled and could not endure expulsion, he thought. He entrusted himself to whatever would happen to him. His grandfather, as a stoker, had longed for a new country, where he would not be nothing, but reality had turned his hope into what becomes of all wishes. It was not the imperfection here that repelled Nagl but the hopelessness that had come of it.

Beyond the bathing cabins on the other side of the street, they could hear the rhythmically roaring ocean. They walked down to the coasting waves with whitecaps, where a concrete wall with a wire fence ran far out into the sea. The sky and the sea met in a thin strip. A child in a yellow raincoat pedaled along the promenade, halted, rolled up its jeans, with the bicycle leaning against a stone bench, and then pedaled away. On the ocean side lay the café with the openwork wooden wall, the terrace, and the wooden grating, and behind it, flagpoles towered naked and lonesome into the sky. Nagl felt as if he could understand everything.

Nothing could have happened to him, but in exchange, all that was left for him was the daily walk to school, and the curriculum, which he had to deal with and teach to the children. On the side, he had led a life of secrecies, loving another man's wife, drinking until he tumbled into bed unconscious, and getting up on time the next day and going to work. He hadn't dared give a hint of anything. Nagl had no desire for his secret life, he merely thought it made up for the life he led on the outside. A blackbird with a yellow beak perched on a white wooden gate, with a palm garden stretching out behind it. Nagl thought of the policeman. He, Nagl, the cause of his pain, had also been the policeman's only confidant, from whom the man had not had to conceal his feelings. He kissed Anna's cold face, felt her warm mouth, and was full of memories.

THEIR COATS WERE SOPPING when they came back to the hotel room. They had the waiter bring a bottle of grappa to the room and they undressed. The grappa tasted sharp and wonderful. They hadn't eaten any supper yet, but the room was warm, and they crept under the blanket and made love. Outside, they could hear the rain. Anna ran hot water into the bathtub, the stockings and her underwear hung from the towel racks and over the backs of chairs. Anna sat on the edge of the tub. While yawning, she absently caressed her lovely white legs. She kissed him, and since they kept their eyes open, they saw one another's dark pupils very big.

They sat down in the bathtub, and he reached tenderly between her legs. The soap was wet, and Nagl let it vanish in her cunt, and squeezed against her belly to make it slide out again. They drained the bottle. Anna started rubbing his penis until it got stiff, then she sat on him and fucked him in the gurgling water. It was uncomfortable, but they were so crazy to make love that they kept moving faster and faster. Her hair had tumbled into her face, and her hands squeezed the faucet so hard that Nagl could see the white knuckles. He asked her to turn around and kneel in front of him. They were half out of the water, Nagl felt he was sweating, veils hung over his eyes and he gasped for air, then he pressed her behind under the water, because he wanted both of them to be in the water when he came. He saw the wet skin on her back in front of him, she turned around deftly so that his penis remained in her, and he felt his testicles bobbing in the water. When his cock slipped out of her, they ran into the room, all wet, wrapped only in towels, and Anna sat down on his face. He had pushed a pillow under his head and now watched her rubbing her clitoris, he saw her breasts rising from below up to the nipples, he saw her childlike face, which was ecstatic and strained. She rubbed, and he licked his tongue inside her, but she was drunk now and fell to the side all at once. Nagl was tired, and he remembered the empty grappa bottle in the bathroom; he stood up, dipped it into the warm water, and pushed it between her thighs. Slowly he moved the bottleneck in and out. The bottle had a widening neck, and Nagl was aroused by the way the bottle moved into her and the labia kept expanding and finally hugged the bottleneck taut and snug.

They were both drunk, and Nagl walked up and down with the white towel around his hips, and spoke about death and leavetaking. He asked Anna if she was asleep. She answered that she wasn't and then fell asleep. Nagl kept talking, he threw two Alka-Seltzer tablets into a bathroom glass and waited until they dissolved in the water. He had seen them lying big and white in his hand when he had shaken them out of the blue glass tube, and now he drained the half-filled glass of water with the dissolved tablets.

In the morning, Anna kissed him until he opened his eyes. His head ached, he felt sick, dizzy, thirsty. He ordered a bottle of mineral water and drained it while lying weary on the bed. Anna showed him his unshaven swollen face in her tortoise-shell mirror, and Nagl remained in bed, stretching out his limbs. Then he felt Anna licking his cock. She licked without letting her hands touch him, and Nagl noticed her face change when she stuck out her tongue or took his cock into her mouth. In the mirror, Nagl could see the inside of his thighs and her head. She crept back into bed with him, Nagl thrust a finger into her behind, and Anna rubbed herself. When she came, Nagl got to his feet, stood over her with spread legs, and squirted on her face, across the closed eyes and into the open mouth. For a while, they lay motionless side by side. Then Anna washed herself, opened the balcony door, and Nagl saw the sun shining. She sat down on the bed with her back to him, played with her toes, and began to put nail polish on them. He watched her as she took one foot into her hand while the other hand dipped the brush into the small bottle of polish and moved it across her toenails. After a while, she asked him when they were going back. Nagl said he didn't know; he said he didn't think about what would happen in a few days. Suddenly, Anna burst into tears. She locked herself in the bathroom, wept, and came out, in her makeup and clothes. Meanwhile, Nagl had gotten up and dressed. After a time, he began talking about volcanoes and the Torfajökull Glacier in Iceland. He said there were cities in Iceland that were black with ashes. Tremendous clouds of smoke rose into the sky. He had read about it, he said. Maybe it was better to travel back into the winter. Anna wept and said she had taken leave of him, yesterday and this morning. When she was with him, she said, he wasn't himself. He described how the sun in Iceland rose over the glaciers, how the ice of the glaciers colored, and how they could see the glaciers from out at sea. He described the volcanic eruptions he had read about in books, but Anna wept, packed the valise, and had it brought to the lobby. Nagl fell silent then.

He carried the valise to the vaporetto, holding it on his lap during the ride. They walked up the steps to the railroad station, Nagl's hand hurt from carrying the valise. The train was ready to leave, and Nagl followed Anna into a compartment where no one was sitting, then he went out again. "If you leave tomorrow, I'll stay," said Anna, hugging him. She yanked down the window and leaned out. He wanted to say he would come back, but the train started moving. He saw Anna waving and he stood there until the train was out of sight.

In the hotel, the clerk asked whether he wanted to exchange his room for one with a single bed, but Nagl said the signora would be coming back. Ah, the signora was coming back, said the clerk. Nagl asked for a bank, where he cashed all his checks.

The narrow streets were so bright in the sun that the moist stone slabs were dazzling and the light shone in people's hair. But it was cold in the shade. He missed Anna. The water in the canals was leaf-green, but wherever it ran out against the sunlight, it shimmered silvery. A woman polished a shop window with squeaking noises. Nagl now focused completely on externals. He took a vaporetto and went to the Accademia. Pedestrians were crossing the canal in the big narrow traghettos. Nagl was freezing. He gazed ahead; at the bend toward the Accademia bridge, the water was so bright that he could only peer at it from the corner of his eye. All at once, he felt physically that Anna was not beside him, and a choking rose in his throat.

Slowly he walked through the Accademia, past the altar-golden paintings of Lorenzo Veneziano and Niccolo di Pietro, he went astray in the building and suddenly found himself at the entrance again. Basically, that was fine with him. He watched as a woman in a fur coat stopped with her little boy, pushed up the wide breeches, unzipped the high-heeled boots, made an adjustment, and then slid her foot back in. The scene had something intimate for him. He remembered sleeping with Anna and felt his abandonment so strongly that he wished he were with someone.

After a time, he came to the sea, to Fondamenta della Zattere, where three big streamers lay at anchor. He had an urge to stroll up the quai with the bare trees and read the names of the ships. A white-and-brown steamer was named *Appia*. Gigantic ropes led to the iron mooring bolts. A sign on a house said that rooms were for rent. He rang, and a bald-headed man showed him a dark room, from which he could see the steamer *Appia* through the window. He paid the rent for one week and sat down in a café under a green linen awning. He thought of Anna, of her moving farther and farther from him, and to take his mind off her, he gazed up at the window of the room and at the ships, on whose ropes seagulls were sitting as if beaded on. Nagl drank wine and felt his head grow heavy. He noticed a child with a bonnet of yellow crepe paper that looked like a marigold. The mother was pushing a black baby carriage with high wheels. Some of the houses in Zattere had their doors and roller shutters closed, reminding Nagl of the winter and of Iceland, but Iceland was now tied to leaving with Anna, and he stopped thinking about it. He took a vaporetto to San Marco. Something within him said that what he was doing was hopeless. A young man sat on one of the stone benches by the wall, a woman stood between his legs, stroking his hair. Nagl thought how nice it would be to have a strange woman stroking him; and at the same time, in his mind, the strange woman was dressed in a velvet coat, like Anna. He heard the flapping wings and the cooing of pigeon flocks, and he walked past the Campanile to the Café Quadri. Gigantic curtains hung between the arcade arches, blocking his view of the stores. Next to a camera that perched on a three-legged stand, a photographer was counting change. Nagl said he wanted a photograph. The photographer reached into a paper bag and threw pigeon feed by Nagl's shoes. Nagl was instantly surrounded by pigeons, who settled on his head, on his arms and shoulders, and swarmed around his feet. "No pigeons!" said Nagl. The photographer stuck his head out of the black cloth and chased away the pigeons. Nagl made an earnest face. After being paid, the photographer gave him a calling card. Nagl wrote down Anna's address, telling him to send the picture to the signora. "But of course," the photographer declared. One of the tremendous, eggshell-colored curtains had the word *Glove* written on it in black script. The Café Quadri had opened. He hurried to get back to the hotel and asked the astonished clerk for the bill. The signora wouldn't be coming back, he said. He took his valise and went to Fondamenta della Zattere.

ONCE HE'D LEFT THE hotel behind him, he felt relieved. In the harsh noon light, the colors of the houses turned pale like crab shells drying in the sun. He rode a bit in the vaporetto, and from the water, the houses looked even paler. Only a palazzo had a radiant golden mosaic with figures and arched windows hung with white. One of the glass panes had the owner's name, SALVIATI, written in gold. The shop windows were empty and covered with linen. Salviati was a well-known glass manufacturer, and now, with the valise on his lap, in the vaporetto, moving through the bright noon light, Nagl thought of his grandfather again. Santa Maria della Salute shimmered pure-white. He realized he had ridden too far, but remained sitting calmly. He had his back to the foredeck and was gazing at the white statues that came out of the canal in front of the Bauer-Grünwald Hotel. Everything looked wan and bloodless, even the gaudy pilings lost their colors in the distance. Opposite him sat a woman with white woolen gloves, holding a furry insect. Nagl leaned forward and realized it was a cricket.

He sat down in a restaurant and put the valise on a chair next to him. He missed Anna. The waiter came and wanted to take the valise to the checkroom, but Nagl wouldn't let him. He had been drinking and felt mysterious. He might be a razor salesman. The entire valise was full of samples in ivory, black plastic, horn, as well as polished wooden handles. Then he had the finest shaving brushes in his valise, badger hair and buffalo tails, heh-heh. Or else the valise was filled with banknotes from an armed robbery . . . He stared at the valise, which was full of dirty underwear, and he wondered why he was carrying it around. What was he supposed to do with the dirty underwear and shirts? But it would make a poor impression if he moved into his new room without baggage. It wouldn't look good having nothing along. He glanced over at the water, which was mercury-colored. It struck him that it was winter, and he gazed pensively into the oily smoke pouring from the room of a vaporetto as it moored at a jetty on the opposite side of the canal. Then he stared at the tablecloth again and thought of Anna. When he thought of her being at home, he believed he had lost her for good. He pictured her sitting asleep in the empty train compartment. Perhaps she would be conversing with another passenger and have forgotten Nagl. The thought pained him, but he felt it was right if that happened. When he looked up again after a time, he noticed it was getting dark and the colors of the houses were deep again. Low-flying clouds drifted across the canal, recalling the veterinarian's funeral, but now he didn't mind remembering. Suddenly, the palazzi were the colors of egg yolks and tea, and through the window of the facing café, he saw blue-and-white-checkered tablecloths. The canal was empty except for the vaporettos, and silver streaks of rain were plunging down. Nagl sat behind the glass pane; outside the open entrance door, people were standing and gazing into the downpour. A winter storm growled far away, and now and then someone hurried past the restaurant. By and by, it stopped raining, and the sky turned the color of ice, with yellow and pale-blue clouds, which Nagl gazed up at. Along the edges of the roofs with strange chimneys that widened toward the top, the sky was a delicate yellow and blue, as though it were evening, yet the afternoon had only just begun. A man carried a child in his arm, it had a cloth over its head so that it looked like a covered bird cage. Nagl paid and stepped out into the cold January air. A man in work clothes came toward him with a big bouquet of roses, alongside him ran a stray mutt that licked one of Nagl's shoes. Nagl was moved by this, he didn't know why, and he turned to look at the dog, which dashed on, snuffling. In front of a dirty café a pregnant woman stood with her hand on her belly, feeling the movements of her child. When she caught Nagl watching her, she stopped in embarrassment and disappeared inside the café. He walked through the dark, cramped house. The bald man opened the door for him and led him into the room, where a mirror with a silver-painted plaster frame hung over a fireplace. Nagl put down the valise, stepped into the next room, and opened the window to the *Appia*. When the man was gone, he lay down on a sofa with a greasy headrest and could thus view the sky, the funnel, and part of the ship's railing. He dozed off for a while, waking up half an hour later. He felt the switchblade in his jacket pocket, took it out, and kept snapping it open and shut for a time. Maybe he would fly to Istanbul. Then he thought it would be best to travel some place where he expected nothing. He felt the valise standing in the next room and went outdoors again.

HE ASKED A GONDOLIER to take him to the railroad station. A mute old man with a lolling tongue helped him into the boat, which the goldolier fitted out with blue leather cushions. The gondola was green on the inside, it had two lovely wide armchairs and two benches. No sooner had the mute with the lolling tongue helped Nagl into the boat than he held his cap out, and the gondolier waited until Nagl threw in money. They moved through reeking side canals, between garbage scows and freight boats, which turned gingerly around a corner. Then they glided under a shady bridge, hearing the chirping and trilling of canaries from an open window. Nagl thought of Anna's bird-tongue, her childlike face, and her presence, and while suffering, he forced himself to see everything. A mailman put letters in a basket, which was lowered from a house, and a woman hoisted the basket up. In a quiet green canal, they moved past a school that emitted the loud screeching of recess din. They turned off to the Canal, and Nagl sat small in the water and looked up at a palazzo, at the Gothic windows and stone balconies. Behind the market halls, there were two old women with black shawls on their heads and black coats, stockings, shoes, and canes. The gondola eased so close to them that Nagl could see one of them opening a clam and putting it into her toothless mouth. The gondolier had to stop and catch his breath outside the Hotel Principe with the black-and-red mottled pilings. The curtains in the hotel were drawn and the high doors were shut.

At the jetty by the railroad station, a dead squid with golden eyes lay on a wooden stairway. Nagl paid and climbed over the animal. He roamed about the station, asked if a train was going to Istanbul, went to the platform from which Anna had left, and then hurried to get out of the station. He walked through narrow, mazelike streets, came to a tiny shop, and watched an old woman repairing umbrellas. The umbrellas lay on shelves up to the ceiling, and the woman was working on an old model with a fine pattern of tiny red roses on a black ground; underneath, there was a dark-blue umbrella with white polka dots.

He hadn't shaved for ten days, and his hair was still greasy and unwashed and stuck together in straggles. He drank a glass of red wine in a bar and ate two cold cuttlefish with lemon. An Italian with a small mustache asked him if he was "Inglese." He bought Nagl a glass of wine, and Nagl shamefacedly left the bar after quickly downing the glass. He found himself in front of a drugstore with frosted panes and a golden male head with a green laurel wreath hanging above them. It was a lovely drugstore with an ornate cast-iron sign giving the proprietor's name. From a window decorated with flowers, he heard a female voice singing coloraturas. He walked toward where he thought the canal was, went past a butcher shop, and reached the jetty of San Simeone. While waiting for a vaporetto, he studied the many gulls in the yellow light and the flowing light on the waves. From the vaporetto, as he glided down the canal, he peered into the golden nervures of the sun between the clouds. He forced himself to look at the sky. Perhaps that was the most beautiful feeling, the teacher thought, he should have told his pupils about it, should have told them that freedom is a state in which they would feel no more fear. A woman in a fur coat and large sunglasses sat ahead of him, and he decided to follow her. They glided between the palazzi, on which the green paint of the shutters had run down the walls, and Nagl stared at the back of the woman's neck. He thought she had to feel his stare. He wanted her to turn around so he could see her face, he also believed she would move her head if only he stared resolutely enough, but the vaporetto kept moving and the woman didn't turn around to him. In his thoughts, Nagl swore to himself that he would try to pick the woman up no matter what she looked like or what happened. The traghetto at the fruit and fish market crossed the canal, and where the fish market had been that morning, pushcarts now stood. The Ponti di Rialto emerged piece by piece, like a white wall, from behind the bend, and they sailed underneath. By the jetty at the Accademia, thousands of golden dots of light quivered in the water, the evening sun made the windows of the palazzi shine honey-yellow and, further away, plantlike green. The woman got out at the next stop, and Nagl saw her face for the first time. It was no longer young. Her hair was dyed blond and well-groomed, and her hands revealed that she was about fifty years old. Nagl followed her into a birreria, where she was greeted by the man behind the counter.

Nagl had to talk to her, but he couldn't find the courage, and he stared into her face when no one was watching. She glanced at him every now and then, but swiftly turned away the instant their eyes met. The birreria slowly filled with people, and since the proprietor paid less and less attention to the woman, Nagl grew more courageous. The woman was Swedish and had married an actor in Venice. But her husband had left her, and her children had moved away. Nagl invited her to dinner, but she begged off. "Then how about a glass of wine?" asked Nagl. Yes, she said, she'd be glad to drink a glass of wine with him. She laughed, and Nagl noticed she had drunk too much. She told him about her life, speaking hectically and giving in to her spontaneous impulses. What line of work was he in? she asked. Nagl answered that he was an Arctic explorer. He told her about the volcanoes in Iceland and the rain of ashes and the glaciers. The woman then wanted to know how long he was going to be in Venice, and Nagl said he was leaving tomorrow . . . Tomorrow already? Yes, tomorrow. That was too bad. Where was he staying? In Fondamenta della Zattere. Aha. He had rented a room there. Would she care to visit him?

He bought a bottle of Merlot and took a boat to the Canale della Giudecca. They didn't speak to one another in the boat, although Nagl tried to talk about something to divert the woman. He asked her what her name was, and she said Luisa. Since she had begun living in Venice, that was what her husband had called her. They sailed up the Canale della Giudecca.

He unlocked the door and took her into the dark room with the fireplace, the mirror, and the valise. "Ah, you've packed already," said the woman. She sat down and glanced at the ship in front of the window and the night sea. "Do you write books?" she asked. She took off her fur coat. Nagl lay down on the sofa and propped his upper body against the wall. He said he wrote books on volcanoes and on Arctic plants. He began talking about those things again, opened the bottle but found no glasses. He apologized for having no glasses, but the woman laughed and told him to switch off the light. Nagl did it, and the woman said: "I can't. You're so young." —"You'll regret it tomorrow," said the woman after a pause. "You mustn't switch on the light." She went to the bed and undressed and slipped under the cover, and Nagl dropped his trousers and followed her. Her bosom was large and solid and her cunt was hot and wet, but she didn't want him to kiss her. She sat up, panting for air, while Nagl embraced her. She had a marvelous way of tightening her cunt and then loosening it again, and her buttocks were soft and gentle, and her breasts, which Nagl reached for, were heavy. She asked him if he would ever come back to Venice. Nagl said yes. When he came back, she'd be as slender as a young girl. She would go swimming and not drink any liquor. She sat on his cock and seesawed up and down until she came and Nagl came, too, and he lay on his side and dozed off. He awoke when the woman was dressing in the semidarkness. He promptly saw that her head had grown small because the hair had been squashed. Her false eyelashes were coming off the lids, and her mouth made a noise like false teeth pressing on gums. Nagl remembered that she hadn't let him kiss her. He stared at the ceiling and heard her rummaging in her pocketbook. After a while, she came toward him, fragrant and made up. She had left her address on the night table in case he came back. She also asked him to lock up after her, unlocked the entrance door, placed the key next to the door, and vanished. Nagl looked out the window, but the woman could no longer be seen. He read her name, Luisa Zanoletti. She lived on Calle delle Veste. He went back to bed, but he couldn't sleep. Being alone didn't bother him. He could think of Anna now without pain. The big ship lay outside. But beyond the darkness, beyond the night, there were spaces, unending spaces. He looked at the dark shadow of the *Appia* in front of his window and imagined sailing it out to sea.

WHEN HE AWOKE the next morning, the *Appia* had vanished from outside his window. It was a beautiful winter day in the south. He remembered taking a trip with Anna to the Grossglockner. He thought of calling her, but he didn't want to tell her any lies. The sea was bluish-green. On the wharf, two policeman were walking in raincoats with rifles slung around their shoulders and pointing downward. Nagl, while dressing, remembered the girl in Rome, lying dead in front of his pensione. And he thought of the man who had come into his room, he thought of the policeman and of Luisa. She was an attractive faded woman, and Nagl wondered what she did in the daytime. He went outdoors, and he felt an urge to be near her. Ships covered with light-brown, washed-out tarpaulins rocked in the canals. He took a vaporetto to Rio della Fava. Steps led from naked brick houses into the water. On the Ponte dei Barcarole he saw a woman in a blue hat and hare-skin coat ringing a doorbell. The door was opened, and the woman went in. An iron balcony loomed above the water; underneath, Nagl read on a plaque that Mozart had lived in this house as a child. Nagl peered at the house, and a woman in glasses came out, stopped in the doorway, and waited to see what Nagl wanted. Nagl wanted nothing, and the woman slowly shut the door. He came to Calle delle Veste, halted, but then strode on quickly to Piazza San Marco, where he sat down in front of the Café Quadri and ordered a grappa, which he quickly drank. The pigeons cooed, and Nagl became drowsy in the sun. Behind pulled-up linen curtains, he could see stores with marble portals and the two cameras on the wooden tripods with the black cloths. A dog was sleeping on one of the long wooden tables, which looked like empty market stands . . . He paid and went into the Doge's palace with a flock of tourists. But he felt a strange emptiness. He passed everything unheedingly, the black sedan with the golden adornment, the golden coffered ceiling, the names scratched into the soot of the old fireplaces, the golden-yellow silk tapestries, and the old chairs—he stopped only once, right at the outset, by the two brown, man-high globes of the world in decorated wooden frames, but he didn't feel like thinking, he merely stood over the wooden spheres and gazed at them. Then he felt an urge to go on, past the black tables with the intarsia of gaudy birds, flowers, grapes, leaves, and animals, past the tar-black pictures by Hieronymus Bosch, the dressers with marquetry of rosewood and mother-of-pearl, the black timbered ceilings with floral garlands, the worn-down cardinal-red velvet chairs with golden leaf ornaments, the lead-framed transparent crown glasses, the walls of tobacco-brown and gilded wood, the Tintorettos and Veroneses on the ceilings, the big peephole on one door, the green, gold, and blue wall clocks, the gigantic gold candelabra attached to the walls, the benches with subdivided seats and arms, the halls redolent with old wood—to a balcony from which he could view the glittering ocean and San Giorgio Maggiore and La Giudecca. It was a vast and lovely sight, as though a man had built this balcony to gather all energy and soar off from there into the universe. He thought of the two large globes of the world and of the ships in Zattere and of the train ride. A bit later, when he had crawled into the prisons—low cells secured with double iron bars—and seen the rock below the bars, a rock which was scoured to an ivory-like shine and in which the names and faces of prisoners were carved: Pirico Camillo and Francesco Sforsa; when he saw the iron rings on the walls and read the dates, he again felt abandonment and loneliness. In the treasure room of San Marco, the gold-framed mosaics were shining and the light was shimmering under the golden cupola of the cathedral as though to comfort him, and Nagl walked in a daze, high over the heads of the people, along twisting stone corridors, saw the mosaics over the doors shining under a glass room, and stepped out on a balcony, from which he saw the pigeons scurry like ants across the ornaments in the stone floor of Piazza San Marco, and the people were as tiny as Lilliputians.

In CALLE DELLE VESTE, he found the house and the nameplate, but he didn't ring. Opposite the house, there was a latteria, in which Nagl saw a middle-aged woman with twisted stockings. She carried a shopping net in one hand, and held a handkerchief in the other. While waiting in the overcrowded little store, she waved the handkerchief in front of her nose. Nagl thought about ringing, then he ambled over to the Ponti di Rialto, found a bar, and drank grappa. The barkeeper wasn't very talkative, he mutely filled a glass for Nagl and worked out a sum on slips of paper. Feeling he owed a conversation, he switched on the radio. Nagl felt himself getting drunk. The sky over Piazza di San Marco was purple now, the water almost black. Nagl went out into the cold and was happy. The sun was a reddish-gold disk setting rapidly behind the palazzi. The purple behind the houses oozed into the sea, pulling along a flow of stringy red clouds. There, where Nagl assumed the Campanile to be, the figure of a golden angel glowed in the setting sunlight, the angel was small and bright, while the heavens turned violet and tinged into green away from the houses. The angel glowed supernaturally bright, and the heavens passed into white-blue and gradually shaded into night darkness. From the vaporetto, Nagl saw the last piece of the sky deep-violet, covered more and more by the blackness of night. But the radiated angel went on glowing, brighter and clearer. They were moving toward it, and Nagl thought: "It's finally like life and not like a dream."

He got out before the Ponte dell" Accademia.

What had he told Luisa?

The glaciers had shimmered over the sea, the icebergs, the snowy wastes.

The valise stood in his room.

Snowstorms raged where the sun went down. But still he felt as if this cold were waiting for him.

He walked through Zattere. An old man, surrounded by cats, sat on a stone bench. The cats roamed at his feet, rubbing against his cane, nestling against him, from behind, under his arm, and on his lap. Nagl halted and watched him. The man had a package wrapped up in a newspaper. He seemed to be waiting for something, peered at his watch, stood up, leaned over. They were filthy alley cats stalking around him, sticking their heads under the handle of his cane and rubbing against him. A woman with plastic bags came out of the next street. She spread some newspapers and fed fish leftovers to the cats. The old man carefully handed his package to the woman, got up, and stood bent over his cane with its rubber stopper, contentedly watching the cats devour his refuse. The woman was also silent now as she sighed and folded the papers together. When the old man saw that all the cats were eating, he trudged, slow, stooping, and alone, into the darkness, where the great ships were anchored. Nagl followed him, but the man went past Nagl's house.

Nagl lay down on the bed and waited. He thought about the ice in the Arctic being called "eternal ice." The ice was blue. He thought of the Spitsbergen Islands in the Arctic Ocean. That was the only place to flash into his mind.

When it grew light, Nagl took a vaporetto to Mestre. He couldn't see the angel against the sky any more. From Mestre he took a bus to Marco Polo Airport and bought a ticket to Fairbanks, Alaska.

The Authors

H.C. (Hans Carl) Artmann (1921–2000) was born in Vienna. During the 1950s, he collaborated with other experimental writers of the "Wiener Gruppe" (Vienna Group); however, he soon followed his own path. His greatest success—the collection of poems, *med ana schwoazzn dintn* (with black ink, 1958)—extends into dialect. Credited as a main proponent of Surrealist literature in Austria, he influenced—both through his translations and his own work—the younger generation of poets; Peter Rosei, for instance, called Artmann his "compañero."

Michael Donhauser (1956–) was born in Vaduz (Liechtenstein) and lived in Vienna from 1976–96; after two years in Paris, he now lives in Maienfeld. He has mostly written poems that have a "prosy" tone and approach life in a way that is reminiscent of Rainer Maria Rilke's "thing poems"; other poems evoke Hölderlin and Trakl. His main concern lies with how language concisely yet completely expresses experience and observation. He was awarded the Ernst-Jandl Prize in 2005.

Barbara Frischmuth (1941–) lives in Vienna and her hometown, Altaussee. She is best known for fiction inspired by autobiographical impulses and focused on gender issues. Combining the serious and humorous, and often transcending realism into the realm of the magical, such as in her *Sophie Silber* trilogy (1976–79), she makes it possible for her female protagonists to use their imagination to explore options for a better society.

Norbert Gstrein (1961–) born in Tyrol, wrote a dissertation on the philosophy of language. He currently lives in Zurich and Hamburg. A major theme in his works has been criticizing the corrosive effect of tourism, especially on his native Tyrol. In his most recent work he has turned his attention to the war in Kosovo.

Josef Haslinger (1955–) is a "new kind of political writer" who fuses the tradition of high "Culture" and trends of popular culture. The resulting atmosphere of political and social authenticity can be seen in his political thriller *Opernball* (Ball at the Opera, 1995), which made Haslinger famous. The author is equally at home in academia; he wrote a dissertation on Hölderlin's aesthetics, held various visiting professorships both in Europe and the United States, and lives in Vienna and Leipzig, where he is professor at the Leipzig Institute for German Literature, Germany's prestigious creative writing institute.

Ernst Jandl (1925–2000) was close to the Vienna Group in the 1950s and became famous for his experimental "sound poems" in which he creates onomatopoetic relationships that are usually tied to meaning, often expressing self-irony or even bitterness. Jandl's later poems sparkle with his typical wit while their tone is more conversational.

Elfriede Jelinek (1946–) her status of a major Austrian writer was confirmed by the 2004 Nobel Prize for Literature. She was born in Mürzzuschlag (in the exact region in which her novel *Die Kinder der Toten* is set). An accomplished musician as well, she published her literary debut in 1970 but is probably best known for her 1983 novel *Die Klavierspielerin*. She combines her political views (criticizing the public's desire to minimize or forget fascism), traditions of serious literature, and elements of pop culture (such as pornography and horror stories) into texts of evocative and controversial quality.

Gert Jonke (1946–) was born in Klagenfurt. After first studying music, literature, and film in Vienna, and then traveling widely, he lives as a freelance writer part of the time again in Klagenfurt. A consistent theme in his writing has been the relationship between reality and illusion, often expressed in a sense of unavoidable necessity or dream logic. Like a "composer," he directly expresses this theme in the dynamics of his sentences, which "cannot be avoided," as Elfriede Jelinek observes. He was awarded the Franz-Kafka Prize in 1997 and the Grosser österreichischer Staatspreis in 2002.

Michael Köhlmeier (1949–   ) comes from (and again lives in) the Vorarlberg region. In addition to writing radio plays, theater plays, and film scripts, he has also explored various narrative traditions, such as the *Kaffeehausliterat*, the author who sits (and, sometimes, writes) in a coffee house. He has enjoyed popular success with his "retellings" of stories from the Western canon; his postmodern novels in which he reconceptualizes the *Odyssey* are the most ambitious examples.

Alfred Kolleritsch (1931–   ), born in Brunnsee, lives in Graz, where he has emerged as a major force on the "scene" of Austrian literature, leading the Forum Stadtpark and editing Austria's most influential literary magazine, *manuskripte*—where, for example, Gert Jonke and Michael Scharang, both represented in this volume, were first published. His own work displays a "crossover" between philosophy and poetry; in a sense, he is a philosopher by training, having written a dissertation on Martin Heidegger.

Friederike Mayröcker (1924–   ) is one of the major women poets writing in German. During the 1950s, she was in contact with the authors of the Vienna Group; her early texts experimented with highlighting the quality of language as material. Her later texts seem more subjective and evoke remembrances of personal experiences but surprise with their objective tone, including those reflecting the illness and death of her partner, Ernst Jandl.

Robert Menasse (1954–   ), a *Poeta doctus* with a dissertation on the outsider in the literary scene, also writes essays on issues of culture and politics. His literary work often shows how individuals respond to social change. He spent the early to mid-1980s in Brazil, where he taught literature at the University of São Paulo. His trilogy of novels—*Sinnliche Gewißheit* (1988; *Meaningful Certainty*), *Selige Zeiten, brüchige Welt* (1991; *Wings of Stone*), and *Schubumkehr* (1995; *Reverse Thrust*)—is set in part in Brazil and in Austria.

Peter Rosei (1946–   ) was born in Vienna, where he studied law before becoming a freelance writer in 1972 and where he still lives. Beginning with his early work, such as *Bei schwebendem Verfahren* (1973), Rosei's prose has been seen as combining lyricism with cool observations and has been compared to the prose of Franz Kafka. Indeed, in 1993 he was awarded the Franz-Kafka Prize.

Gerhard Roth (1946–   ) was born in Graz. His monumental seven-volume cycle of book-length texts *Die Archive des Schweigens* (The Archives of Silence), published 1980–91, expresses the central theme of his writing—human isolation—while clearly identifying the political character of this isolation. This political character of writing has become more evident over the years in the author working to preserve the memory of his country's past that includes National Socialism.

Michael Scharang (1941–   ) was born in Styria and now lives in Vienna, where he attended university and earned his Ph.D. in 1965 with a dissertation on Robert Musil's theater plays. While he also writes radio plays and film scripts, he is best known for his fiction. Social criticism has remained a major theme in his writing.

Raoul Schrott (1964–   ) grew up in Tunis and Tyrol, and now lives in Ireland. After studying literature and linguistics in Norwich, Paris, Berlin, and Innsbruck, and teaching in Naples, he became a freelance writer of poetry and prose, as well as translator, with a breadth of learning that led H. C. Artmann to call Schrott a Poeta doctus.

Joseph Zoderer (1935–   ) was born in Meran, grew up in Graz, and attended university in Vienna; he now lives in South Tyrol (Italy). Although his involvement with literature began in the late 1950s, he has been a freelance writer only since 1981. Many of his works bear the mark of his native region; for example, in 1974 he published a collection of dialect poems, and often his novels deal with issues of being "at home" in a particular region.